SOME KEY PROVISIONS OF THE
CANADA-CHINA INVESTMENT DEAL

- Chinese investors, including state-owned companies, have a general right to buy anything they wish in Canada — but Canadian investors do not have the same right in China.
- Chinese investors can challenge the decision of any public entity in Canada, including provinces and municipalities, and seek generous compensation for the decision.
- Instead of going to court, these investors can take the dispute to a three-person arbitration panel made up of private lawyers, not judges.
- The arbitrations may take place entirely in private, before lawyers who depend on investors for their ability to earn lucrative pay as arbitrators, and are open to little or no review in any court anywhere. The arbitrators' decisions in favour of foreign investors can be enforced all over the world against the losing country.
- The federal government can keep any challenge against Canada secret, allowing the government to settle a case, by paying out public money or changing its decision as the Chinese investor prefers, without any public knowledge or hearing.
- Chinese investors have rights not available to any domestic investor in Canada — including the right to be compensated for some changes in laws or policies that affect the value of their assets, even if that decision applies to everyone in the country and is made for a public purpose, such as to promote jobs or to protect health or the environment.
- Chinese investors have powerful rights to use Chinese managers and workers in their Canadian operations, including extracting Canadian resources. And   way, they are given a special av   :ion.

"Through meticulous and painstaking research, Van Harten blows open the doors on the largely unknown and misunderstood world of investment arbitration ... Every concerned citizen—and, more importantly, those who are unaware of these developments—should read this book."

— David Schneiderman, Professor, Faculty of Law,
University of Toronto

"Van Harten's authoritative book shows us how little trade there is in these 'trade' agreements, and how much other factors have invaded these secretive and unbalanced negotiations."

— Harry Swain, former Deputy Minister, Industry Canada

"Authoritative, accessible and very important, *Sold Down the Yangtze* is essential reading for every Canadian who values democratic governance, access to information, indigenous rights, a clean environment, as well as their own health. This book will change the way you think about the role of government and the power that governments can hand multinational companies in a globalised world. It will also help you to protect your rights."

— Dr. Margot E. Salomon, Associate Professor,
Law Department and Centre for the Study of Human Rights,
London School of Economics and Political Science

"*Sold Down the Yangtze* is a primer on what is at stake for Canada under the new treaty, as well as a masterful display of how to render the complexities of a highly technical area of law accessible. *Sold Down the Yangtze* should be required reading for Canadian officials, serious journalists, scholars and, most important — an informed public."

— Alec Stone Sweet, Leitner Professor of International Law,
Politics and International Studies, Yale Law School

"Van Harten's path-breaking book reveals how Canada negotiated an investment deal with China that elevates the rights of Chinese firms over those of the Canadian government and its citizens . . . a model that skews the incentive structures of market economies and threatens the gains in governance and democracy that have evolved over the past century."

— Kevin P. Gallagher, Associate Professor, Pardee School for Global Studies, Boston University

"Written in a conversational tone, using highly accessible language and with the treaty's 'legalese' stripped out, Van Harten explores what the treaty's implications will be for everyday Canadians."

— Barnali Choudhury, Senior Lecturer, University College London

"Van Harten's *Sold Down the Yangtze* offers a powerful analysis of the content and implications of Canada's historical trade agreement with China . . . While, I am sure, there are many in Canada that do not want to hear what Van Harten has to say about the Canada-China FIPA, all should."

— Federico Ortiño, Reader in International Economic Law, King's College London, University of London

"The treaties are often dealt with as if they were merely technical or economic in nature. It is extremely important that their consequences to democracy are clearly laid out. Nobody does this better than Gus Van Harten."

— Martii Koskenniemi, Professor, University of Helsinki, former member of the UN International Law Commission

Dear Norah,

Thank you for caring about our
beautiful country!

Gus Van Harten

GUS VAN HARTEN

SOLD DOWN THE YANGTZE

Canada's lopsided investment deal with China

GUS VAN HARTEN

James Lorimer & Company Ltd., Publishers
Toronto

James Lorimer & Company Ltd., Publishers acknowledges the support
of the Ontario Arts Council. We acknowledge the support of the Canada
Council for the Arts which last year invested $24.3 million in writing
and publishing throughout Canada. We acknowledge the Government of
Ontario through the Ontario Media Development Corporation's Ontario
Book Initiative.

Cover modified from design by Jennifer Griffiths.

Library and Archives Canada Cataloguing in Publication available.

James Lorimer & Company Ltd., Publishers
317 Adelaide Street West, Suite 1002
Toronto, ON, Canada
M5V 1P9
www.lorimer.ca

Printed and bound in Canada.

CONTENTS

ACKNOWLEDGEMENTS

There are many people I would like to thank for helping me write this book. I am grateful to the thousands of Canadians who responded to the China FIPA so far. I also acknowledge my colleagues who have helped me to see the importance of speaking openly about investor-state arbitration. Those who stand out in my immediate memory, in no particular order, are Martin Loughlin, Deborah Cass, Sol Picciotto, Muthucumarswamy Sornarajah, David Schneiderman, Kyla Tienhaara, Nathalie Bernasconi-Osterwalder, Howard Mann, Robert K. Stumberg, Scott Sinclair, Douglas C. Hay, Harm Schepel, and Martii Koskenniemi. I am also indebted to Hong-Hai Bi, Douglas Hay, Kirsten Mikadze, Scott Sinclair, and Sara Slinn for their comments on parts of the manuscript.

From what I saw, there were some politicians who responded actively to the concerns about the FIPA. I am sure there were others with whom I did not have contact. While I do not wish to be partisan in this book, I think it right to name those who seemed to do the most to study the FIPA critically and respond. The order reflects only the sequence in which I became aware of their commitment on the issue: Green Party Leader Elizabeth May, NDP Member of Parliament Don Davies, Liberal Member of Parliament Wayne Easter, NDP Leader Thomas Mulcair, and Yukon NDP Leader Liz Hanson. I am grateful to these politicians, and the others who did not come to my personal attention, for their work on this file.

Many journalists took on the difficult task of trying to digest and communicate the FIPA's importance. I think there were too many to single out any by name, but I would like to pass on my respect for their ability to turn a complicated and dry subject into an engaging story that people can understand. I have tried to learn from them in writing this book, for better or for worse.

This is the first time I have self-published a book instead of submitting a manuscript for publication by an academic or trade publisher. The main reason for doing so was to avoid delays in getting the book out and to have more control over how it is distributed. Self-publication also allowed me to donate more of the proceeds of the book to organizations that are working to spread awareness about the FIPA or investor-state arbitration. Self-publication backed by further online referencing was a way to achieve a balance between public access and academic detail. However, self-publication only worked well because of the expert support of Trena White and Megan Jones at Page Two Strategies, who among other things organized the graceful copy edit by Michelle MacAleese, creative cover design by Jennifer Griffiths, efficient typesetting by Press Books, and diligent checking by Chelsey Doyle and Kristen Steenbeeke. If nothing else, the experience of writing this book has confirmed that no book is ever created by the author alone.

The book draws on aspects of my research on investment treaties that received financial support from Osgoode Hall Law School and York University, Canada's Social Sciences and Humanities Research Council, and the Law Commission of Ontario. This funding allowed me to employ the many research assistants who contributed to the research behind the book. They include: Constance Abebreseh for research on types of decisions reviewed by arbitrators, Rana Arbabian for background research on arbitrators, Sean Aherne-Beisbroek for spreadsheet management and research on NAFTA cases, Sarah Colgrove for research on NAFTA cases and regulatory chill, Joslyn Currie for transcription and analysis of interviews, Ryan De Vries for spreadsheet management and research on China, Kelly Goldthorpe for statistical analysis and quantitative project design, Heather Krause for statistical analysis and quantitative project design, Kerrie Lowitt for research on NAFTA cases and MMT in gasoline, Pavel Malysheuski for research on size and wealth of claimants, Kirsten Mikadze for fact-checking and research on issue resolutions and NAFTA cases, Alexandra Monkhouse for research on issue resolutions, Nikki Petersen for research on FIPA promotion, Yuxi Sun for research on NAFTA cases and regulatory chill, and Sounithtra Vongsaphay on actuarial modelling of investment treaties.

There is no way this book—or my public criticism of the FIPA and investor-state arbitration—would have been possible without the patience and kindness of my wife Susanne and children Olivia and Mattias. Words cannot capture the fullness of my love and appreciation. I also thank my other family members and friends for offering feedback and am especially grateful to my parents Peter and Sandy for their guidance and support.

PREFACE

I wrote this book to present a full picture of what's wrong with the Canada-China investment deal, also known as the Canada-China Foreign Investment Promotion and Protection Agreement, or simply the FIPA. The book is for those who have heard of the FIPA and for those who haven't. Anyone should be able to use the book to understand flaws in the deal and see how Canadians were misled in the media blitz to sell it. All may find ways to work with the ideas I propose to help Canada in the FIPA era.

Despite a public campaign to stop it, the FIPA was ratified by the Harper Government in September 2014 without a proper review of what it meant for the country. By that point, the FIPA had been sold to Canadians by painting its critics as fearful, hysterical, or ill-informed. This sales pitch for the FIPA was so misleading I thought it a priority to respond and to show what was lost in the rush to finalize this long-term deal.

I have done so in five steps in this book. First, I explain how the FIPA is lopsided and decidedly to China's advantage. Second, I reveal the threat posed by the FIPA's system of foreign investor protection to democracy and governments in Canada and other countries. Third, I outline the FIPA's impact on the courts and the weaknesses of the Federal Court of Canada's limited review of the FIPA in response to a legal challenge by the Hupacasath First Nation. Fourth, I debunk line by line the claims of the FIPA's promoters. Fifth, I offer an explanation for why the FIPA appears to have gone so wrong, and suggest what can still be done to protect Canadians.

The book is for a public audience, not just academics. Some say that academics shouldn't write for the public because of the risk of over-simplifying complex topics. As I see it, I am a publicly funded academic and it is mostly the public that gives me the opportunity to develop my expertise and to speak freely. I see it as one of my roles—and a very rewarding one—to tell members of the public, as clearly as I can, if I find things in my research that appear to threaten them. Rarely have I seen anything so fitting that description as the China FIPA and, more broadly, the Harper Government's push to lock in an obscure system of foreign investor protection.

The foreign investor protection system of which I speak is called, technically, "investor-state arbitration" or "investor-state dispute settlement." The threat that it poses in the China FIPA and other trade and investment deals is institutional and financial. Basic powers of legislatures and judges are being shifted to multinational companies and the international lawyers who serve them. The shift in power is anti-democratic because it will legally be very difficult for governments to reverse. It is being pursued quickly and unnecessarily by the Harper Government in a few new deals, including the China FIPA and the still-pending Canada-Europe Comprehensive Economic and Trade Agreement (CETA) and U.S.-led Trans-Pacific Partnership (TPP). The reach of investor-state arbitration would be expanded even more by a proposed Europe-U.S. trade deal called the Transatlantic Trade and Investment Partnership (TTIP). These deals would take things far beyond what has happened in more familiar trade agreements, such as the North American Free Trade Agreement (NAFTA).

Why are so many investment treaties—and the confusing acronyms that they create—being rushed through so quickly? I fear it is so people won't have time to find out how much they stand to lose.

At its core, this book is a condemnation of the federal government's negotiation and acceptance of a lopsided investment deal with China. It is certainly not an attack on China or the Chinese people, whose history and achievements I very much respect. If anything, I think China comes out well in this book for besting Canada in the FIPA negotiation and for getting an agreement that fits China's economic strategy. Canada, on the other hand, appears to have accepted a deal that jeopardizes our economy, environment, and sovereignty, all in one go.

I admit that I have written the book from a "patriotic"—to borrow a term used more by my Chinese colleagues and friends than my Canadian ones—perspective. I think that investor-state arbitration is a threat to people in all countries, but am also sympathetic to realistic perspectives on Canada's relationship with China and other powerful countries. For example, Matthew Fisher's perspective: "China does not buy or invest because it likes you. It does so because it is in its national interest and makes economic sense to do so." Or, Charles Burton's: "I just don't think we have the degree of faith in the goodwill of the Chinese side to engage in reciprocal concessions. It seems that most of China's interaction with the West in terms of trade is to serve their own interest." Or, William Watson's: "The Chinese government may not be nearly as fickle as the Canadian media but do we really want to found our economic strategy on the assurance of its everlasting goodwill?"

I have read a lot of investment treaties and as a whole they expose the tough rivalries at the heart of the global economy. Upon careful examination, the China FIPA suggests that Canada can be far too eager to compromise long-term, in the hope of a quick buck now.

Still, my most important message is that the FIPA shows how governments are betraying Canadians and Chinese alike, by pushing hard for the expansion of—in effect—a world supreme pseudo-court whose purpose is to protect the property rights of foreigners, meaning essentially the wealthiest companies and individuals in the world. Absurdly, this institution has been staffed not by judges but by private lawyers, working as for-profit arbitrators, and many of its activities are not even open to the public. Few people in Canada or China know that they are financially backing a costly scheme to insure foreign investors against the general risks of democracy and politics. This fast-expanding system is called investor-state arbitration; the name is a turn-off for a reason. Many who benefit from it don't want you to learn more. In this book, I explain why.

PART 1.

THE TREATY AND THE PITCH

CHAPTER 1.

A PRIME MINISTER BENDS THE KNEE

In 2012, in Beijing's Great Hall of the Peoples, Prime Minister Stephen Harper agreed to a Foreign Investment Promotion and Protection Agreement—or FIPA—with China.

Canada's federal government has concluded twenty-seven FIPAs with other countries, none nearly as big and powerful a country as China. Compared to the other FIPAs, the China FIPA is more one-sided, more secretive, and more enduring. Shocking as it sounds, the FIPA will bind Canada for at least thirty-one years.

In this book, I show how the FIPA is lopsided, how it gives Chinese investors an enclave legal status in Canada, and how its promoters misled Canadians about the deal. In other words, I explain how Canada got sold down the Yangtze.

It began with a compromise on human rights. In 2006, Prime Minister Harper made an official trip to Asia. He was asked by Chinese officials to limit the discussion to trade alone. Harper refused and was denied a meeting with the Chinese president, Hu Jintao. Harper said admirably, "I don't think Canadians want us to sell out important Canadian values. . . . They don't want us to sell out to the almighty dollar."

Five years later, Harper had changed his tune. *Globe and Mail* correspondent Mark MacKinnon called it Harper's Chinese lesson: "Within three years of that 'almighty dollar' comment, Mr. Harper reversed course in his China policy. . . . By 2011, Mr. Harper had buried the human-rights agenda so deeply that he refused to even utter the name of jailed Nobel Peace Prize winner Liu Xiaobo while he was on an official visit to China."

But there was more to Harper's Chinese lesson than a compromise on human rights. In the summer of 2011, the Harper Government moved to concede important Canadian goals and values in a FIPA with China that had been stymied for over a decade. By early 2012, the FIPA was finalized for Canada, long-term.

For China, the FIPA fits a strategy. The strategy is to buy into other countries' resources and extract as much value from them as possible. It is to maximize profits and wages for Chinese companies and workers from the extraction of resources abroad. It is to transfer raw materials to China for processing and to capture foreign technology in order to fuel China's factory of the world. It is to use a strong economy at home to nurture globally competitive companies, and to open up the home economy only after those companies are ready to dominate markets abroad. This is a familiar plan used by powerful countries since the nineteenth century.

For Canada, the purpose is less clear and more of a gamble. Canada may benefit from Chinese investment in Canada, but takes an economically dependent position as mostly a supplier of raw materials to China. The FIPA's terms make it more difficult for Canadians to benefit from value-added activity that comes from the relationship with China. The FIPA also makes it potentially very costly for governments in Canada to change course if things go badly.

Most importantly, the FIPA concedes Canadian priorities for its economy, democracy, and sovereignty. How is this so?

First, the FIPA is economically unequal. Strikingly, it gives a right of market access to Chinese investors, but not to Canadian investors. That is, it requires Canada to open its economy and resources to Chinese companies in general, but lets China keep a closed economy if it chooses to do so. China can also keep favouring its companies at home in areas like intellectual property, approvals, or tax levels, even if doing so hurts a Canadian company in China. Thus, the FIPA is more about giving Chinese investors the freedom to buy what they want in Canada—such as natural resources and infrastructure—than it is about protecting Canadian investors in China.

Second, the FIPA puts a potentially huge price tag on Canadian democracy. It lets Chinese investors decide if any Canadian law will be reviewed outside of Canada's courts, in an exceptionally powerful system of international arbitration that is skewed in favour of foreign investors and very risky for taxpayers. For large multinationals, this new power can be a useful tool to pressure decision-makers behind the scenes, especially when there are hundreds of millions or billions of dollars at stake. Because the FIPA applies to all Chinese investors, whether they are state-owned or not, China itself now has a special status to bring supersized lawsuits against Canada.

Third, the FIPA transforms Canadian sovereignty. It shifts powers from Canadian legislatures, governments, and courts—whenever a Chinese investor wants the shift to happen—to a tribunal of three powerful "arbitrators," who have the supreme authority to order Canada to pay compensation. Ominously, a handful of arbitrators has ordered billions of dollars in compensation against countries in the last few years alone, and the arbitrators themselves earn more fees as more foreign investor lawsuits are brought. Worse, the FIPA makes special allowances for secrecy in these arbitrations. As a result, the federal government can keep a Chinese lawsuit against Canada entirely secret, so long as the government settles the lawsuit before the arbitrators issue their award.

For Canada, many of these aspects of the FIPA were entirely new. Yet, no one outside of the Harper Government could know how much Canada had given away when the FIPA was announced in early 2012. It took seven months for federal officials to release the treaty text, which they finally did in September 2012.

After the FIPA's text was released, some commentators, including me, criticized the FIPA's lopsidedness. We called for a thorough, independent, and public review in Canada before the deal was finalized. As the clock ticked toward expected ratification of the FIPA, a public controversy ensued. Ratification was delayed, but the government never organized a proper review.

Instead, a media blitz to sell the FIPA began in late October 2012, involving the federal government and prominent voices in the media. As usual, some Canadian lawyers who work in investor-state arbitration also pushed for the deal. The media blitz was built on two simple tactics. The first was to smear critics of the FIPA as alarmist, fear-mongering, or xenophobic. The second was to avoid a serious discussion of the treaty's concessions to China and of the Harper Government's reasons, whatever they might be, for the concessions.

As an academic specialist in investment treaties, I watched this debate with a mixture of disappointment and alarm. From what I saw, many Canadians were trying to make sense of a complex deal. Meanwhile, the government, investor-state lawyers, and other promoters ran interference by saying misleading things about what the treaty meant.

Eventually, the Harper Government finalized the FIPA in September 2014. Legally, this step required the government to send a ratification letter to China announcing Canada's consent. Apparently China had given a similar letter to Canada in early 2013 and later pushed Canada to follow suit.

When it came, Canada's ratification was done quietly. The

Harper Government announced it in a short press release on a Friday afternoon. With that, Canada was locked in until 2045.

It is impossible to predict the FIPA's impacts precisely. However, the deal clearly undermines the ability of Canadian voters to change laws and policies in Canada if the change would interfere with the business priorities of a Chinese investor. One can also expect that Canadian taxpayers will have to pay compensation to China, possibly in huge amounts, if Canada loses or settles a dispute with a Chinese company.

Like other investment treaties, the FIPA expands a costly and controversial system to resolve conflicts between foreign investors and countries. For-profit arbitrators are given immense powers to protect foreign investors from virtually any decision by a country. No court has so much power to discipline a sovereign. No one except foreign investors is protected in an international forum that is nearly as powerful.

Since the late 1990s, there has been an explosion of investor lawsuits against countries under investment treaties like the FIPA. The general public is not aware of it, but global law firms certainly are. The biggest beneficiaries of the lawsuits have been very large companies and very wealthy individuals, by which I mean companies that have over USD$1 billion in annual revenue and individuals who have over USD$100 million in net wealth. More than 90 per cent of the money awarded to foreign investors under these treaties appears to have gone to these corporate giants and tycoons.

Of course, the explosion of investor lawsuits has also benefited the lawyers and arbitrators. They have earned billions of dollars in fees over the last decade. Not surprisingly, members of the investor-state legal industry have also promoted the treaties actively, and some of them even stepped up to defend the China FIPA after it became controversial.

Personally, I think the FIPA comes pretty close to a capitulation by Canada, as I explain in detail in part 1 of this book.

Assuming for the moment that I am right about this, why would the prime minister choose to bend the knee so far?

My best guess is that the Harper Government's overriding commitment to oil sands expansion made the government dependent on China to open its markets to Canadian oil and to loosen Chinese purse strings for investment (meaning ownership) in Canada's natural resources. I think China saw the government's vulnerability and played its hand well. With the FIPA, China avoided any enforceable commitments to open its markets or invest in Canada, in the oil sands or anywhere else. On the other hand, China obtained a long-term treaty with highly enforceable obligations that clearly favour China.

It can be depressing to think about Canada being locked into a lopsided deal. However, there are ways to limit the damage and draw out more of the truth about the FIPA. It starts with Canadians informing themselves and each other about the deal and taking what steps they can to respond. With this book, I try to do my part by explaining the FIPA's terms and highlighting its implications. I also explain the significance of investor-state arbitration, and why the deal should have been reviewed more closely before it was locked in. I offer an explanation for why the Harper Government agreed to the FIPA and ideas about what to do next.

Among these ideas, I suggest that governments should establish an independent process to track the FIPA closely. Laws should be enacted to require officials to tell the public about how the FIPA is being used. The federal government must commit to rigorous use of the Investment Canada Act to screen Chinese takeovers of companies in Canada. To safeguard Canadian democracy, no more investment treaties should be allowed with such long lock-in periods. Canada should contribute to reform of investor-state arbitration instead of pushing to expand a system that lacks independence, fairness, openness, and balance. Lastly, I suggest that Canadians have good reason to vote for and support, at all levels of government, whoever they think will take the FIPA's problems seriously.

CHAPTER 2.

PROTECTING CANADIAN INVESTORS, WITH A CATCH

Probably the hottest pitch for the FIPA was the protection it offered for Canadian investors in China.

For example, when the FIPA was signed, the prime minister announced that it would "provide stronger protection for Canadians investing in China." On this, he was right, but only because he fudged the point. "Stronger" protection is not the same as strong. And, it is hard to say the FIPA's protections for Canadian investors are strong.

Undoubtedly, Canadian investors could use strong protection in China. Like other foreign investors, they confront a myriad of laws and rules that sometimes disfavour them. They must often agree to joint ventures with local companies as a condition of entry to the Chinese economy. They risk losing their technology and know-how when intellectual property rights are not enforced. The challenge of running a business in China includes having to deal with an extremely powerful government. A foreign investor who runs afoul of high-level decision-makers may not last long.

That said, it is important to keep in mind that this central-ized power and planning follows from an effective strategy not unique to China. The strategy is to attract foreign investors with the promise of cheap labour, with an eye to capturing their technology. The technology and know-how can then be used to build Chinese companies. The Chinese companies are protected for as long as possible until they can compete globally. To ask China not to favour its own companies, therefore, is really a demand that China retreat from a strategy that has delivered something approaching an economic miracle, at least until now, and that has been exploited by Canadian and other Western companies for their own purposes.

Not surprisingly, China did not pull back from this strategy in the FIPA with Canada. In fact, the FIPA fits China's strategy very well.

For Canadian investors to have strong protections under the FIPA, it is sometimes said they need a "level playing field" with Chinese companies. For the FIPA to deliver this goal, China would have to commit to removing discriminatory laws, regulations, and practices against Canadian companies. It would also have to loosen protectionist restrictions on Canadian access to China's economy. However, the FIPA does neither of these things, not even a little.

The FIPA does give other kinds of protections to Canadian investors. Those protections turn on a new right of access to investor-state arbitration, if there is a dispute about a Canadian investor's treatment by Chinese officials. That is, Canadian companies can bring a claim to a tribunal, outside China's courts, and get a compensation order against China if the tribunal decides in their favour.

Like other investment treaties, the FIPA gives the investor-state arbitrators a lot of discretion to order compensation, if they think that a Canadian investor has not received "fair and equitable treatment" or "full protection and security" or has had its assets expropriated in direct or indirect ways. Similarly, compensation can be ordered if a Canadian investor has been blocked from transferring money out of the country or has been required to use Chinese suppliers in its business (although Canadian investors would presumably want to take advantage of China's cheaper labour anyway).

What this means in any particular dispute depends on a lot of things. Obviously, one has to ask, what are the facts? As importantly, who is the arbitrator and is he (there are few women) a hawk or a sheep when it comes to protecting foreign investors? Even so, the ability of Canadian investors to go to arbitration will give some of them an option that was not available before the FIPA, even if the FIPA does not deliver "strong" protection because of various catches.

What are these catches? Here are a few.

First, a savvy Chinese official may be aware that the FIPA lets China keep discriminating against Canadian investors, based on any existing law, rule, or practice in China. If the official wanted to harm a Canadian business in China, he or she could avoid more obvious kinds of mistreatment and instead apply discriminatory rules—such as a requirement for the Canadian business to get special approvals or pay higher fees that don't apply to Chinese companies—without violating the FIPA.

I suppose the question is, how much does the federal government think Chinese officials will know about what the FIPA allows?

Second, even if a Canadian investor has a strong argument under the FIPA, it is a long and costly struggle to mount an arbitration against a power like China. Worse, doing so may raise the ire of the Chinese government, which appears much more able than a government in Canada to single out and punish particular companies who fall into disfavour because they invoked the FIPA.

There is a third downer for Canadian investors. For the FIPA's promoters, it was an inconvenient fact that China has never been ordered to pay compensation to a foreign investor in a known case under any investment treaty. Indeed, China has virtually never been sued by foreign investors, despite having signed more investment treaties than almost any country.

On the other hand, Canada has about thirty investment treaties and has been sued dozens of times under one of them, NAFTA. Indeed, Canada has been sued more often than all but four countries *in the world* and has had to pay compensation in a significant number of cases. So, it may be that a series of intrepid Canadian companies will one day fight China and win under the FIPA. Lawyers who make their fortunes under investment treaties would have us believe that, but I am not holding my breath.

The last catch is the most important one: the FIPA's protections for foreign investors cut both ways. Chinese investors get legal protections too, from whatever a Canadian legislature, government, or court might do to them. They have the same access to a powerful arbitration tribunal, outside of the courts, and they can use this power to attack any law, policy, or other decision in Canada.

For these reasons, the prime minister was right to avoid saying that Canadian investors get "strong" protections under the FIPA. And, even if a Canadian investor one day does what no foreign investor ever has—sue China and win—it will still be the case, as I discuss in the next few chapters, that Canada as a country has given up far too much in exchange for this "win" for Canadian investors in China.

CHAPTER 3.

CHINA CAN KEEP ITS DISCRIMINATORY LAWS

I mentioned that the FIPA lets China keep all of its existing laws, rules, and practices that allow for discrimination against foreign investors in favour of domestic companies. Canada keeps the same right, but appears to have far fewer "existing" discriminatory measures to start with. Therefore, while the FIPA looks like it applies equally to Canada and China in this respect, in fact, it favours China.

I elaborate on this lopsided effect of the FIPA in detail in this chapter because it so obviously contradicts claims by the FIPA's promoters. For example, when he announced the FIPA in February 2012, Prime Minister Harper said that the deal would protect Canadian investors from discrimination in China: "This agreement is an historic step forward. . . . What a Foreign Investment Promotion and Protection Agreement does is *it ensures non-discriminatory treatment* in terms of national firms in application of the law (emphasis mine)."

On this point, it appears that Harper was misinformed. The FIPA does not "ensure" non-discriminatory treatment of Canadian companies in China because it carves out and thus preserves all of China's existing discriminatory measures, as they affect all Canadian investors going forward. Yet, at the time Harper made his declaration about the FIPA, no one could fact-check the claim because the FIPA's text was not publicly available.

Foreign businesses sometimes complain that they suffer from unfair discrimination in China. They report that they are subject to permits when Chinese companies are not. They may face higher tax rates than Chinese competitors. They are confronted with a maze of unwritten rules and find it hard to know how to meet the requirements. Rules may change at the discretion of officials. The rule of law, as it is understood in Canada, does not exist.

Investment treaties are often said to address these issues. How is it then that the FIPA could allow a country that commonly uses discriminatory measures as part of its economic strategy—by giving advantages to domestic companies that are not available to foreign companies—to keep all of those discriminatory measures in place?

The FIPA's endorsement of this situation is not easy to see. The treaty does not clearly say for example that China can continue discriminating against Canadian investors. Even so, the legal effect is precisely the same, based on a provision buried in Article 8(2)(a) of the treaty. The provision in question says simply, "Articles 5, 6 and 7 do not apply to: . . . any existing non-conforming measures maintained within the territory of a Contracting Party." The effect of this provision is to exempt any existing "measures"—meaning any law, regulation, policy, or practice—that are discriminatory according to the FIPA's rules (Articles 5 and 6) which would otherwise disallow discrimination against a foreign investor. Thus, Canada and China can keep discriminating in favour of each country's own companies and against the other's, so long as the discriminatory power existed at the time of the FIPA.

Some other investment treaties let countries keep some of their discriminatory measures, such as limits on the ownership of oceanfront land or certain kinds of subsidies. Creating these carve-outs can be a way to facilitate the bigger deal. However, the China FIPA goes much further than most deals by exempting *all* existing discriminatory measures, at all levels of government.

Most importantly, in practice the FIPA gives this green light to continued discrimination in a lopsided way. China likely has far more existing discriminatory practices than Canada. Also, in China, these practices may be more opaque and thus harder for Canadian investors to identify as "existing" at the time of the treaty.

To illustrate, based on a survey of its members, the US-China Business Council in 2013 made this report on doing business in China:

> Respondents most frequently claimed to have experienced protectionism in licensing and regulatory approvals, while also noting discriminatory enforcement and preferential policies favoring domestic Chinese companies in many forms.
>
> Fundamentally, there continues to be a significant difference in how foreign companies are treated, both formally and informally, versus their domestic Chinese counterparts. As one respondent noted, "As long as the term 'foreign-invested company' exists [in Chinese policies and regulations], the competition will not be very fair and the discrimination will exist in some way."

According to the Business Council's report, 61 per cent of foreign businesses in China had challenges with administrative licensing, 49 per cent saw tighter enforcement of rules for foreign companies than Chinese companies, and 33 per cent reported laws or regulations that specified differential treatment for domestic competitors. Remarkably, under the FIPA, China can keep discriminating against Canadian companies in all of these ways.

Worse (for Canada), the FIPA requires Canada and China to

lock in each other's approach and to not become more discriminatory in the future. Obviously, this hamstrings Canada more than China if Canada is less discriminatory now. China can keep an uneven playing field for Canadian companies, while Canada must maintain a relatively even-handed approach for Chinese companies in Canada.

About a year after the FIPA was announced, a Canadian trade official was questioned about the deal in a legal challenge to the deal. The official indirectly confirmed the problem for Canada:

> [Y]ou have to look at the two economies as they exist at the time that the treaty comes into force. And when you look at the Canadian economy, it's relatively open, in terms of protectionist measures and discriminatory measures. You look at the Chinese economy, and they are more protectionist and they do have rules in place that allow them to discriminate in favour of Chinese investment....
>
> So . . . at the time that this comes into force, you will have a relatively open Canadian economy locked in place, in terms of its ability to discriminate, and a less open, more closed [Chinese] economy locked in place at the time it comes into force.

China's interest in keeping its ability to discriminate and thus to protect its economy is not surprising. China is doing what other countries did to industrialize. In the late 1800s, the U.S and Germany followed similar practices to compete with Great Britain and, from the 1950s, Japan, South Korea, Singapore, and Taiwan used the same strategy to develop their economies.

Many countries champion free markets after their companies have grown and can succeed globally. In the FIPA, oddly, Canada has opened the door to China's companies, even if China does not return the favour. In turn, our Canadian small and medium companies are vulnerable to takeover by larger foreign competitors, while Canadian companies are frustrated by discriminatory treatment abroad.

The only defence I saw to the FIPA's cementing of an uneven playing field came from media commentator Andrew Coyne in the *National Post*. After dismissing concerns about the FIPA's non-reciprocity as "at best half-issues," Coyne said: "It's probably true, for example, that we did not extract fully reciprocal terms from China. So what? The value of any such deal lies in persuading us to remove protectionist restrictions in our own market; anything we get from the other side is gravy."

So, according to Coyne, the FIPA will always have value because it will make it costly for governments in Canada to stop Chinese takeovers of Canadian firms, even if the government is responding in kind to Chinese protectionism or discrimination. Taken to its logical conclusion, this argument would seem to mean that Canadians should not have expected any commitments at all from China in the FIPA.

At best, Coyne's position is naive. Even if having an open economy always works better than a selectively closed one—which is doubtful—why should Canada give up the latter option unilaterally, for decades? Why not pursue the benefits of an open economy simply by using Canadian laws to create one, without taking on risky obligations to China?

Coyne's approach entails a strange penitence from Canadians. We must take on potentially crippling costs, to protect us from ourselves. We must make it hard for Canadians ever to change their minds.

This is a peculiar position for Coyne to take, since he has presented himself as a champion of the role of Parliament. In a parliamentary democracy, shouldn't voters be able to change the government, and the government to change the policies, without facing impossibly costly obligations that were locked in by an earlier government?

On the contrary, Coyne seems to be saying, Canadians should be blocked from responding democratically, even if China keeps a closed economy and discriminatory policies and even if this bankrupts Canadian companies and costs Canada dearly. In the long run, we are perhaps to believe, greater Canadian companies will emerge from the ashes stronger than their competitors. I worry, as the economist John Maynard Keynes once said, that in the long run we are all dead.

With the FIPA, the Harper Government has forced Canadians to swallow a bitter pill. It endorsed a deal that gives China a sharp whip with which to sting Canadians for doing things that China itself has a legal right to keep doing with impunity. In a world of tough economic competition, that giveaway alone made the FIPA a bad deal.

CHAPTER 4.

CANADA PLAYS THE CAPITAL-IMPORTING LOSER

The main purpose of investment treaties is to give new rights and protections to foreign investors. On the other hand, the treaties do not create any actionable responsibilities for foreign investors.

Indeed, investment treaties arguably protect foreign investors more powerfully than any other kind of treaty protects anyone else. For example, because they allow for investor-state arbitration, investment treaties are much more powerful than all of the treaties whose purpose is to fight corruption, protect public health, or defend human rights. They are also vastly more powerful than the handful of agreements that put (voluntary) obligations on multinational companies. Put differently, international law is weak, except when it comes to protecting foreign investment and trade.

This lopsided situation came about mainly because the rich countries that originally pushed investment treaties tended to dominate the countries with whom they signed them. In the 1960s and 1970s, the former European empires used the treaties to keep their big companies safer in Asia and Africa, after the colonies gained their independence.

Basically, the treaties were legal weapons to substitute for or complement other kinds of intervention, such as coups and invasions. The United States put out an especially broad version of the treaties in the 1980s, and Canada followed suit in the 1990s, starting with a handful of FIPAs with Eastern bloc countries transitioning to a market economy.

Why would the United States and European former colonial powers want the treaties to be so favourable to foreign investors, compared to legislatures and governments? One important reason is that, when they wrote the first treaties in the 1960s and 1970s, these countries were unlikely even to be subject to the rules. For example, it was easy for Dutch officials to push an aggressive investor protection deal with Indonesia—a former Dutch colony—when Indonesians did not own major assets in the Netherlands.

On the other hand, with one significant exception, Western countries did not sign investment treaties with each other. As a result, they avoided the risk of massive liability under the treaties. The one exception was Canada, which lamely consented to investor-state arbitration with the United States in NAFTA, and has now done so again with China. Thus, Canada is presently consolidating the dubious honour it has held since the 1990s of being the only Western developed country whose foreign-owned economy is heavily subject to investor-state arbitration.

I shall backtrack a little. In Canada's other FIPAs—all of them concluded in the last twenty-five years—Canada has played the role of the "safe country." This is because all of the FIPAs, before the one with China, were with countries whose investors did not own much in Canada. As such, there was never a serious risk of Canada being sued and constrained under FIPAs.

On the other hand, there were often big Canadian investments—especially by resource companies or banks—in the other FIPA country. As a result, Canada's FIPAs were in effect one-sided in favour of Canada and against an economically weaker country in Africa, Asia, Latin America, or Eastern Europe.

The big exception for Canada was NAFTA. In NAFTA, in the early 1990s, the federal government accepted an investment chapter that allowed for investor-state arbitration as part of a trade agreement with the United States. Canada was the loser in agreeing to the NAFTA investment chapter because U.S. investors owned more assets in Canada than vice versa. The investor-state arbitration mechanism also appeared to favour the U.S. in other ways. For instance, it gave default arbitrator appointment powers to officials at the World Bank in Washington, D.C. Because the World Bank was established after the Second World War, it operates in the political orbit of the U.S. more than any other country.

Indeed, one could say that, when NAFTA came into force in 1994, Canada gave up a slice of its judicial sovereignty—by agreeing to investor-state arbitration in a situation where Canada was likely to be sued—for the first time since Canada's sovereignty was made whole, in 1982, when Canada's constitution was repatriated. That is, the time between 1982 and 1994 was arguably the high water mark of Canadian sovereignty. In that period, (1) the Supreme Court of Canada had final and effective authority over any dispute, between a private party in Canada and the state, over the legal boundaries of Canadian sovereignty, and (2) Parliament and provincial legislatures were the supreme lawmakers, subject only to the supreme court's decisions and the Canadian constitution.

That isn't true anymore. Under NAFTA and the China FIPA, U.S. and Chinese investors can now decide to give a few lawyers—sitting as arbitrators—the ultimate authority to decide what a Canadian legislature, government, or court can do in law, and what happens when Canada is found to have violated the law. The arbitrators' authority is meaningful, and it extends in principle over much of the Canadian economy, because of the size of U.S. and Chinese assets in Canada. This change to Canada's formal sovereignty is an important development.

In NAFTA's case, but not the FIPA's, the federal government could defend its decision to accept investor-state arbitration while Canada was in the weaker position relative to the United States. It could do so by pointing to other benefits of the trade deal, which weighed against Canada's concessions in NAFTA's investment chapter. At least, the debate over NAFTA's costs and benefits goes beyond NAFTA's investment chapter to include its chapters on other economic issues.

Also, Canada agreed to NAFTA before the explosion of investor-state arbitration began. This explosion of foreign investor lawsuits started only in the late 1990s (triggered largely by NAFTA's entry into force in 1994). Thus, the federal government's early acceptance of investor-state arbitration came before anyone could really say what it would entail.

The China FIPA is different. It is not part of a larger trade agreement and deals only with foreign investment. Unlike in NAFTA, Canada did not get any new access to China's market for exports of Canadian goods, in exchange for Canada's concessions on investment. Canada simply accepted powerful protections for foreign investors, in a situation where Chinese investors own more assets in Canada than the other way around.

When the FIPA was signed, Chinese assets in Canada outstripped Canadian assets in China by about three to one. Thus, one could say loosely that Canada took on about triple the risk that China did. Until the China FIPA, Canada had never before agreed to a FIPA while Canada was in the capital-importing position and the host to large amounts of assets owned by investors from the other country.

Also, the value of Chinese assets in Canada appears likely to grow much faster than Canadian assets in China. For example, Chinese investment in Canada rose from about CDN$334 million a year (in the period between 2001 and 2005) to CDN$10.7 billion a year (between 2008 and 2012). If that growth rate continues, Chinese assets in Canada will be worth hundreds of billions of dollars by 2020. At that point, they will have outstripped Canadian investments in China—extrapolated on the same basis—by about 26 to 1. By the mid-2020s, Chinese assets in Canada would be worth more than U.S. assets in Canada, also extrapolated on the same basis. This potentially far-reaching penetration of Canada's economy would come about one quarter of the way through the FIPA's minimum lifespan.

Of course, these predictions are only informed guesses. A lot can happen to affect investment flows, all the more so when they can be guided by a centralized decision-maker like the Chinese government. Yet, Canadian officials themselves have signalled their expectation of major growth in Chinese ownership of assets in Canada, especially in the resource sector. For example, in debates about the FIPA, Canadian trade officials reported in 2012 that China's outflows of investment may reach USD$1 trillion globally by 2020. This compared with USD$64 billion in 2011. If a significant share of China's new outflows came to Canada, this would transform Chinese ownership of the Canadian economy.

Also, under the FIPA, the Harper Government gave Chinese investors a general right to buy assets in Canada, without insisting on a similar right for Canadian investors in China. Why? As I discuss in chapters 6 and 41 of this book, it seems likely that the government was actually expecting a Chinese buy-up of assets in Canada and that the FIPA's lopsidedness on this issue was part of the deal.

On the other hand, the expectation of more Chinese investment in Canada was contradicted by other events. In 2012, before the FIPA was finalized, the Harper Government said that it would limit Chinese state-owned companies from buying majority stakes in more companies in the oil sands and perhaps elsewhere in the economy. The policy suggested that Chinese investment in Canada may not be allowed to reach U.S. levels.

At any rate, Canada clearly is the loser under the China FIPA, in the sense that the benefits of investor protection in an investment treaty go mostly to the country whose nationals have more investments covered by the treaty.

Incidentally, the Harper Government was apparently aware of this disparity when it agreed to the FIPA in early 2012. In July 2011, according to the *Vancouver Sun*, Foreign Affairs Minister John Baird said that in the previous five years Canadian investment in China had gone up by 167 per cent. Meanwhile, he said, Chinese investment in Canada had gone up by 1,400 per cent. I doubt that Baird and other Harper Cabinet members made the mistake of assuming that the FIPA would reverse this trend. More likely, they expected the FIPA to open the door to more Chinese ownership in Canada.

What risks and constraints does Chinese ownership create for Canadians, under the FIPA?

Think first of Canadian companies in Canada. They are disadvantaged relative to Chinese companies because they cannot go to a powerful outside tribunal, and use the threat of doing so, to lobby Canadian governments behind the scenes. To have the same leverage, a Canadian company would need to sell a share of its ownership to a Chinese investor. Some resource companies in Canada have done so already. The Canadian companies that do not will be left on an uneven playing field in their own country. In this way, the FIPA actually creates an incentive for big Canadian companies to link up with Chinese investors.

A similar disadvantage affects anyone else in Canada who has interests that may conflict with a Chinese investor. There are a lot of people in that group. Canadian workers may be squeezed by imported Chinese labour. Canadian companies may lose out in bids where a larger Chinese firm opts instead for Chinese suppliers. Canadian municipalities may come under pressure from Chinese developers. Canadians in general may suffer from environmental damage that is more risky for a government to regulate because it comes from a Chinese source.

All of these groups of Canadians may have reason to complain about the business activities of a Chinese investor. The FIPA leaves fewer options for governments in Canada to respond. And, if these groups are unhappy with how a government responds to their concerns, they must settle for Canada's courts. Meanwhile, Chinese investors can go to Canadian courts, or they can go to a FIPA tribunal whose overriding purpose is to protect them. That can be a powerful advantage.

What about Canadian taxpayers?

Under the FIPA, Canadian taxpayers assume new risks of financial liability to foreign investors. If FIPA arbitrators decide that a country treated an investor unfairly, the country would usually be ordered to pay compensation. Depending on the value of the affected assets, the compensation can run to hundreds of millions or even billions of dollars. If the government does not pay, the country's assets can be seized abroad to make good on the award.

If we take a step back and look at the FIPA, it is basically a taxpayer subsidy for foreign investors and a windfall for investor-state lawyers. Foreign investors get more financial assurance against the risk that a legislative, government, or court in Canada will make a decision that disrupts their business plans. The lawyers get lucrative fees from the new opportunities for litigation. All of these costs are underwritten by the public because foreign investors would rarely (if ever) bring FIPA claims, without some prospect that the targeted country will have to pay compensation.

Thus, the subsidy for foreign investors is financial because taxpayers pay for their country to defend the lawsuits and pay the awards. It is also administrative and political because a responsible government now has to vet its decisions in order to manage the new financial risk of the FIPA. Whenever the FIPA causes a government to change its decisions, the FIPA has hurt everyone who is disadvantaged by the change. It is difficult to evaluate these effects on taxpayers and citizens from outside of government. Yet, treaties like the FIPA certainly have such effects, because they always involve some cost to the public and they sometimes lead to changes by governments that hurt others in order to help a foreign investor. The big unknowns are, how often and how much do these things happen?

Similarly, the FIPA waters down the rights of Canadian voters by limiting what elected governments can do, in an exceptionally powerful way. More precisely, the FIPA is an obscure back-door way for one government to make firm commitments on behalf of future governments in Canada, for decades to come. In Canadian law (based on the English common law), there is a democratic principle called the no-fettering rule that bars one elected government from making commitments to bind another. However, this principle does not exist in international law and the FIPA—as an international agreement—cannot be trumped by the laws of Canada or China. Thus, because of their uniquely powerful constraints, treaties like the FIPA undermine Canadian democracy.

One might say, we could vote the bums out, except they've fixed the toilet so it can't be flushed.

In response to these concerns, those who pushed the FIPA in Canada sometimes pointed out that all treaties limit voters' choices because all treaties require one country to make commitments to another. That is right in principle, but deceptive in practice. The crux of it is that investment treaties put far more effective constraints on countries than other treaties do. In Canada's case, the only real comparison is the World Trade

Organization (WTO). Even then, WTO agreements do not impose the same degree of constraint as investment treaties because, at the WTO, foreign investors cannot bring one-way lawsuits against countries and because countries do not face a risk of unavoidable and massive financial liability.

A big part of the story of investment treaties is the extraordinary degree to which they put countries and their people in a straightjacket, compared to other treaties. With that in mind, in the final chapter of this book I suggest ways to stop governments from committing Canada to treaties with long lock-in periods, as a defence of Canadian democracy. Unfortunately, the Harper Government has already used the China FIPA to commit our country, long-term, to this undemocratic arrangement with China.

In these ways, Canada plays the loser under the FIPA. Canadians assume more of the risk and constraints because Chinese companies own more in Canada, making Canada the capital-importer in the relationship. By implication, the FIPA's negative impacts on taxpayers and voters, companies and workers, fall more heavily on Canadians.

CHAPTER 5.

THE MAGICAL FIPA: ATTRACTING CHINESE INVESTMENT WITHOUT ANY ENVIRONMENTAL IMPACT!

Promoters of the China FIPA sometimes justified its risks for Canada as a necessary evil to attract more Chinese investment to Canada's economy. For example, Andrew Coyne said: "As for the complaint that we should not be entering into such a deal because the Chinese invest so much more in Canada than we do there, it is quite frankly bizarre. . . . It is the point of the agreement to bring in more."

Coyne's dismissal of the disparity in the investment flows between Canada and China is based on a convenient claim about investment treaties that is familiar to researchers in the field. The claim is that the treaties encourage investment in capital-importing countries, rather than simply protecting the assets of stronger countries and multinational companies. Promoters of the treaties would have you believe the treaties are a win-win situation.

The first problem with this claim is that, for a long time, it was never based on actual evidence. The second problem is that, as the available evidence was tested over the past decade or so, it proved very hard to confirm the claim.

Let's assume for a moment that more Chinese ownership of Canada's economy is always a good thing, for whatever reason. It may be that Chinese companies would not invest in Canada without the FIPA in place. On the other hand, it may be that they would invest, regardless of the FIPA. As researchers, we do not know whether investment treaties actually make a significant difference in foreign investment decisions. The research on this issue is mixed and plagued by limitations in the data on cross-border investment flows. However, it appears that most companies decide where to invest without considering investment treaties much, if at all.

What about the China FIPA? Surely, the federal government would not lock Canada into a long-term treaty, with major concessions to China, while flying blind on whether the treaty would deliver on, as Coyne put it, "the point of the agreement."

Sadly, no serious Canadian research of this sort exists on the China FIPA or any other FIPA. The federal government has not done it, at least publicly. Instead, the government has simply asserted that FIPAs encourage investment and (even more dubiously) jobs and growth. Its policy of giving up Canada's sovereignty—at least on this rationale—has been remarkably evidence-free.

Why might the federal government want to avoid proper research on whether FIPAs encourage investment? It seems to me that, in an evidence vacuum, a government is more able to assert or deny links between FIPAs and investment, according to its spin goals. The Harper Government played the spin game repeatedly with the China FIPA. For example, when the FIPA was signed, the Prime Minister's Office declared,

> the Canada-China FIPA *will facilitate* investment flows, contributing to job creation and economic growth in Canada (emphasis mine).

Meanwhile, the federal government's environmental assessment of the China FIPA—by federal trade officials—said, new flows of investment from China into Canada (or Canada into China) *cannot be directly attributed to* the presence of a FIPA (emphasis mine).

As I discuss in further detail below, on the basis of the latter claim, the government's environmental assessment of the China FIPA actually denied—ridiculously—that the FIPA would have any environmental impact at all in Canada.

Which claim should we believe: the one that the FIPA will contribute to more Chinese investment, or the one that it won't? Both came from the federal government. Each contradicted the other.

I would say that neither had any value. Both were just self-serving assertions. The government could pretend that the FIPA did not carry an environmental cost, while the Prime Minister's Office was trumpeting the deal's assumed benefits. It was the magical FIPA that would attract Chinese investment, without any environmental impact.

It is especially telling that the government, in its environmental assessment of the China FIPA, discounted *entirely* the possibility of environmental impacts of new Chinese investment in Canada. This discounting was premised on the government's assumption that there was not enough proof of a causal relationship between the FIPA and any new Chinese investment. According to the environmental assessment,

> As new flows of investment from China into Canada (or Canada into China) cannot be directly attributed to the presence of a FIPA, there can be no causal relationship found between the implementation of such a treaty and environmental impacts in Canada. It is for this reason that the claim made in the Initial [environmental assessment], that no significant environmental impacts are expected based on the introduction of a Canada-China FIPA, is upheld.

By taking this narrow approach to causation, the government

neatly avoided the ways in which the China FIPA clearly does affect environmental decision-making in Canada. For example, the government ignored how the FIPA's new rights for Chinese investors can be used to pressure governments against enforcing or tightening Canadian environmental laws.

The discounting of environmental impacts was doubly silly because governments in Canada (and other countries) had already pulled back from environmental decisions, after getting sued by foreign investors under treaties like the FIPA. Any careful assessment would have looked at all the past foreign investor lawsuits that involved a country's decisions related to health or the environment.

To illustrate just how frequently investment treaties have been used to attack health and environmental decisions, as part of a public comment process for the FIPA's environmental assessment, I sent the federal government a list of foreign investor lawsuits that appeared to have involved a country's decisions in matters of health or the environment. The sheer length of the list of cases involving such decisions pointed to the importance of a thorough review of possible environmental impacts from the China FIPA: *Aguas del Tunari v. Bolivia, AIG Capital v. Kazakhstan, Andre v. Canada, AWG v. Argentina, Azurix v. Argentina, Baird v. United States, Bayview Irrigation v. Mexico, Bishop v. Canada, Biwater Gauff v. Tanzania, Burlington Resources v. Ecuador, CCFT v. United States, CGE/ Vivendi v. Argentina No 1, CGE/ Vivendi v. Argentina No 2, Chemtura v. Canada, Chevron v. Ecuador No 1, Chevron v. Ecuador No 2, Clayton/ Bilcon v. Canada, Commerce Group v. El Salvador, Dow v. Canada, Ethyl v. Canada, Frank v. Mexico, Gallo v. Canada, Glamis Gold v. United States, Grand River v. United States, Greiner v. Canada, Howard/ Centurion Health v. Canada, Kenex v. United States, Lucchetti v. Peru, Metalclad v. Mexico, Methanex v. United States, Pacific Rim v. El Salvador, Philip Morris v. Australia, Philip Morris v. Uruguay, Plama v. Bulgaria, SD Myers v. Canada, Signa v. Canada, Suez & InterAguas v. Argentina, Suez & Vivendi v.*

Argentina, Tecmed v. Mexico, Vattenfall v. Germany No 1, Vattenfall v. Germany No 2. Remarkably, the government's environmental assessment did not even mention, let alone evaluate, any of these cases.

Simply, both the environmental assessment and the prime minister's statement on the FIPA should be understood as spin devices. They do not help anyone to understand the FIPA and its implications.

As an aside, the federal government has also avoided the environmental impacts of other FIPAs. Usually, it could do this by turning a blind eye to any environmental impacts that come from Canadian investment in other countries. For example, in its environmental assessment of Canada's FIPA with Peru, the federal government looked at potential environmental impacts of investment from Peru to Canada, but not from Canada to Peru. Thus, any environmental impacts from activities of Canadian investors in Peru—such as Canadian mining companies—were ignored. And, lo and behold, Peruvian investors did not own much in Canada, so it was also easy to say that the Peru FIPA would have no environmental impact.

The China FIPA posed a challenge for this charade. For the first time under any of Canada's FIPAs, the other country's investors owned a lot of assets in Canada. So, to deny any environmental impact from the China FIPA, the government needed to manipulate the assumptions in a different way. Evidently, it chose to claim that there was no direct causal connection between the FIPA and new Chinese investment in Canada, meaning there were no proven environmental impacts.

With creative accounting like that, it would be better if the government didn't do environmental assessments of FIPAs. It would save a few trees, at least.

As for the government's flip-side claim—that the FIPA will

attract Chinese investment to Canada—this also avoided deeper questions. What will more Chinese investment mean for Canada? Will it create jobs or displace them? Will it deliver an overall benefit, after accounting for the real environmental costs? Even if the FIPA does promote Chinese investment, obviously one should not assume that such investment will be good for Canada.

By itself, the word "investment" has positive connotations. It conjures up the idea of people and companies committing money, talent, and energy to make money and improve the world in some way. However, as it is defined in Article 1 of the FIPA, the word "investment" has a different and much broader meaning. The FIPA's definition of investment includes shares, stocks, bonds, and loans. It includes intellectual property rights and "any other tangible or intangible . . . property and related property rights." Somewhat ominously, for Canada, it includes Chinese investors' "concessions to search for and extract oil and other natural resources."

By including such a wide array of activities and assets in the concept of "investment," the FIPA reduces that concept to mere ownership, with no requirement that the ownership involve any actual risk to the owner or any commitment of capital. So, the FIPA may encourage investment. But it will do so in the sense of ownership of assets, and not necessarily because that ownership actually contributes to jobs, growth, or anything else Canadians might want.

With this in mind, the FIPA is more accurately called a Foreign Ownership Protection Agreement or, more specifically, An Unequal Agreement to Open Canada's Economy to Chinese Ownership.

Alternatively, if one were to focus on the financial transfers that have taken place so far under these types of treaties, then the FIPA would be called an Agreement to Transfer Public Funds to Foreign Companies, Lawyers, and Arbitrators. With a name like that, I wonder if the FIPA would still have made it past the federal Cabinet.

The breadth of the FIPA's coverage of owned assets means that Canada will be more on the hook, if its decision-makers do something that a Chinese owner of assets—and two of three arbitrators on a FIPA tribunal—condemn.

The FIPA will be most risky when the Chinese owner's assets are worth a lot of money. In those situations, the pressure on governments to not upset a Chinese owner will be considerable. If a government were to go ahead with a decision opposed by a Chinese investor, it would have to account for the risk of a potentially very large and unavoidable cost down the road.

Why do I say the future cost would be unavoidable? The special design of investor-state arbitration means that countries do not get an opportunity to avoid having to pay compensation to a foreign investor, after they have been found by the arbitrators to have done something wrong. This risk is especially challenging for governments to manage because the treaties' rights for foreign investors are typically vague and open-ended.

As a result, the FIPA is especially dangerous for Canada in the case of Chinese assets worth billions of dollars, such as in the resource sector. The problem is not that Chinese companies might be too big to fail. It's that the FIPA makes the big ones too risky to regulate.

CHAPTER 6.

MARKET ACCESS FOR CHINESE INVESTORS, BUT NOT FOR CANADIAN INVESTORS

The FIPA, on its terms, is clearly more about opening Canada's resources to Chinese investors than it is about encouraging investment flows between the two countries. I say this because the FIPA obliges Canada, but not China, to open its economy to the other country's investors. A concession like that is so extremely rare (if not entirely unique) in investment treaties, I was astonished that Canada agreed to it. I stress that it was a huge concession for the Harper Government to accept such inequality of treatment under the deal.

More technically, Chinese companies have a general right in the FIPA to buy into Canada's economy, which is then subject to limitations in some cases. On the other hand, Canadian investors have no general right to buy into China's economy and, even if they did have that right, the FIPA would subject it to more limitations than in the case of Chinese investors in Canada.

No other investment treaty of Canada's allows market access by one side, but not the other. I have never come across another investment treaty that is lopsided in this way.

Many investment treaties require countries to provide each other's investors with a reciprocal right of market access to their economy. The right allows foreign investors to buy what they want, as long as the existing owners are willing to sell. The right often has limitations, so countries can protect key parts of the economy. However, as a general right, it allows foreign investors to enter the country in any area not specifically carved out of their right of market access.

On the other hand, a lot of investment treaties do not provide for market access at all. They do not require either country to open its economy. They allow both countries to continue to decide whether to open up, case by case, and then they give powerful protections to the foreign investors that are admitted.

Historically, the United States has usually insisted on market access in its investment treaties—albeit with carve-outs for large areas of the U.S. economy—and the Western European powers have not. Since NAFTA, Canada favoured the U.S. approach. Which approach is better? This leads to a debate about the expected costs and benefits of foreign investment, when measured against a country's economic strategy. In general, countries that have a more developed economy, and companies that are more able to compete globally, tend to want market access commitments.

The striking thing about the China FIPA is that it gives market access to China's investors, but not Canada's. In thousands of other investment treaties, foreign investors from both countries get a right of market access or neither gets it. Either way, the rules are reciprocal. Considering this context, the approach to market access in the China FIPA heavily favours China.

This inequality of market access in the FIPA is hard to find in the FIPA's text. Indeed, it is buried in so many layers of legalese, I suspect it might have been designed to mask

Canada's giveaway. For those who are interested in the details, I explain them next. It is heavy going, so feel free to skip ahead.

The China FIPA's inequality of market access comes from the interaction of the deal's different rules on non-discrimination. There are two key provisions.

The first, called the national treatment provision, requires Canada and China to treat each other's investors no worse than *its own* investors. Each country can favour foreign companies and discriminate against their own companies, but neither can disfavour foreign companies unless the treaty carves out its right to do so.

Investment treaties almost always have a rule of national treatment that applies to foreign investments *after* they are established in a country. This is partly what makes the broad carve-out in the China FIPA for existing discriminatory measures very significant. This broad carve-out in the FIPA means that, even after being allowed market access in China, Canadian investors still will not receive protection from many forms of discrimination.

Less typically, investment treaties have a rule of national treatment that applies to foreign investors *before* they are established in a country. In Canada's case, only some treaties—including NAFTA, a few other trade agreements, and about a dozen FIPAs—provide for national treatment at the pre-establishment stage of a foreign investment. This way of applying national treatment is the usual way for investment treaties to give a general right of market access to foreign investors.

For its part, the China FIPA has a rule of national treatment, but that rule does not apply at the pre-establishment stage; it applies after, not before, a foreign investor is admitted to the country. One can see this in the definition of the FIPA's national treatment rule (Article 6 of the FIPA). For both Canada and China, the rule does not apply to an investment's "establishment" and "acquisition." Rather, the rule is limited to the investment's "expansion, management, conduct, operation and sale or other disposition." As a result, no market access is given to foreign investors in the usual way, based on national treatment.

However, there is a second provision on non-discrimination in investment treaties. It is called the most-favoured-nation (MFN) treatment provision. Basically, MFN treatment creates a rule against a country giving a better deal to one country's foreign investors than another country's. According to this rule, Canada and China have to treat each other's investors at least as favourably as they treat investors from third countries.

MFN treatment is an extremely complex obligation whose application has bedevilled lawyers and led to conflicting decisions by arbitrators on important issues. For present purposes, the key and fairly basic point is that MFN treatment—like national treatment—usually applies in investment treaties only at the post-establishment stage, after a foreign investor has been admitted to a country. Sometimes, it also applies at the pre-establishment stage. Canada, in its investment treaties, has taken both approaches to MFN treatment.

If you're still reading this technical background, please bear with me. We're getting to the punch line.

Remarkably, in the China FIPA, MFN treatment *does* extend to the pre-establishment stage of foreign investment. Thus, unlike for the FIPA's national treatment rule, the deal requires Canada and China to give each other's investors no less favourable treatment than investors from third countries, at the establishment and acquisition stages of investment. Put differently, the FIPA gives foreign investors a general right of market access *only if* Canada or China has otherwise given that right to investors from another country.

This complicated set-up is unique for Canada's investment treaties, none of which extends MFN treatment to the pre-establishment stage without doing the same for national treatment. Indeed, I have never come across any investment treaty that takes this approach to its rules on non-discrimination. I would guess that the China FIPA is the only investment treaty in the world that takes this approach.

And it is this aspect of the FIPA that leads us to Canada's big giveaway. Simply, Canada has given market access rights to foreign investors from other countries in other FIPAs and China has not; Canada has done so by including a national treatment rule in some of its other FIPAs which extends to the pre-establishment stage, while China has never done the same in any of its investment treaties.

As a result, the China FIPA gives Chinese investors a general right—derived from other FIPAs of Canada—to buy whatever they want in Canada. The original right, from which the Chinese one is derived, is held by foreign investors from a few other (small) countries that have FIPAs with Canada. Chinese investors automatically get the same general right because they are entitled to no less favourable treatment than that received by these other investors in Canada.

In contrast, China does not have to give a right of market access to Canadian investors because, as is well known among researchers in the field, China—like Western European countries—has never given such a right to foreign investors from any other country. There are no "more favoured" foreign investors for Canadian investors to complain about.

I regret the complexity of all this. I have put the mechanics on paper for those who may doubt that the FIPA could be one-sided in this way. Sadly, it is. The FIPA lets Chinese investors own assets in Canada that no Canadian investor can own in China. The deal may appear reciprocal on a superficial review of the text; in fact, it is not.

Obviously, giving market access to China without getting the same in return was a huge concession by Canada. When I described it to colleagues in the field, they were, like me, surprised, if not shocked. Why would Canada do it?

The government has not explained why this aspect of the treaty was thought to be a good idea. However, to my knowledge, it has never denied the point either. The point is so complex, I doubt that many government officials are even aware of it. In any event, we have to guess at an explanation.

One troubling possibility is that Canadian negotiators did not realize that the FIPA had this effect. However, one has to assume the negotiators did their job and informed the prime minister and others about the concession. Assuming that Cabinet was properly informed, why would it agree to a deal that requires Canada to open up unilaterally?

Another possibility is that the government hoped that China will agree to a right of market access—for the first time—in a future investment deal with the United States. Presently, China and the United States do not have an investment treaty, though they have been discussing one since 2008. So, it is possible that Canadian investors may one day get market access to China based on the MFN treatment rule in the FIPA, if they can piggyback on Chinese concessions to the United States.

That's a big if. There is a lot of uncertainty about the proposed China-U.S. investment treaty, and market access goes to the heart of it. It is hard to accept that Canada would concede to the inequality of market access in the FIPA, for decades, based on mere hopes about what China will do in the future. It is especially hard to accept because, legally, it would have been straightforward to make Canada's market access commitments conditional, like China's are, on what happens down the road between China and the United States. Was the Harper Government really so desperate?

Another possibility is that the government wanted to open Canada's economy and didn't really care if China did the same. That is the penitence point I talked about in chapter 3 of this book, in response to Andrew Coyne's comments in the *National Post*. As I explained in that chapter, penitence is a lousy excuse for a lopsided FIPA. This explanation—an intentional, unilateral giveaway of market access rights—suggests that the Harper Government was in so much of a rush to sell Canada's resources to Chinese investors that it did not even care to ensure the long-term conditions for Canadian companies to compete, in China or Canada. Such a cave-in to China's priorities could not be revisited for a generation.

Ironically, when the FIPA was announced in early 2012, Prime Minister Harper was reported to be seeking reciprocity on market access from China. He was again reported to be seeking market access for Canadian investors when the federal government reviewed—and eventually approved—the Chinese National Offshore Oil Corporation's takeover of the Canadian oil firm Nexen, in late 2012. Again and again, I found media reports about Harper's quest for the holy grail of market access for Canadian investors in China.

The irony was that, when these media reports came out, the federal government had already given up on a reciprocal right of market access in the FIPA itself. Its best chance to ensure reciprocity had come and gone. Yet, the government still presented itself as fighting for Canadian investors to get access to China. It seemed to me that black was white and white was black, according to the government's spin.

By opening Canada's economy to Chinese investors, the FIPA fits nicely with China's strategy. It gives China access to Canada's resources to feed China's industrial machine. Raw materials can be extracted in Canada, ideally by managers and workers from China, and used to create economic value in China.

Canadians will also see benefits from Chinese resource extraction in Canada, under the FIPA. However, Canada risks selling low, by giving up the value-added benefits of processing and developing its resources at home. Even worse, Canadian companies will not have a reciprocal entitlement to buy up resources in China.

A few months before the FIPA was announced, China's consul general shared his view of Canada's role in an interview with the *Vancouver Sun*. "Hurry up," he said. "Don't only look south of the border. Look across the Pacific. You are rich in natural resources and natural gas." That sounded like the role played by many other countries—in Asia, Africa, and Latin America—that supply resources to China, and import manufactured goods in return. Obviously, China would like to be able to buy the resources it needs from as many suppliers as possible, to bargain for a better price and ownership stake.

In this context, the FIPA looks like a hasty leap into the classic trap of a resource-based economy. Sell the resources, watch others develop them, and import the finished product at a higher cost. Is this what's happening? Even before the FIPA, it sure looked that way. In 2013, Canada exported CDN$20.5 billion, mostly in raw materials, to China and imported CDN$52.7 billion, mostly in manufactured goods. So yes, Canada and the FIPA seem to fit right in.

CHAPTER 7.

FAITH IN THE INVESTMENT CANADA ACT

Promoters of the FIPA often stressed—albeit without mentioning the FIPA's lopsidedness on market access in general—that Canada could still control its economy and resources by using the Investment Canada Act to block Chinese investments. This was a fair point, but misleading.

It is true that the FIPA has a carve-out for the Investment Canada Act. This carve-out lets the federal government block specific Chinese takeovers of Canadian companies. On the other hand, the Investment Canada Act is not nearly as powerful a safeguard as was often claimed.

Also, even for this part of the FIPA, the deal was clearly lopsided in favour of China. That is, Canada's power to block specific investments is limited in ways that China's equivalent power is not. For a reliable protection of Canada's economy and resources, the federal government should have insisted on the same language that China secured in the FIPA.

Once again, the full explanation of why the FIPA is unequal in this way is pretty technical. However, it is important to lay it out, for the record.

The FIPA preserves the Investment Canada Act's role in a carve-out of "investment screening" decisions by Canada and China. The effect of this carve-out is to let each country block investments by the other's investors, on a case-by-case basis. However, the carve-out is broader for China than for Canada.

This example of the FIPA's inequality is found at the end of the treaty's text, but is easy to see. In Annex D.34, the FIPA removes investment screening decisions by Canada and China from the treaty's dispute settlement processes, meaning that such decisions can't be taken to investor-state arbitration (or country-to-country arbitration) under the FIPA. According to Annex D.34:

> 1. A decision by Canada following a review *under the Investment Canada Act*, an Act respecting investment in Canada, with respect to whether or not to:
> (a) initially approve an investment that is subject to review; or
> (b) permit an investment that is subject to national security review;
> shall not be subject to the dispute settlement provisions under Article 15 and Part C of this Agreement.
> 2. A decision by China following a review *under the Laws, Regulations and Rules relating to the regulation of foreign investment*, with respect to whether or not to:
> (a) initially approve an investment that is subject to review; or
> (b) permit an investment that is subject to national security review;
> shall not be subject to the dispute settlement provisions under Article 15 and Part C of this Agreement(emphasis mine).

How is this preservation of investment screening powers broader for China than for Canada? I have italicized above the key words creating this inequality. With those words, Canada keeps its ability to screen investments based only on the Investment Canada Act, while China does the same for *any* of its "Laws, Regulations and Rules relating to the regulation of foreign investment."

Obviously, China's carve-out is much bigger. It protects investment screening by China without specifying any single law under which the screening has to occur. As a result, China has more flexibility to block Canadian investments, even if

Canadian investors one day were to get a general right of market access to China.

That is, China's carve-out is more flexible because it does not include various limitations that come with the Investment Canada Act, as that act stood when the FIPA took effect. And, all of the existing limitations in the Investment Canada Act are now locked in by the FIPA for Canada—but not for China—because only Canada restricted its power of investment screening to a specific law that is incorporated into the FIPA.

What are these limitations for Canada but not China?

Well, the Investment Canada Act lets Canada's federal government block foreign investments if they involve the takeover of a Canadian company, but not if they involve the establishment of a new business. Thus, if Chinese investors were to buy farmland in Canada and put it to a new use, they could skirt the Investment Canada Act.

Also, except on national security grounds (which we can expect won't be invoked very often), the federal government can block foreign takeovers under the Investment Canada Act only if the value of the Canadian company being taken over by a Chinese investor exceeds roughly CDN$350 million. By the way, the Harper Government plans to raise this threshold to CDN$1 billion, as of 2018, but has said it will leave the threshold where it is now for foreign state-owned companies.

Of course, there are major businesses in Canada that are worth less than CDN$350 million. Presumably, many Canadians would not want them to be owned by Chinese investors—and possibly the Chinese government—without a careful review by the federal government. With the FIPA, the government gave up Canada's sovereign right to block Chinese takeovers of such businesses, whether by going beyond or by changing the Investment Canada Act.

In June 2014, the *Globe and Mail* reported on China Oil and

Gas Group's takeover of a private Canadian energy company, Baccalieu Energy, for CDN$236 million. This takeover was described as an example of "a trend in Asian buyers launching takeovers for small firms since the Harper Government imposed tougher rules on deals in late 2012."

The takeover was finalized before the FIPA's ratification. Even so, it showed how, without a possibility of review under the Investment Canada Act and now the FIPA, a Chinese investor "could [scoop] up a company that produced 4,244 barrels of oil equivalent a day in the first quarter of this year. . . . In 2013, it earned CDN$20-million on revenue of CDN$74.7-million." The Canadian company that was taken over also had "stakes in 469 square kilometres in the Pembina, Ferrier, Sylvan Lake and Harmattan areas of west-central Alberta, where its proved and probable reserves are pegged at 22 million barrels of oil equivalent."

I am not saying that this particular takeover was bad or good. But it does illustrate how, in spite of the Investment Canada Act, the federal government will not be in a position to block Chinese purchases of significant resources in Canada, under the FIPA.

There are other ways for Chinese investors to avoid the Investment Canada Act. A review of a takeover under the act can be evaded by making step-by-step purchases, each of which falls below the monetary threshold for review. Also, in circumstances where a Chinese-owned company is expanding an existing business in Canada, the act does not apply. Official Opposition and NDP Leader Thomas Mulcair highlighted this last loophole in 2012 when the federal government approved the takeover of Canadian oil company Nexen by the China National Offshore Oil Corporation (CNOOC). Mulcair's concern—denied by Prime Minister Harper—was that the government's approval of the Nexen deal, combined with the FIPA, would open the door to more takeovers of Canadian assets by CNOOC, without any further review under the Investment

Canada Act. Personally, I found Mulcair's concern to be credible and precise.

In any event, there are specialized lawyers in Canada who are able to advise Chinese companies about how to structure their entry into Canada's economy so they avoid or limit review under the Investment Canada Act.

There is another blind spot in the Investment Canada Act, as a means to watch over Chinese investments. Under the act, only the federal government—not a provincial government or any other level of government—can block a Chinese takeover of a Canadian company. In contrast, under the FIPA, any level of government in China can block a Canadian investment. To do so, a Chinese official needs only to point to any Chinese law, regulation, or rule that relates to the regulation of foreign investment and that authorizes the official's decision to block. The decision could be made by a mayor, for example, so long as the local government had a rule requiring foreign investors to meet special requirements before investing. China's FIPA right to screen foreign investments, unlike Canada's, is not limited to its national government.

Does this lopsidedness really matter for Canada? It certainly does, if you think that you might disagree with future Chinese takeovers of Canadian companies. Under the FIPA, the federal government took the liberty of surrendering the power of other governments in Canada to screen Chinese investments. Worse, it did so without getting a similar commitment from China.

The importance of this concession was illustrated by a report from the European Union Chamber of Commerce in China, which observed in 2013, "China has used the vast size of its domestic marketplace to protect domestic companies and to place conditionalities on market access for foreign companies." The importance of the concession was also confirmed by David Fung, a FIPA promoter who was a vice-chair of the Canada-China Business Council: "There are lots of horror stories about Canadian investments in China . . . In Canada, our cities don't go and destroy somebody else's investment. But in China, a mayor has a lot more power than our mayors in Canada." At the time he said this, Fung was trying to encourage Canadians to support the FIPA. He did not mention, and I suspect may not even have known, that the FIPA itself lets mayors in China discriminate against, or block, Canadian investments.

These observations by the Chamber of Commerce and by Fung show the importance of the federal government's acceptance of unequal limitations on Canada's investment screening powers. To summarize the concessions, the FIPA requires Canada to open its economy to Chinese investors, and to keep it open. That requirement is subject to a limited power of the federal government to block investments, case by case. Meanwhile, China can keep its protectionist approach to Canadian investors in general and—if needed one day—in specific cases too.

If that doesn't undermine the sales pitch for the FIPA, I'm not sure what could.

CHAPTER 8.

POSSIBLE CONFLICTS OVER CANADIAN JOBS, HEALTH, AND THE ENVIRONMENT

With Canada's economy open to Chinese investors, what will they buy? Well, they will buy whatever they want, if the price is right for them. No government in Canada will be able to block them, beyond the federal government's limited powers under the Investment Canada Act.

What's more, some Chinese investors, because of their special access to low-cost financing from the Chinese state, can buy a lot of things that others in Canada cannot. In a book on China's economic expansion into Asia, Africa, and Latin America, called *China's Silent Army*, the Spanish journalists Juan Pablo Cardenal and Heriberto Araújo highlighted how China "uses its astonishing financial clout to serve the country's national strategic objectives." As Cardenal and Araújo put it, the almost limitless funds of Chinese development banks "represent an incalculable advantage in an era otherwise dominated by empty coffers and a dwindling cash flow." Access to such funds allows Chinese companies to "buy strategic assets, secure long-term supply contracts and develop projects to exploit natural resources" and in turn "gives 'China, Inc.'—the triumvirate formed by the party-state, the banks, and the state-owned companies—the ammunition needed to blow their competitors out of the water."

Why is this possible for China but not for other countries? Cardenal and Araújo concluded that it came from the situation of Chinese savers, who earn artificially low interest on their deposits in China and cannot put their money elsewhere because of controls on capital outflows from China. Whether this policy has hurt or helped the Chinese people is a question for another book. The key here is that it makes Chinese investors more able to buy what they want in Canada because of their access to low-cost state financing back home. In turn, that advantage can be put to good use under the FIPA because of the relative openness of Canada's economy and Chinese investors' right to market access.

When the FIPA was announced in February 2012, according to the *Globe and Mail*, Chinese premier Wen Jiabao "was blunt about China's desire to buy Canadian oil." Likewise, China's official Xinhua newswire reported that the Chinese premier told Canada's prime minister that China was ready to expand imports of energy and resource products from Canada.

Months later, when the FIPA was signed in September 2012, the Prime Minister's Office acknowledged that "Chinese firms have also expressed a desire to invest in Canada. Sectors of interest include mining, and oil and gas extraction." The federal trade ministry also cited sectors in which Chinese investors may invest under the FIPA. Resources were first on the list.

These reports indicated that Chinese companies will want to buy in to Canada's resource sector, especially if it fits China's wider strategy. Chinese companies have a pattern of buying into resources and associated infrastructure, in Canada and other parts of the world.

China's strategic interest in Canada's resources makes China a natural partner for resource companies in Canada (and their Canadian and foreign owners). Such companies may be keen to bring in new capital, to access China's market, to diversify risk, or sell out at a profit. But it is another matter whether these interests fit the priorities of Canadians to boost the economic benefits of resource extraction in Canada, while managing the environmental costs.

In this context of Chinese investment, what areas of possible conflict—between Chinese investors and Canadian decision-makers—could emerge under the FIPA? There are lots of possibilities.

One area of possible conflict comes from the likelihood that Chinese investors may want to use Chinese managers and workers for their operations in Canada. The case of the Chinese-owned coal mine in Murray River, British Colombia, is an example. Chinese investors, through a company called HD Mining, were allowed by the federal government to hire 201 temporary foreign workers from China, after the company put a Mandarin language requirement in its job advertisements in Canada. Reportedly, jobs at the mine, based on federal approvals, are not open fully to Canadians until 13 years into the project.

Without evaluating the details of this example—which were disputed in litigation after two BC labour unions tried to challenge the federal approvals—it's clear that the scenario it portrays is very troubling. The case indicates how Chinese investors may be allowed to use Chinese labour to extract unprocessed resources in Canada, for export abroad. For a resource-dependent country like Canada, this flies in the face of the goal of maximizing the benefits of resource exploitation in the country's own economy.

Incidentally, we know of details about this case only because the labour unions pursued access to information requests, and fought it out in court, to expose what the federal government approved. The episode indicates how the government can downgrade the interests of Canadian workers. It is hard to say how many cases there are like this, and how many more we will see under the FIPA.

I stress this last point because the Alberta Federation of Labour has tried to use access to information requests to expose details about the use of temporary foreign workers in Canada. It has uncovered information about how widespread the program was allowed to become; for example, the workforce of one major Chinese oil company in Alberta—Sinopec Canada Energy—consisted of more than 50 per cent temporary foreign workers, according to documents produced by the federal government. However, the documents in question did not reveal how many foreign workers were hired by Sinopec, nor at what job classifications or wage levels.

Now consider, what if Canadians demanded their government take a tougher stand on the use of foreign workers by all companies in Canada? How might Chinese investors react, with their new FIPA rights in mind?

At one point in the controversy over the coal mine in Murray River, the *Globe and Mail* reported an interesting statement by a spokesperson for the Chinese owner of the coal mine: "Our company, and others too, are watching very closely to determine if goalposts can be changed after a company has invested much time and CDN$50-million on a project in this country." From this statement, it appears that some Chinese investors will expect the federal government to keep on approving the use of Chinese workers by Chinese investors in Canada and, if the law or policy changes, Chinese investors will not be happy about the lost profits for them. To me, this sounds a lot like the arguments that investor-state lawyers have made, often successfully, under investment treaties.

Another area of potential conflict under the FIPA relates to the health and environmental consequences of Chinese investment in Canada. As I explained in chapter 5, the federal government used dubious assumptions to ignore the risk of environmental impacts in Canada from Chinese investment. But any serious study of the issue would find cause for concern.

To illustrate, here is how the U.S. journalist Craig Simons summarized the impact of Chinese investment and consumption on forests in other countries:

> Until the late 1990s China was largely self-sufficient in lumber. Then, in the summer of 1998, heavy rains flooded the Yangtze River, killing more than three thousand people and causing billions of dollars in damages. China's leaders realized that widespread logging had caused massive erosion and increased runoff, damaging the nature buffers to heavy storms. With the power wielded only by single-party states, Beijing banned logging across most of the nation.
>
> Like squeezing a balloon, that decision forced demand outward and forests began to fall across Asia. Today, most of the natural forests of Southeast Asia are gone. Russia's—the world's largest remaining tract of temperate forest—are falling at record speed. China takes growing quantities of African hardwoods: 90 per cent of Mozambique's log exports; 70 per cent of exports from Gabon and Cameroon. In total, *nearly half* of all the tropical logs and pulp made from tropical logs, which is traded for use in paper, passes through a Chinese port (emphasis his).

Simons relays other examples of "the great environmental costs of China's manufacturing success," ranging from water to air quality to species diversity to climate change. Clearly, China faces tremendous pressure to meet the needs and wants of its people, and this can have huge environmental consequences for other countries.

For our purposes, the key issue is that the Harper Government discounted the FIPA's potential impacts on health and the environment in Canada. As a result, it seems likely that future Canadian governments will have to cope with the problems and clean up the mess. This is another area of potential conflict with Chinese investors: the tightening and enforcement of environmental laws in Canada.

These are two examples of potential hotspots under the FIPA. There are other possibilities, ranging from energy subsidies to securities regulation to workplace safety. The common theme is that Chinese investors can use the FIPA, in almost any area, to pressure governments to water down Canadian rules and regulations.

Of course, not all Chinese investment in Canada is objectionable. Yet, for many Canadians, it seems possible that Chinese investment will undermine their priorities when it comes to jobs, health, or the environment. Whatever the future holds, one thing is sure. The FIPA gives Chinese investors a powerful new tool to get their way.

CHAPTER 9.

THE SPECIAL STATUS OF CHINESE INVESTORS

Foreign investor lawsuits under investment treaties are so powerful—compared to other kinds of lawsuits against countries—I would call them supersized. In turn, the right to bring such lawsuits gives foreign investors a special or "enclave" status in a country. Only they can bring the supersized lawsuits against the country's decisions, with a potential cost to the country of hundreds of millions or billions of dollars.

As a result, under the FIPA, Chinese investors now have a power to sidestep Canada's legal system by starting a lawsuit under the FIPA. Or, they can go to the courts in Canada to attempt to strike down a decision, while using the FIPA to seek compensation that would not otherwise be available under Canadian law. For instance, under the FIPA, Chinese investors can seek full compensation for the economic impact of a new law on their business, including their future profits; this would not be possible under Canadian law, to preserve the role of elected legislatures.

By the same token, arbitrators under the FIPA have immense power to condemn Canada by ordering compensation, without any monetary limit, for a Chinese investor. The arbitrators' awards are enforceable against a losing country's assets around the world, and are more enforceable than any court judgment against a country in its role as the sovereign.

However, the power of investor-state arbitrators can easily get hidden or drowned in detail, especially by lawyers who promote investment treaties. Below, I highlight ten points that give a sense of how far their power goes and how it can be used. My hope is to help readers make up their own minds about what this special status of Chinese investors means for them.

1. After a FIPA lawsuit is filed by a Chinese investor, the arbitrators can review almost anything that Canada has done in its sovereign role, that is, on behalf of its people. There are complex exceptions in the FIPA that safeguard some aspects of Canada's authority, but in general the arbitrators' power is very broad.
2. Likewise, Chinese investors can dispute—and the arbitrators can review—decisions by governments as well as legislatures and courts. The usual principles of Canadian law that the rule of law requires such disputes to be decided ultimately in a court, and that one elected government cannot bind another, simply do not apply under investment treaties or, in general, under international law.
3. FIPA lawsuits against Canada are not limited to the federal government. Decisions of a province or territory—whether by a legislature, government, or court—or a municipal or First Nation council can also be challenged. In international law, all of these bodies, because they exercise public powers, are part of Canada as a whole.
4. FIPA arbitrators operate at a different level from Canadian courts. A decision by a court, up to and including the Supreme Court, is a sovereign act of

Canada. Thus, court decisions are also subject to review by the arbitrators, if challenged by a Chinese investor.

5. Because they operate at the international level, FIPA arbitrators are not limited by Canada's constitution or other parts of Canadian law; rather, they are subject to the FIPA and relevant rules of international law.

6. To a far greater degree than other treaties, investment treaties like the FIPA lay out elaborate rights for private parties (albeit only foreign investors). They also make those rights highly enforceable.

7. Meanwhile, investment treaties give investor-state arbitrators a broad power to condemn countries for how they treat foreign investors, and to order compensation. Foreign investors' rights in the treaties are often described using vague language, which arbitrators have typically interpreted broadly. For example, in numerous cases, arbitrators have used the right of foreign investors to receive "fair and equitable treatment" to order a country to compensate a foreign investor for changing its laws or other decisions, even when the change applied to everyone in the country, came from a democratic or judicial process, or responded to a pressing public need.

8. The arbitrators are largely a power unto themselves. Their awards are subject to little or no review in any court. In some cases, they can be reviewed on limited grounds by a panel of other arbitrators, all of whom are chosen by the president of the World Bank in Washington, D.C. In other cases, they can be reviewed (also on limited grounds) in a court in a place that is chosen by the arbitrators themselves. After that, the awards are automatically enforceable in dozens of countries, including Canada.

9. If Canada did not pay a FIPA award, a Chinese investor could take the award to other countries that have agreed

to enforce arbitration awards through other treaties that facilitate enforcement of international arbitrations. These other treaties—especially the New York Convention of 1958 and the Washington (or ICSID, for International Centre for Settlement of Investment Disputes) Convention of 1965—were originally negotiated to give force to arbitration awards under contracts, not investment treaties. Under these enforcement treaties, commercial assets of Canada in other countries would be subject to seizure to make good on an unpaid FIPA award.

As an example, money owed by U.S. customers to a Crown corporation like BC Hydro or Hydro-Québec would typically be subject to seizure because they are commercial assets of Canada. The assets would be vulnerable to seizure, even if the FIPA award came from a decision by the federal government or a province other than BC or Quebec, as the case may be. Again, this is because, under international law, the assets of any level of government in Canada are treated as assets of Canada as a whole.

In other words, the FIPA is backed by an exceptionally flexible and powerful system to enforce the arbitrators' awards.

10. Critically, FIPA arbitrators have the power to order countries to pay backward-looking compensation to foreign investors. That is to say, the compensation against a country is calculated from the time of the original decision that is later found to have violated the treaty. It is not calculated from the time of the arbitrators' decision itself. So, countries can rack up massive liability without knowing if the original decision actually violated the treaty. This risk of liability can give powerful leverage to a large multinational that has deep pockets to fund an investor-state lawsuit.

Foreign investor lawsuits have exploded since the late 1990s, leading to billions of dollars in awards against countries. Even so, it often seems as if the investors and arbitrators are still just getting going.

For example, in recent years, foreign investors have brought lawsuits in a range of new areas. Arbitrators have made larger and larger awards, peaking in 2014 with an astounding USD$50 billion award against Russia. Whatever one thinks of Vladimir Putin, an award of this size against a sovereign country was totally unprecedented in international law. In time, the risk of massive awards may put so much pressure on countries that they will have to choose between appeasing big multinationals or bankrupting their economies. In either case, investment treaties would have drastically changed the options available to governments.

For Canadians, this ability of Chinese investors to bring these powerful lawsuits means that we, as a country, cannot avoid liability if the FIPA arbitrators decide that Canada has violated the FIPA's rights for Chinese investors. Such decisions by the arbitrators can wreak havoc with public budgets, long after the country's original decision was made. This aspect of FIPA arbitration is very different from court decisions in public law and policy, which would not use compensation as the primary remedy for an injured party. In rare cases when courts do order compensation against the state, in its sovereign role, they put tight checks on the amounts that can be awarded.

Slowly or abruptly, decision-makers in Canada can be expected to learn about the FIPA's risks. Increasingly, they may adjust their decisions to favour Chinese investors over others who have a conflicting interest. Usually, governments would face pressure to settle a Chinese lawsuit behind closed doors. For this reason, Canadians should be alert that a government may change a decision to appease a Chinese investor—especially a big company—in secret. I suggest ways to respond to this predicament in the final chapter of this book.

With this in mind, it was worrying to see Prime Minister Harper say, before his government approved the 2012 takeover of Nexen by the China National Offshore Oil Corporation, that "the most important thing is that we have rules in Canada that are respected." He continued, "[i]t is up to the Chinese to display a willingness to play within our rules." To me, these statements suggested a lack of basic understanding about how the FIPA allows Chinese investors to challenge Canada's rules in an extraordinarily powerful way.

In contrast to their elaborate rights, a Chinese investor in Canada could not itself be sued under the FIPA. Investment treaties are rigged one way in that they give special rights to foreign investors, with no actionable responsibilities. Thus, for a Chinese investor, the financial downside of a FIPA lawsuit is the cost of the lawyers and arbitrators. In some cases, a Chinese investor might be ordered to pay Canada's costs if the lawsuit is dismissed and, for many investors, this will be a significant deterrent. However, for a large Chinese company—backed by the Chinese state—it is not a significant barrier in a dispute about major assets.

This imbalance is a political choice. A treaty can be written to put clear responsibilities on foreign investors, for example to avoid corrupt activities or respect workers' rights. But the governments that drive the treaties—in Washington and Western European capitals but also in Ottawa and Beijing—have not done so.

CHAPTER 10.

DOES CANADA'S RULE OF LAW PROTECT US?

Promoters of the FIPA often downplayed the risk of Chinese lawsuits against Canada. Frequently, they claimed that Canada's rule of law would protect us. The treaty was important to protect Canadian investors in China, but not the other way round.

For example, writing in the *Globe and Mail*, investor-state lawyers Milos Barutciski and Matthew Kronby argued that "the benefits of a predictable, rules-based environment for investment under the [FIPA] are far more likely to accrue to Canadian investors in China than to Chinese investors operating in Canada, who already take a predictable, rules-based environment for granted."

The problem with this argument is that it was contradicted by the evidence of actual claims by foreign investors against Canada and China. In all known cases to that point, Canada had been sued over thirty times, while China had been sued only once!

All of the investor lawsuits against Canada so far have been under NAFTA, and they were all brought by U.S. companies.

In defending these lawsuits, Canada has a mixed record. The cost to Canadian taxpayers for awards and settlements has been significant—about CDN$180 million—but not as serious as for other countries that have faced billions of dollars in awards. Various NAFTA cases against Canada are ongoing.

In a recent report, the Canadian Centre for Policy Alternatives provided a summary of the NAFTA cases that Canada has lost or settled, which I reproduce below with updates and modifications (e.g. all amounts have been adjusted to include any pre-award interest ordered on top of base compensation, and rounded to the nearest million).

1. *ETHYL V. CANADA* (LAWSUIT FILED IN 1997)

Amount awarded: CDN$19 million, as part of a settlement.
Why Canada lost: The U.S. chemical company challenged a Canada-wide ban on import and trade of the gasoline additive MMT, a suspected neurotoxin and threat to emissions control systems in cars. After a preliminary decision went against Canada, the government repealed the ban, issued an apology, and paid a settlement.

2. *SD MYERS V. CANADA* (LAWSUIT FILED IN 1998)

Amount awarded: CDN$8 million, as part of an award by the tribunal.
Why Canada lost: The U.S. waste disposal company challenged a Canadian ban on the export of toxic PCB wastes, which was passed after the U.S. unexpectedly opened its border to the import of PCB wastes. The Canadian ban was connected to Canada's obligations under an international environmental treaty. The tribunal ruled that the ban violated NAFTA's rules on investor protection because it helped a Canadian competitor of the U.S. company.

3. *POPE AND TALBOT V. CANADA* (LAWSUIT FILED IN 1998)

Amount awarded: under CDN$1 million, as part of an award by the tribunal.

Why Canada lost: The U.S. lumber company challenged Canada's lumber export rules that implemented the country's commitments under the Canada-U.S. Softwood Lumber Agreement. The tribunal ruled that Canada violated NAFTA's rules on investor protection, but awarded only a small amount of compensation.

4. *MOBIL INVESTMENTS/ MURPHY OIL V. CANADA* (LAWSUIT FILED IN 2007)

Amount awarded: CDN$17 million plus, as part of an award; damages will continue to accrue as long as the violating guidelines are in effect.

Why Canada lost: ExxonMobil and another U.S. oil company argued that Canada's rules requiring oil companies to invest in research and development in Newfoundland and Labrador were inconsistent with U.S. investor rights under NAFTA, and not covered by a NAFTA carve-out. A majority of the tribunal agreed, adopting a surprisingly narrow interpretation of the NAFTA carve-out.

5. *ABITIBIBOWATER V. CANADA* (LAWSUIT FILED IN 2009)

Amount awarded: CDN$130 million, as part of the largest NAFTA-related settlement to date.

Why Canada lost: The pulp and paper company closed its last mill in Newfoundland and Labrador in 2008, and the provincial government enacted legislation to return the company's timber and water rights to the Crown and expropriate some of its lands and assets associated with water and hydro-electric rights. AbitibiBowater (now known as Resolute Forest Products) was to be paid compensation in a process required under the legislation, but the company launched a NAFTA lawsuit instead, and the federal government settled without defending the claim.

6. *CLAYTON/ BILCON V. CANADA* (LAWSUIT FILED IN 2008)

Amount awarded: Not yet decided, although Canada was found to have violated NAFTA.

Why Canada lost: The company's proposal to build a quarry at Whites Point, Nova Scotia, was rejected based on a recommendation by an environmental assessment panel. The company argued, and a majority of the tribunal agreed, that the environmental assessment was unfair. The dissenting arbitrator warned that the decision would create a chill in environmental assessment.

7. *ST. MARYS V. CANADA* (LAWSUIT FILED IN 2011)

Amount awarded: CDN$15 million, as part of a settlement.

Why Canada lost: The company argued that its Canadian subsidiary was the victim of political interference when it tried to open a quarry near Flamborough, Ontario, after residents grew concerned about the groundwater. The Ontario government passed a zoning order to prevent the site from being converted into a quarry, and the company claimed that this decision was unfair. As part of a settlement, the company withdrew the lawsuit in exchange for compensation from the Ontario government.

This record of investor-state lawsuits against Canada is hard to fathom if, as FIPA promoters often said, Canada's rule of law is supposed to protect us. If Canada is immunized from FIPA lawsuits for this reason, why have we been sued and lost these cases under NAFTA?

Indeed, under NAFTA, U.S. investors have sued Canada

about twice as often as they have sued Mexico. Canada has been sued more often in investor-state arbitration than any other developed country, and more often than all but four developing or transition countries.

How could Canada get in trouble so often? For a start, one reason is that the rights of foreign investors under the treaties are very broad, and have been interpreted even more broadly by many arbitrators. They go well beyond obvious cases of abuse, allowing lawsuits against general laws, regulations, and other decisions that were adopted in good faith and are not discriminatory. A country with democratic elections and independent courts is far from immune.

What about China? FIPA promoters often claimed the deal was vital to protect Canadian investors because China does not deliver the rule of law. Yet, China had been sued only once under an investment treaty, despite having signed more such treaties than almost any other country. Furthermore, China has about a dozen investment treaties with significant capital-exporting countries, whereas, before the China FIPA, Canada had just one such treaty, with the United States.

Why is China sued so rarely? One likely explanation is that China is a powerful country with a huge economy. This makes it daunting for foreign investors to sue, thereby risking being forced out of the Chinese market. If a foreign investor did sue, China's government is well-positioned to punish the investor regardless of the treaties.

Whatever the explanation, Canada has been a much more inviting target for foreign investor lawsuits, regardless of the rule of law. The FIPA promoters' reassurances about the threat of Chinese lawsuits should be taken with a grain of salt.

PART 2.

THE TROUBLE WITH ARBITRATOR POWER

CHAPTER 11.

THE EXPLOSION OF FOREIGN INVESTOR LAWSUITS

The first known lawsuit under an investment treaty was filed in the 1980s. It was brought against Sri Lanka, after a military campaign by the Sri Lankan government destroyed a U.K. company's shrimp farm, which the Sri Lankan army thought was a Tamil Tiger base. Two of the three arbitrators decided that Sri Lanka did not protect the U.K. company adequately and ordered about USD$610,000 in compensation. The dissenting arbitrator thought the other two arbitrators went too far in scrutinizing decisions of battlefield commanders.

This was a very small case and it attracted little attention. Only in the mid-1990s did foreign investor lawsuits take off, beginning especially with NAFTA lawsuits against Canada. Since then, the explosion has been remarkable.

Up to 1995, there had been just three foreign investor lawsuits, worldwide, under investment treaties. These three were started in 1987, against Sri Lanka as just mentioned, in 1993 against the Congo, and in 1995 against Burundi. Then, from 1996 to 2000, anywhere from five to twelve new lawsuits were started *each year*, for a total of forty-one lawsuits in that five-year period. Of these lawsuits, eighteen were filed under NAFTA. Since the late 1990s, there have been hundreds of foreign investor lawsuits against countries, including dozens against Canada.

For our purposes, this explosion of litigation helps us to understand the FIPA in two useful ways. First, it suggests strongly that there will be Chinese lawsuits against Canada, some leading to an award or settlement that favours a Chinese company. Second, it shows that it is reasonable to expect that some lawyers who actively promoted the FIPA may in time benefit from the fees generated by FIPA lawsuits and settlements.

On this second point, it is no exaggeration to say the explosion of litigation under investment treaties is probably the biggest boon for international lawyers in modern history. I can think of no other context in which so much international litigation, with comparable amounts of fees, has taken place. For example, litigation at the World Trade Organization is comparable to investor-state arbitration because of the rise of WTO litigation since the 1990s. Yet, WTO litigation seems unlikely to create as much business for lawyers because it occurs exclusively among states. Much lower fees are paid to WTO arbitrators than investor-state arbitrators and, at the WTO, government lawyers and diplomats play more integral roles than private sector lawyers. Crucially, WTO litigation does not lead to backward-looking compensation orders against a country. Instead, it leads to trade sanctions, and only after the country has had a chance to comply with the WTO rules, as interpreted by WTO adjudicators.

Because of the high fees and high stakes, the explosion of investor-state arbitration has been extremely lucrative for lawyers and arbitrators who specialize in the field. The average cost of an investment treaty arbitration, in legal and arbitration fees, is about USD$8 million. Extrapolating from that, several billion dollars, at least, has been billed to countries and investors in hundreds of known cases. Even this is a conservative estimate of what the lawyers have billed because it does not account for fees billed outside of actual arbitrations. Basically, since the late 1990s, investment treaties have been a huge windfall for law firms.

Not surprisingly, it is very rare for anyone in the investor-state legal industry to offer any fundamental criticism of the system in public. One can imagine why. A lawyer who does so may put his or her clients in jeopardy, at the hands of the arbitrators. An arbitrator who does so may find it harder to get agreement from the other arbitrators who sit on tribunals with him or her. Both may suffer in future work. Even many of the academics in the field typically work, or aspire to work, as lawyers or arbitrators in the industry (I am among those who do not). Boards of academic journals in the field are typically dominated by investor-state lawyers and arbitrators.

That is not to say that everyone who works in the system agrees with how it is designed. Some lawyers and arbitrators are privately sympathetic to criticisms of its non-judicial process, for example. Likewise, some specialists who are not earning a lot of income from the system nevertheless support it. However, in my experience, most academics who have knowledge of investor-state arbitration, and no financial stake in its expansion, express significant reservations and often strong criticism. In contrast, many members of the legal industry, including academics, have been very active in promoting the system. I highlight this aspect of the explosion of litigation because I think the public should be aware of it, when considering the debate about investment treaties.

What does the explosion of investor-state arbitration tell us about how Chinese investors will use their FIPA power to bring supersized lawsuits against Canada? Will governments censor themselves to avoid disputes? Who will win and lose, at the hands of the as-yet unknown FIPA arbitrators in each case—one to be appointed by the Chinese investor, one by the federal government, and a third, if the investor and the government do not agree, by an outside appointing body?

These are some of the questions that follow from the FIPA's change to the status of Chinese investors in Canada. They are difficult questions to answer reliably because, of course, they depend on predictions about the future. Perhaps recognizing this, FIPA proponents often shifted the debate about the FIPA to these sorts of questions, and then supplied selective facts and rosy assessments to dismiss concerns about the FIPA as hysterical, alarmist, or overblown.

This rhetorical tactic allowed promoters to dodge the FIPA's clear changes to the status of Chinese investors in Canada. The tactic also often helped boost promoters' own claims of expertise in the debate, by directing attention to a thicket of uncertainty that no non-expert could hope to navigate without doing a major research project. In other words, it was a convenient way to sell a dubious deal.

That said, it is still important to anticipate how Chinese investors and FIPA arbitrators may use their new powers. To me, the best way to do so is by looking at how investors and arbitrators have used their powers under other investment treaties that protect foreign investors in very similar ways. But when I offered forecasts about the FIPA on this basis, federal trade officials argued that experiences of other countries in investor-state arbitration were not relevant to what might happen to Canada under the FIPA. "Canada is not Ecuador!", they seemed to be saying.

This struck me as an odd approach to the questions and the evidence. It is true that there are differences among the treaties, but the differences can be accounted for when the evidence is weighed. Meanwhile, virtually all investment treaties have a common set of rights and protections for foreign investors, and rely on the same rules and processes of arbitration. Most importantly, only a few dozen lawyers sit regularly as arbitrators across the treaties. Typically, they are men who have a history working as corporate lawyers, commercial arbitrators, or law professors (often, as all three).

In light of the common features of the treaties, the experience of other countries in the hundreds of foreign investor lawsuits under other investment treaties is clearly a useful source of evidence in trying to predict what may happen to Canada under the FIPA. The FIPA promoters who did not consider this evidence were being selective, not thorough.

Foreign investor lawsuits have come fast and furious in the last fifteen years. They have come against countries of varying sizes in all parts of the world. They have involved disputes in different situations of investment and regulation. They have been brought by investors of different sizes and incomes, though the biggest-money awards have gone to large multinationals and tycoons.

To make strong claims about this recent history would require a close study of hundreds of cases. One would also need to research what happened beyond the actual arbitrations and beyond what was reported in the arbitrators' awards. Even then, one would not be able to capture the many arbitrations and settlements that are secret. For this reason, any credible commentator will make clear that there is a lot of debate about what has happened, and a lot of uncertainty about what will happen, as a result of investment treaties.

In this part of the book, I aim to summarize research in the field—focusing on examples of the best evidence in my view—to help readers get a clearer picture of what has happened since the explosion of foreign investor lawsuits against countries began. I offer the summary as an academic who has followed investor-state arbitration closely since the early 2000s. I should make clear that during that time I have, among other things, criticized the absence of safeguards of judicial independence and fair process under the treaties. Partly to preserve my objectivity in evaluating the system, I have also declined to do paid work as an arbitrator, lawyer, or expert in investor-state arbitration. Of course, my findings and views are still open to debate.

Some of the chapters in this part of the book provide numbers drawn from my research, and numbers should always come with disclaimers. For example, there are significant limitations on our ability to research investor-state arbitration because of the role of researcher discretion in coding information and in the choice of methods, the need for time cut-offs in tracking and analyzing awards, and the existence of confidential cases that cannot be researched reliably. For these reasons (and others that are described in the studies I cite), all the numbers should be treated as approximate. And, unless I describe them as "statistically significant," the numbers reflect what's happened so far under the treaties, but do not give reliable predictions about the future. Often there is not enough data for the latter.

In this part of the book, before turning to what may happen in the future under the FIPA, I outline—in chapters 12 to 14—some problems with the process of investor-state arbitration that give cause for serious concern, especially under the FIPA. In chapters 15 and 16, I offer an overview of the rights that investment treaties create for foreign investors and the implications for democracy in Canada. This discussion of the FIPA's process and substance sets the stage for chapters 17 to 21, which point to what may happen in the future.

CHAPTER 12.

FOR-PROFIT ARBITRATORS INSTEAD OF JUDGES

On its face, investor-state arbitration looks even-handed. After a foreign investor brings a lawsuit, the investor and the country each appoint an arbitrator. If they cannot agree on the third (presiding) arbitrator, he or she is chosen by an outside body, such as the World Bank. Trusting this outside body to be independent, though there are reasons to doubt that, the process appears fair.

Concerns about a lack of independence emerge as one scratches the surface more deeply.

Investment treaty arbitration is not based on a judicial process and, unlike other kinds of arbitration, it is not subject to judicial review. Some describe the arbitrators as "judges," or part of a "court," but that's wrong. They are lawyers, not judges. They operate for profit and, partly as a result, they do not have the usual safeguards of independence and fairness that characterize courts.

What's the trouble with arbitrators working for profit? Lots of activities are for profit, to encourage hard work and innovation. In many situations, the profit motive is an important source of accountability to customers and shareholders. However, in investor-state arbitration, the profit motive is a fatal flaw because of the decisions that the arbitrators make and how they make them.

Imagine if judges worked for profit; that is, imagine if they were paid by the case and made more money if there were more cases. Each judge who wanted to sit in future would have a financial incentive to encourage more litigation. Presumably this would not be the only driver of how the judge made decisions, but even the possibility of this incentive affecting the judge's decisions would raise doubts about his or her impartiality in all cases. For example, if criminal trials were decided by for-profit judges, judges could reasonably be suspected of favouring the government—at the expense of accused people—as a way to encourage more prosecutions.

To avoid this problem, judges have institutional safeguards of their independence. They are paid a set salary to remove any financial interest in encouraging litigation. They have secure tenure to limit economic dependence on powerful actors in government and the marketplace. They are supposed to be assigned to cases in an objective way, so no one can say a sensitive case was kept in so-called safe hands. They are not allowed to work on the side as lawyers, so no one can say they interpreted the law to favour a paying client in another case.

It's not enough that individual judges commit personally to being fair and impartial. That is only the start of it. Judicial independence also depends on institutional safeguards to remove reasonable appearances of bias. According to the Canadian Judicial Council (quoting a Supreme Court of Canada decision called *Valente*):

> [J]udicial independence involves both individual and institutional relationships: the individual independence of a judge, as reflected in such matters as security of tenure and the institutional independence of the court or tribunal over which he or she presides, as reflected in its institutional or administrative relationships to the executive and legislative branches of government.

> . . . [J]udicial independence is a status or relationship resting on objective conditions or guarantees as well as a state of mind or attitude in the actual exercise of judicial functions. . . .
>
> The objective conditions and guarantees include, for example, security of tenure, security of remuneration and immunity from civil liability for judicial acts.

Now, consider the arbitrators who decide the lawsuits under investment treaties. They are paid by the hour or by the day. The more appointments they get, the more they earn. The longer the case goes, the higher the fee. The more cases are brought by foreign investors, the more opportunities for appointment.

Similarly, the more an arbitrator is approved by the lawyers and officials who make appointments in individual cases, the more he or she can expect more appointments. The more an arbitrator supports the investor-state legal industry, the more he or she can expect support from senior players in the industry. The more a powerful country benefits from the system, the more that country can be expected to support the key treaties that give the arbitrators their power and income.

And so on. The system is tainted because it is not judicial. Unlike the domestic and international courts that resolve disputes involving sovereign countries, there is no security of tenure, no set salary, no objective means of case assignment, no rule against arbitrators working on the side as lawyers.

These problems are unique to investment treaty arbitration because of its peculiar structure and function. In other kinds of arbitrations—under a contract or a collective agreement, for example—each side can in principle sue the other. This basic reciprocity is thought to help keep the arbitrators honest.

In contrast, only foreign investors can sue under investment treaties; the countries cannot themselves initiate a case. Thus, the system is not reciprocal in the usual way of arbitration. In turn, the arbitrators have an apparent incentive to favour foreign investors—especially deep-pocketed ones—to grow the arbitration business. This suggests they will interpret the treaties in a way that encourages claims. Or, they may favour a powerful government—or its investors—that is needed to support the treaties that give the arbitrators their power.

Whether or not this happens in fact, and who ends up further ahead, is not the point. The point is that it is unfair to allow a case of importance for an entire country to be decided by someone who has a financial interest in how issues under the treaties are worked out. I suggest that the institutional set-up creates what lawyers in Canada would call a "reasonable apprehension of bias" in favour of some and against others. It gives rise to unavoidable conflicts of interest.

This unfair arrangement may well have suited the Western European countries that originally created investment treaties that allow for this kind of arbitration. The system was slanted in their favour. That is, it seems to work better for the country with more political and economic clout. Both forms of power set up the right sorts of dependencies among the arbitrators, from the point of view of those countries.

For Canada, the arrangement has not worked out too well so far. Canada's main experience has been under NAFTA. Canadian investors have filed seventeen lawsuits against the United States and not won a penny in compensation. The Canadian investor lawsuits were not all duds, compared to U.S. investor lawsuits that have been successful against Canada and Mexico. Also, in my systematic review of NAFTA awards, it emerged (albeit tentatively) that NAFTA arbitrators were significantly more likely to take a restrictive, country-friendly approach if the lawsuit was against the United States instead of Canada or Mexico. I am not saying these numbers prove an actual bias on the part of any arbitrator. Rather, they support the existing reasons to doubt the independence and fairness of investor-state arbitration because of its institutional design.

Under the Canada-China FIPA as well, the institutional design appears more likely to work in China's favour than Canada's. It's fair to say, China has more clout. For example, the size and the wealth of its companies offer a more lucrative opportunity for investor-state lawyers and arbitrators. The companies are especially deep-pocketed because they are backed financially by the state. They own more in Canada than Canadian companies do in China. Perhaps most simply, if the process were slanted one way historically, wouldn't we expect it to favour the more powerful country?

For Canada, this is a cause for concern in a long-term deal that, on its terms, is already lopsided in China's favour. Even so, the key issue is not which country comes out ahead under which treaty. Investor-state arbitration is just as tainted when Canada benefits from it, in a treaty with a small and poor country. The system should be fair for everyone.

In chapter 20 of this book, I say more about a leading Canadian investor-state arbitrator named Yves Fortier. As an aside here, I will mention one of Fortier's experiences as an illustration of why institutional safeguards are important, and of how their role may not be fully appreciated.

While sitting as an arbitrator in one case, Fortier was challenged (unsuccessfully) by Venezuela on grounds of alleged impartiality, related to his past conduct in the arbitration. In response to the challenge, he gave this statement to the World Bank official who dealt with the challenge:

> For more than 10 years now, I have been practising law exclusively as an arbitrator. I consider arbitration a very noble profession and I am extremely proud to be a member of that profession.
>
> When I ceased, after many years at the Bar, to act as counsel, I no longer represented clients. I became an adjudicator who, whether as party appointed or chairman of arbitral tribunals, had no case to win or lose. I pledged to myself that I would always be independent and impartial and decide all cases submitted to tribunals on which I sat strictly on the basis of the factual evidence and the applicable law. I am convinced that I have always honored my pledge.

The statement conveys that Fortier has a strong sense of his own integrity. I don't doubt his sincerity or pride. Yet, it does precious little to address the real problem of whether Fortier or any other arbitrator will "always be independent and impartial:" the absence of the usual safeguards that would otherwise back up these personal claims. "Words are wind," as George R.R. Martin put it in *Game of Thrones*.

As things stand, *all* of the decisions of investor-state arbitrators are open to doubt because of the absence of judicial safeguards: secure tenure, a set salary, an objective method of case assignment, and so on. Those safeguards are needed—above all, when a country's sovereignty and solvency are ruled upon—because they reassure everyone that a judge has not succumbed to inappropriate bias, regardless of what the judge says about his or her goodwill.

CHAPTER 13.

NO STANDING FOR CANADIANS

Imagine that your community opposes a Chinese investor's project. The federal government supports the investor. You succeed in blocking the project, after years of court battles. The investor then sues Canada under the FIPA.

Your community would have no right to standing—meaning a full right to participate in the arbitration process—even if the Chinese investor's FIPA lawsuit smeared people in the community, even if it led to an award that affected the community's reputation, and even if it prompted a settlement in which the government agreed to change course and force the project through after all. Your community would not even have a right to know that the lawsuit existed.

That is Canada now, brought to you by the FIPA. Arbitrators can make decisions that affect Canadians, without ever hearing from them.

Arbitrations under the FIPA may affect actors besides the foreign investor. They may also affect governments other than the federal government. Yet, the process does not allow these other parties to participate fully and to the extent of their interests.

This exclusion of others from the process is a basic flaw

in investment treaties. The treaties use arbitration, based on principles of private litigation, to decide disputes that affect third parties and the public. But they raise only foreign investors, not other private parties, to the same level as sovereign countries in international disputes. Only the foreign investor that brings the claim and the national government of the country that is sued get to have full standing.

This selective approach to participation violates a fundamental rule of fairness. The rule is captured in the common law by the maxim *audi alteram partem*, the other side must be heard. It's in Latin because it's an old rule.

Many actors other than the foreign investor and the national government can be affected by the arbitrators' decisions. For example, private individuals may be accused of involvement in government corruption, as happened in the *St. Marys* NAFTA lawsuit against Canada. A local company may have bid on the same government contract as a foreign company, which then challenges the bidding process under an investment treaty, as happened in a case called *Eureko v. Poland*. A province may be accused of violating the FIPA, and have different interests from Ottawa, as seemed true in the NAFTA case of *AbitibiBowater v. Canada*, involving Newfoundland and Labrador. An indigenous people may have a land claim or cultural traditions that are the subject of findings by the arbitrators, as happened in the cases of *Pezold v. Zimbabwe* and *Glamis Gold v. United States*.

In each of these cases, a party could not seek full standing in the arbitration, even though the arbitration affected the party's interests. The party did not have a legal right to access the record and make fulsome factual and legal submissions to the extent of its interests, as a fair process must allow all affected parties to do.

Tying the hands of others in this way may suit the foreign investor and national government involved in a FIPA arbitration. It can help things go faster and cheaper. There is little risk of having to confront another party's point of view. It might be easier for one or the other side to win the case, or for both sides to settle their dispute on terms that hurt an excluded party.

None of that should matter at all. The process is fundamentally unfair. Like in a court process, it can be made fair only if all of those who have an interest in the outcome can seek a full right of standing.

Promoters of investor-state arbitration sometimes claim that this unfairness in the process was solved by letting the arbitrators grant amicus curiae or "friend of the court" status to parties other than the foreign investor and the government. The China FIPA, like some investment treaties, allows for this accommodation, saying:

> A Tribunal, after consultation with the disputing parties, may accept written submissions from a person or entity that is not a disputing party if that non-disputing party has a significant interest in the arbitration. The Tribunal shall ensure that any non-disputing party submission does not disrupt the proceedings and that neither disputing party is unduly burdened or unfairly prejudiced by it.

However, this response is clearly inadequate to solve the problem of unfairness. If a party has "a significant interest in the arbitration," as the FIPA says, then the party should be given full standing to the extent of the interest. Full stop. That is fair; the alternative—a possible opportunity to make a limited "written submission" at the arbitrators' discretion—is not.

It should not matter if the other party's participation may "disrupt the proceedings," as the FIPA says, or if it means a Chinese investor or the federal government is "unduly burdened." That is another way of saying that the process is an exclusive system for foreign investors, at the expense of anyone else who is affected by the dispute.

There are other problems with this limited right of participation under the FIPA. An affected party's right to participate is entirely at the arbitrators' option and can be limited in all sorts of exceptional ways, as it has been under other treaties that include the procedural accommodation now in the FIPA. The FIPA itself only lets other parties file one twenty-page document, in a context where the documents submitted by the foreign investor and national government regularly run into thousands of pages. There is no right of the affected party to make submissions on relevant issues or even to review all of the documents put before the arbitrators. There is no requirement for public notice of FIPA lawsuits, so that others are given an opportunity to apply for standing.

The FIPA is basically a licence to be unfair.

CHAPTER 14.

SECRET DEALS WITH CHINA

Another troubling thing about the China FIPA is its special allowances for secret lawsuits and secret settlements. In this chapter, I outline this problem and why it is so serious under the FIPA.

Secrecy is widespread in investor-state arbitration, as compared to the courts that would otherwise resolve disputes about what a legislature or government is allowed to do. Why is secrecy widespread? It is because investment treaties rely on arbitration procedures that were designed for private, commercial disputes, and so are more open to confidentiality than a court process would ever be. All arbitration rules used in investment treaties allow confidentiality, to varying degrees. Some arbitration "houses"—such as the International Chamber of Commerce—have rules that require blanket secrecy for all information, in all cases. Others—such as the International Centre for Settlement of Investment Disputes—have rules that allow publication of most information, in most cases. Even so, none of the rules and houses are as open as a court's. In the courts, all documents are presumed to be public, subject to specific exemptions for business confidentiality or national security, for example.

Promoters of investor-state arbitration have defended

secrecy in the system. Usually, they argue that the "disputing parties" to an arbitration should be allowed to keep a dispute secret, unless both of them agree to "their" dispute being made public. They invoke the idea of consensual dispute settlement to justify this. It is a good argument in commercial arbitration, where the dispute affects two parties and not any other parties or the public.

However, when the principle of consensual secrecy is applied to disputes under investment treaties about what a country can do on behalf of its people, the public is always affected. Ultimately, it is the public's legislature, government, and money that are on trial. With this kind of dispute, secrecy is unacceptable because it makes public accountability impossible.

Imagine the idea of consensual secrecy applied to other kinds of disputes that affect the public. How many accused criminals would prefer to keep secret that they were accused and put on trial? How many big polluters would prefer to challenge regulations they don't like in private courts?

Personally, I suspect a reason why some members of the investor-state industry support secrecy in investor-state arbitration is precisely because it lets investors or governments hide their dirty laundry. In turn, secrecy makes arbitration more competitive, compared to courts.

After investor-state arbitration began to explode in the late 1990s, it quickly became clear that the arbitrations could be kept totally secret. Arbitrators in various cases decided to favour secrecy, even when the sued country wanted a case to be made public. Canada, Mexico, and the United States responded in the early 2000s by issuing a joint statement under NAFTA. The statement made clear that nothing in that treaty prevented the governments of these countries from publishing documents in the arbitrations and that the arbitration hearings could be open to the public. Canada and the

United States followed up by including clear rules for openness in their new investment treaties.

Reflecting this historical position, in 2010 the Harper Government told a UN body working on the issue of openness in arbitrations under investment treaties:

> Canada's Foreign Investment Promotion and Protection Agreements (FIPAs) and Free Trade Agreements (FTAs) contain provisions protecting and promoting investment. Over time, these treaties have included increasingly explicit provisions concerning the transparency of treaty-based investor-State arbitration . . . .
>
> With respect to dispute settlement, the [FIPA] model [of Canada] was revised to promote transparency. Article 38 of the updated model *requires that all documents submitted to or issued by the Tribunal, including hearing transcripts, be made public* subject to redaction for confidential, privileged or third party business information. Further, *all hearings are to be open to the public*, subject only to closure when necessary to protect confidential business, privileged or third party information (emphasis mine).

That was then.

The China FIPA is a disheartening move away from Canada's position on openness in investor-state arbitration. The FIPA says that arbitration *awards* will be public, but leaves it to the sued country to decide if any other documents or the hearings should be public. According to the FIPA:

> Any Tribunal award . . . shall be publicly available, subject to the redaction of confidential information. [Where the sued country] determines that it is in the public interest to do so . . . all other documents submitted to, or issued by, the Tribunal shall also be publicly available, subject to the redaction of confidential information.
>
> [Where the sued country] determines that it is in the public interest to do so and notifies the Tribunal of that determination, hearings . . . shall be open to the public . . . .

These provisions create a presumption that any documents, other than an award, and all of the hearings in FIPA arbitrations are strictly confidential, unless the sued country makes any of them public.

So, in the case of a Chinese lawsuit against Canada, the federal government now has a broad power to keep everything about the lawsuit secret, until an award is issued. No one in Canada would even know of a FIPA lawsuit against Canada, unless an award was issued. For this reason, especially, the new approach in the FIPA marks a considerable expansion of the federal government's secrecy power.

Was this change demanded by China? Or was it preferred by the Harper Government? Maybe it was a bit of both. The key is that the federal government accepted the change, with knock-on effects for accountability in Canada.

My biggest concern about the FIPA's allowances for secrecy is that the federal government—faced with an embarrassing Chinese lawsuit—now has a clear right under the FIPA to cover up the lawsuit, by settling it before an award is issued. That is troubling because FIPA settlements may involve changes to regulatory decisions and payouts of public money. Canadians now have reason to wonder if the FIPA played a role whenever a government in Canada makes a decision that favours Chinese investors.

In response to this criticism, the federal government said that it plans to disclose lawsuits by Chinese investors on a website, as it does for NAFTA lawsuits. I assume that this commitment was made in good faith. Still, it is a very weak assurance.

As a Canadian voter and taxpayer, I ask, firstly, if Canadians can really trust that governments over the next three decades will not give in to the temptation to keep a sensitive Chinese lawsuit secret. The Harper Government has locked in a right for all federal governments to hide such lawsuits under the FIPA. On the other hand, the Harper Government is unable to commit future governments to a policy of openness, since future governments can always change the policy. The obvious way to cement a commitment to openness would have been to include it in the FIPA.

Second, the Harper Government should explain why it changed Canada's position on openness. If the answer is that China wanted to keep lawsuits secret, why not ensure that the FIPA at least required lawsuits against Canada to be public automatically, instead of on the say-so of the federal government? The FIPA is one-sided in other ways. Why not make it one-sided in this way too?

Third, if China is not committed to openness in investor-state arbitration, shouldn't we worry that China may pressure the federal government to keep Chinese lawsuits against Canada a secret? The Harper Government has not shown much backbone so far in defending Canadian values from Chinese pressure, as evidenced by other terms of the FIPA. Just as likely, the government would want a Chinese lawsuit kept secret too.

Fourth, under NAFTA, the federal government has not always disclosed documents from U.S. lawsuits in a timely way. There are murky cases of apparent settlements based on payouts by provincial governments. If that information has not been revealed, why should Canadians expect it to be any different under the FIPA?

As I discuss in the final chapter of this book, if the federal government is committed to releasing information on FIPA lawsuits, then a requirement to release such information should be put into law. Also, it must be enforced by an independent agency that has the powers needed to ensure maximum and timely disclosure to the public. Otherwise, Canadians have a credible reason to suspect—based on the text of the FIPA—that pressure has been brought to bear by Chinese investors and FIPA lawsuits have been settled, entirely in secret.

CHAPTER 15.

WHAT DO THE TREATIES PROHIBIT?

An essential part of the arbitrators' power lies in the vagueness of the terms of investment treaties. This vagueness shifts power to those who decide how the treaties should be interpreted: the arbitrators.

For example, investment treaties prohibit "expropriation without compensation." That is an important protection, but it also raises a lot of questions. For example, does it apply to general laws that incidentally reduce the profitability of a business? If so, the cost to the public may be huge. And, why give foreign investors this wide-ranging insurance without giving it to everyone else who loses out from a general law? Pretty soon, governments may not have any money left for anything else.

Even in clear cases of direct expropriation—meaning a complete taking of property by the state—it is not always obvious how much compensation should be paid to a foreign investor. For example, should the amount of compensation be lowered, or should access to investor-state arbitration be restricted, because of a foreign investor's own bad conduct?

Investment treaties also give foreign investors a right not to be discriminated against, relative to domestic companies. But how far should that right go in situations where a foreign investor experiences some less favourable *effect* of a law or regulation, instead of explicit and intentional discrimination? And, might it be good sometimes for a government to favour local companies, if doing so helps a disadvantaged region, for example, or encourages support for an important environmental policy?

The treaties also include a right of foreign investors to receive "fair and equitable treatment." This one has become notorious. Arbitrators have taken the concept in all sorts of new directions. They have said it should include a right to "a stable legal framework" for doing business, even when an elected legislature changes the law. They have said it preserves foreign investors' "legitimate expectations," which can mean all kinds of things.

Critically, these new rights are not written in the treaties. They were read into them by arbitrators who, in the explosion of investor-state arbitration, took the vague idea of fair and equitable treatment far beyond its closest pre-explosion comparator, i.e. the widely understood meaning of the customary "minimum standard of treatment" in international law.

I have reviewed several hundred decisions by investor-state arbitrators and studied many of them closely. Overall, I think the arbitrators have taken foreign investors' rights much too far. In turn, they have tilted the treaties even more in favour of foreign investors at the expense of others. I think it's fair to say the arbitrators in some cases have turned the treaties into a catch-all insurance policy for foreign investors, albeit with a long and arduous process for getting paid on a claim.

The expansions of the treaties' vague protections for foreign investors have a corresponding impact on voters who want a government to be able to change its policies, or on taxpayers who want public money to be managed responsibly.

With this in mind, what rights does the China FIPA give to foreign investors? And what expanded protections might the arbitrators bring into the picture based on their interpretations of similar treaties?

Some FIPA promoters in Canada appeared to have a poor understanding of these issues. For example, they said that investment treaties only protect foreign investors from discriminatory and arbitrary treatment, and from uncompensated expropriations. That's definitely not true, based on the terms of the treaties. Yet, the myth lives on.

In fact, the FIPA, like other investment treaties, provides a wide range of powerful rights for foreign investors. They include the right:

- to fair and equitable treatment and full protection and security,

- to make free transfers of money in and out of the country,

- to be compensated for expropriations, including indirect expropriations that do not involve any actual taking of title to property,

- to be treated no less favourably than domestic or third-country investors (including both intentional and de facto discrimination), although with wide exceptions in the FIPA, and

- to be free from requirements to use local goods or suppliers, and other local content requirements.

If Canada was found by FIPA arbitrators to have violated any of these rights, Canadians would normally be on the hook to compensate the Chinese investor in full for its economic losses. It's unclear just how widely the rights will be interpreted by FIPA arbitrators, however, making it that much harder for a government to know in advance if it risks violating a Chinese investor's rights.

Obviously, foreign companies would like to be compensated for whatever a legislature, government, or court decides, if the decision has costs for them. Just as obviously, they would like to reap the benefits of any decision that gives them a windfall. Who wouldn't want a cushy deal like that?

Yet, in any democracy, voters must have the right to change the rules. By requiring special compensation for foreign investors when the rules do change, investment treaties erode the value of voting rights. Even in an undemocratic country, governments still have a responsibility to respond to the needs of their people.

For example, any government may face a financial crisis, mass unemployment, new health or environmental threats, or a corrupt decision by another government. In each context, sometimes the government needs to make difficult or urgent decisions, free from the risk of massive liability to foreign investors. Yet, in each of these contexts, investor-state arbitrators have already required a country to compensate a foreign investor because of how the country responded to a major crisis, a new threat, or evident corruption.

What about the FIPA's exceptions to foreign investors' rights? Don't these protect the "right to regulate" in Canada and China?

For some kinds of government decisions, the FIPA includes protections that go by various names: exceptions, reservations, carve-outs, and so on. They are pretty boring. I deal with them here because FIPA promoters seem to love them. In a nutshell, exceptions are a weak response to the FIPA's constraints on Canadian voters and taxpayers.

Exceptions in an investment treaty give some reassurance that a government's decisions are less likely to lead to liability. The exceptions in the China FIPA thus give a modest breathing room for FIPA arbitrators to balance the rights of Chinese investors against the rights of Canadians. However, even assuming that a balance like this is needed—beyond all the other protections that foreign investors enjoy outside of the

FIPA—the FIPA's exceptions do not deliver a balance. There are four reasons why.

First, exceptions in an investment treaty make the country's right to regulate foreign investors an "exception" to the primary rule, which is to protect foreign investors. They do not establish the right to regulate as an equal partner. To make it an equal partner, the treaties would need a clear statement of the right to regulate alongside a country's many treaty obligations to protect foreign investors. The China FIPA doesn't have a statement like that. This omission is typical in investment treaties, reflecting the imbalance they create.

Second, the exceptions in investment treaties often do not extend to all of the treaties' rights for foreign investors, and arbitrators can almost always find some other basis to order compensation for a foreign investor, if an exception gets in the way. For example, exceptions often don't apply to foreign investors' right to fair and equitable treatment, even though arbitrators have used this rule more than any other to condemn countries for making policy decisions that went against the interests of a foreign investor.

Third, exceptions are often limited to a narrow area of regulation. This exposes other areas of regulation to the risks that the exception was supposed to counter. For example, exceptions may protect a government's flexibility in competition matters but not in health or environmental matters. One may ask, why does investor-state arbitration pose an unacceptable risk to competition policies but not to these other priorities?

The China FIPA has a lot of gaps like this. For example, in Article 33(2), it includes general exceptions for health, environmental, and conservation measures, which are borrowed from a historical trade deal, the General Agreement on Tariffs and Trade of 1948. However, one exception that was in the historical trade deal—for a country's decisions "relating to the products of prison labour"—was not put in FIPA. Why exclude that exception from the FIPA, if not to help any foreign investors whose business relies on prison labour?

Fourth, exceptions always have conditions that limit their relevance. For example, arbitrators have sometimes decided that a decision was not strictly "necessary" (as is required by the terms of some exceptions) if a less restrictive option was open to the country, even if the other option was more costly or otherwise less feasible. Similarly, where an exception says that the FIPA does not "prevent" a new environmental law, the arbitrators can order full compensation for a foreign investor on the basis that the law could still be enacted—even if at huge cost to taxpayers—and so was not technically "prevented." These are some of the loopholes that let arbitrators put trade values ahead of other valid concerns, as they have often chosen to do.

Let's accept for a moment that foreign investors should be privileged over everyone else, by having a special process to balance their interests against those of everyone else in a country. The FIPA's exceptions simply do not achieve such a balance. They are not a substitute for a clear affirmation of the country's right to regulate. Indeed, they actually undermine the right to regulate because they suggest that the FIPA's key purpose is to protect foreign investors, unless the country can make an exceptional case for regulating. That is prioritizing, not balancing.

In broad strokes, I have painted a picture of the arbitrators' power to condemn countries and re-direct public money. Ultimately, the importance of this power amplifies other concerns about the arbitrators' role. FIPA arbitrators are not accountable, like a legislature. They do not have to balance the interests of many people and groups, like a government. They are not independent, like a court. On this basis, it is wrong to give the arbitrators the final power to review what these other institutions in Canada decide.

CHAPTER 16.

THE PRICE TAG FOR DEMOCRACY

Chinese investors can use the FIPA to challenge anything that a legislature or government or court in Canada does. They may not win, but the ability to sue in this way is a powerful tool by itself. It is also a special opt-out from the country's usual democratic process under the Canadian constitution. And, if a Chinese investor does win, the cost to taxpayers could be huge. It almost goes without saying that this is an important development for the future of Canadian democracy.

As a defensive step, promoters of investor-state arbitration sometimes downplay the arbitrators' role in reviewing elected legislatures. For example, they have relied on a study by two U.S. political scientists, Jeremy Caddel and Nathan Jensen. In their study, Caddel and Jensen said that "there are only 14 cases of legislatures taking actions leading to disputes" (in 163 World Bank arbitrations under investment treaties). In turn, they recommended that "democratic legislatures should embrace investor-state arbitration as an additional check on executive branch misbehaviour."

For me, this finding and recommendation were surprising to see. They were especially surprising because I had previously analyzed 162 investment treaty cases—most of which overlapped with those reviewed by Caddel and Jensen—and found 60 cases, not 14, in which a legislative decision was challenged by the foreign investor. Many of the cases were against countries that had established democratic institutions, such as Canada and the United States, suggesting that Caddel and Jensen's reassuring recommendation to legislatures was hasty, at the very least. I also wondered how our numbers could be so different, especially because my findings had been reported (and the data made public) about six months before Caddel and Jensen released their study.

A closer look at Caddel and Jensen's methods revealed the answer. They filtered out of their numbers all the cases in which a foreign investor targeted a legislative decision *alongside* an executive (i.e. government) decision, wherever they thought the latter decision was the investor's main target. By coding for these "primary" decisions only, the number of cases involving a legislative decision fell dramatically. By comparison, my numbers accounted for all the decisions challenged by foreign investors, whether legislative or executive, as described in the investors' submissions to the arbitrators. This led to the findings that 60 (37 per cent) of the cases involved a legislative decision—compared to Caddel and Jensen's 14 (9 percent) of the cases—and that virtually all cases involved an executive decision.

Each of these methods has value and I don't mean to challenge Caddel and Jensen's focus, which investigated a legitimate question. My concern is that they did not mention the effect of their method on the numbers when they presented their numbers publicly. Then, based on the misleading numbers, they made a dubious recommendation that legislatures should embrace investor-state arbitration, as I quoted above.

Because I have seen it happen before, I was not surprised when Caddel and Jensen's study—soon after it was released in the spring of 2014—was fed into the seemingly endless campaign to promote investor-state arbitration. This time, the campaign was picking up steam in Europe, focusing on the

Canada-Europe CETA and Europe-U.S. TTIP, two massive proposed trade deals. A report commissioned by the Netherlands trade and foreign affairs ministries, and submitted to the Dutch parliament in the summer of 2014, used Caddel and Jensen's study to downplay concerns about possible "regulatory chill" created by investor-state arbitration (which in Europe is called ISDS, for investor-state dispute settlement). It was stated in the report:

> The second argument against regulatory chill is that most ISDS claims do not challenge legislative acts. Instead, the vast majority of "regulatory" challenges are administrative in nature. . . . In a study published in April 2014, researchers Jeremy Caddel and Nathan Jensen concluded that the vast majority of investor-state claims arise from executive branch decisions instead of legislative decisions.
>
> After analyzing all concluded ICSID decisions, the researchers found that 47 per cent of disputes were associated with ministries or agencies while only 9 per cent (14 total cases) resulted from legislative acts. According to the [Caddel and Jensen] study: "Given the low rate of disputes involving legislative branch activity, arguments that investor-state arbitration may encroach on the legitimate prerogatives of domestic governments appear to be overstated. Instead, democratic legislatures should embrace investor-state arbitration as an additional check on executive branch misbehavior."

Thus, a dubious recommendation based on misleading numbers was quickly used to spin investor-state arbitration in an overly positive light. Indeed, it was used in this instance, intentionally or not, to misinform a country's parliament on basic questions about the relationship between investment treaties and democracy. For our purposes, this was a follow-up to how the FIPA was sold to Canadians in all sorts of questionable ways, as I discuss in part four of this book.

Promoters of investor-state arbitration have also claimed, misleadingly, that foreign investors bring lawsuits to challenge decisions that targeted a foreign investor specifically, but rarely to attack general laws or regulations.

However, after testing this claim in a systematic review of known cases, I found that about half of foreign investor lawsuits involved challenges to a decision that appeared general. By this, I mean that the decision appeared to affect lots of people besides the foreign investor. For example, many cases involved the following areas.

- *Environmental decisions* to limit mining activities, regulate hazardous wastes, or prohibit chemicals.

- *Health decisions* to put controls on tobacco or supervise a communal water system.

- *Economic decisions* to change a system of agricultural subsidies, put a windfall tax on resource companies, or require oil companies to put money into local research and development.

- *Infrastructure and resource decisions* that involved conflicts, often involving local communities, about a dam, mine, pipeline, or other big project.

The disputes in these cases involved a foreign investor, but they appeared to affect other actors too. Even cases that looked very specific to the situation of a foreign investor sometimes seemed to have implications for other people. For example, some "specific" cases involved a contract between a government and a foreign company that seemed important for the country's economy.

A related finding from the systematic research was that the arbitrators usually reacted negatively, when they were faced with decisions that were connected to a democratic process. I researched this issue by searching for terms like "election," "accountability," and "democracy" in all known investor-state awards. I found that arbitrators—in cases in which the dispute was linked to an election—typically left this fact out of their reasons for the decision, or approached the role of the election and surrounding politics with suspicion. As well, arbitrators sometimes referred to public protests as a reason to doubt a government's decision, if it went against a foreign investor. On the other hand, they rarely examined the reasons for public concern in the first place.

For example, in a case called *Tecmed v. Mexico*, the residents of local communities protested against the continued operation of a hazardous waste facility. The dispute came to involve the federal government and the courts in Mexico. Eventually, the foreign owner of the facility brought an investor-state lawsuit against the country. In deciding this lawsuit, the tribunal focused on whether the Mexican government had done enough to suppress the protests "in accordance with the parameters inherent in a democratic state," as the tribunal put it rather ominously, and to protect the foreign investor's assets. Even after finding that the government had done enough in this respect, the tribunal awarded compensation because the government had not renewed the investor's operating permit. The tribunal suggested that the government's decision about the permit was an irrational response to the public protests, though the tribunal did not elaborate on any of the reasons for public opposition. In passing, the tribunal said that residents of a nearby town had objected to shipments of waste in open trucks through the community. Pray tell us more?

The essential point I am trying to highlight is that the FIPA poses a challenge for Canadian democracy. It lets Canadians change the rules that govern their country, but with a new proviso: Chinese investors may have to be compensated for their losses. Thus, new laws in Canada may now have a price tag, with the size of the sticker shock yet to be determined by FIPA arbitrators.

CHAPTER 17.

SETTLEMENTS OF LAWSUITS, KNOWN AND UNKNOWN

What will happen under the FIPA if a Chinese investor objects to something that a Canadian legislature or government is proposing to do? This question is hard to answer partly because—based on the FIPA's terms and Canada's experience under NAFTA—one has to be wary of what governments say about foreign investor lawsuits.

As I discussed in chapter 14, the FIPA goes beyond other investment treaties of Canada, by allowing for secret settlements of foreign investor lawsuits after the lawsuit is launched. As a result, Canadians need to be wary that the FIPA will play a behind-the-scenes role in government decision-making about Chinese investors. To what extent this will happen in practice, no one outside government, and probably few inside, can know for sure. In my experience, officials in Canada are coy about how the treaties have affected their internal decisions.

At least, it seems that governments in Canada may be tempted to hide controversial Chinese lawsuits from the public. Without public access to the record, we can never reliably know the real story. In this chapter, I elaborate on an example of a murky NAFTA settlement in order to illustrate why there is cause for concern about what will happen under the FIPA.

To backtrack, when U.S. investors brought the first NAFTA lawsuits against Canada in the late 1990s, Canadian trade officials reportedly tried to keep one of the cases secret, when they were asked if it existed. The case was exposed at the time because federal environmental officials did not play along. (These events occurred at a meeting with organizations from outside of government, according to a confidential source who was present at the meeting.)

A few years later, the federal government rightly pushed for more openness under NAFTA, and adopted a policy of releasing most of the documents in NAFTA investor-state cases. This change in policy was important, and its rollback in the China FIPA very unfortunate. Yet, even under NAFTA, the policy did not deliver the level of openness one would find in a Canadian court. Also, the terms of NAFTA settlements—and sometimes their mere existence—were not always made public. In some cases, federal officials appear to have used this lack of openness, and the selective release of information, to downplay negative NAFTA developments for Canada.

The example I would like to highlight is the NAFTA case of *St. Marys v. Canada*. The NAFTA lawsuit was brought by a Brazilian-owned U.S. quarry company. The company's proposed quarry near Flamborough, Ontario, was blocked by the Ontario government after years of public opposition that focused on its environmental impacts. At the time, the quarry's water impacts in particular had not been approved by environmental regulators.

The NAFTA case puttered along for about two years, drawing in numerous officials from the federal and Ontario governments. It touched on important areas of policy, such as public health and fiscal responsibility. In March 2013, the case was settled. Unfortunately, the terms of the settlement were not made public, but we can piece together the basics of what happened from press releases.

To begin, the federal government issued a press release that presented the settlement as a victory for Canada and for NAFTA. According to this version of events, the U.S. company "agreed to irrevocably and permanently withdraw its NAFTA claim" and acknowledged that "it lacks and has always lacked standing to bring this claim under NAFTA." "Therefore," the press release said, "no payment has been made by the Government of Canada in the settlement of the dispute." Thus, federal trade officials painted the *St. Marys* case as a frivolous NAFTA lawsuit that was rightly withdrawn, without any compensation paid by Canada.

The U.S. investor—St. Marys Cement—issued a press release that told another part of the story. It said that St. Marys agreed to withdraw "any current litigation," obviously including the NAFTA lawsuit, and that, as part of the deal, it was in fact paid CDN$15 million toward the costs of the project (which the company claimed had reached CDN$22 million).

Lastly, the Ontario government issued a press release that said it had reached an agreement with St. Marys that would "ensure a quarry near Flamborough will not be built and protect local wetlands and water supply." The release also confirmed that Ontario agreed to pay St. Marys CDN$15 million, and that St. Marys "agreed to withdraw all current or future litigation." Thus, Ontario evidently paid a substantial sum to get rid of the NAFTA lawsuit.

Oddly, neither Ontario nor St. Marys mentioned the NAFTA lawsuit, and the federal government did not mention the CDN$15 million payment. Why would that be? And was the settlement favourable to Ontario taxpayers, or did it give a windfall to the U.S. investor that would have been next to impossible under Canadian law?

Well, St. Marys would be extremely unlikely to win a financial award at all, let alone an award of that size, in the courts.

Usually, in judicial review, the primary remedy in a case like this one would not involve compensation. A court might quash the government's decision to block the quarry, but it would not order millions of dollars in compensation for the unhappy owner of an unapproved project.

There are other reasons that might help to explain the way in which this settlement was presented. For example, the Liberal government in Ontario may have wanted to avoid another embarrassing story about a cancelled project. Not long before, the government had reached a costly settlement with other companies after cancelling two controversial power plants.

For our purposes, the important point is that the press releases about the settlement suggest an attempt to understate NAFTA's role in driving Ontario to pay compensation to a U.S. company, and to spin the NAFTA settlement as an unqualified win for Canada. The federal government has a track record of portraying investor-state arbitration favourably. By doing so, it defends Canada's decision to be the first (and only) Western developed country to agree to accept investor-state arbitration with the United States in NAFTA. Furthermore, it helps the federal government's current push for more deals that will lock Canada into investor-state arbitration more extensively than under NAFTA. The most important of these deals are the FIPA with China, the Canada-Europe CETA, and the U.S.-led Trans-Pacific Partnership.

In addition, the Ontario government may have wanted to avoid any implicit acceptance of responsibility for future NAFTA or FIPA awards. This last point is a little bizarre. Mostly, it comes from a loose end since NAFTA was concluded over twenty years ago: if a province's actions lead to an award or settlement under NAFTA, should the province have to pay? Or should the federal government have to pay, since it was the federal government that committed Canada to the deal without asking for provincial approval? This quandary comes from governments in Canada pushing for trade deals without first addressing the constitutional issues that such deals create for Canadian federalism. The issue of which level of government has to pay for Canada's obligations to compensate foreign investors under NAFTA has been on the back-burner for about twenty years.

More broadly, it is troubling that NAFTA allows for confidential settlements. It is even more troubling that the FIPA allows the federal government to cover up the mere fact of a Chinese lawsuit by settling it before an award comes out. The *St. Marys* case shows how the government can play with secrecy to cast settlements in a favourable light. Meanwhile, the FIPA's allowances for secrecy make it impossible for Canadians to track how Chinese investors are using the FIPA. None of this is a good sign.

CHAPTER 18.

AN EXAMPLE OF REGULATORY CHILL

Opponents of investor-state arbitration have long warned that it may lead to so-called "regulatory chill," by creating financial risks for countries that deter responsible regulation of foreign investors. Promoters of investor-state arbitration have denied the charge, calling on others to provide specific evidence that investment treaties have led governments to change their decisions because of the threat of a foreign investor lawsuit.

My reaction to this debate is that it is a government's responsibility to investigate the issue—since it is the government that controls most of the relevant information—and to reassure the public that foreign investors are not privileged unfairly in a country's decision-making. From outside, usually one can only guess at how changes to government decisions may have been caused by NAFTA or other investment treaties.

However, in some cases there is reliable, public information that connects an investment treaty to changes by a legislature or government. In those situations, promoters of investor-state arbitration usually say two things: (1) something else, such as political pressure or a court judgment, must have led to the change, (2) any change from an investment treaty was in any event positive.

These responses seem to me to reflect clever techniques

of argument in the debate about regulatory chill. The first response puts a high burden of proof on anyone claiming a link between a treaty and regulatory change, but puts a low burden on those saying that other factors caused the change. Basically, it moves the goalposts according to which side has the ball.

The second response is different. It shifts the debate from the question of whether regulatory change happened to the question of whether a change was good or bad. Obviously, the merits of any regulatory change—whether linked to an investment treaty or not—can be debated for a long time. Some people might like the original decision, some might not, and there may be evidence to support both views.

Really, by shifting the debate in this way, promoters of investor-state arbitration are accepting that the arbitrators—instead of a legislature, government, or court—should have the final word on the merits of a country's decisions, whenever they are challenged by a foreign investor. By implication, promoters are accepting that a country's decision-making processes should be changed to make sure that foreign investors are privileged or subsidized. By themselves, these strike me as radical propositions, from the point of view of Canadian constitutional democracy.

A good example of regulatory chill, and the threat to democracy, comes from one of the early NAFTA lawsuits against Canada: *Ethyl v. Canada*. This case was started by a U.S. company, Ethyl Corporation, after the federal government proposed in 1997 to ban MMT, a gasoline additive. Ethyl was one of the main manufacturers of MMT. The proposed ban responded to concerns from the auto industry that MMT interfered with new emissions technology in cars. There were also apparent health risks linked to inhalation of MMT in gasoline fumes.

At the time, MMT was banned or not used in nearly all

the United States, due to health and environmental concerns, although Ethyl pushed repeatedly in the 1980s for MMT to be approved in the United States. Meanwhile, the federal government in Canada had approved MMT in the 1980s on the self-assured basis that there was not enough evidence of health risks.

When the federal government moved to ban MMT in Canada, in 1997, Ethyl launched a lobbying campaign against the proposed ban. This campaign was reminiscent of Ethyl's earlier one against the banning of lead in gasoline, which Ethyl also manufactured.

In its later fight for MMT, Ethyl was joined by Canadian oil refineries who opposed the ban because it would bump up their costs; the estimated cost to re-tool refineries in Canada for an MMT-free world was reportedly around CDN$115 million. The refineries and Ethyl lobbied provincial politicians, some of whom joined the fight for MMT. Meanwhile, the auto industry supported the proposed ban, as did environmental groups and academic researchers tasked with investigating the health effects of MMT.

Most importantly, for our purposes, Ethyl's fight to keep MMT was helped by two new trade deals, both of which came into effect a few years before the federal government's proposed ban. One of the trade deals was NAFTA, the other was an internal Canadian deal called the Agreement on Internal Trade. The latter deal was modelled on NAFTA, and is a good example of how a foreign trade deal can have knock-on effects in Canadian law. Both deals gave Ethyl new options that were not available in its earlier campaign to keep lead in gasoline.

Ethyl took advantage of the NAFTA option by invoking its obscure investor-state arbitration mechanism to sue Canada for the proposed ban. Ethyl argued provocatively—from the perspective of Canadian law—that its status as a U.S. company under NAFTA required that it get full compensation for its losses from Parliament's proposed ban, including for claimed damages to its reputation as an MMT manufacturer. A NAFTA tribunal was established and, in a decision that seemed to surprise Ottawa, the tribunal let Ethyl's claim go ahead. This was the first formal foreign investor lawsuit against Canada and one of the first under any investment treaty.

Meanwhile, Alberta used the Agreement on Internal Trade (AIT) to bring a separate claim against the federal government. And, before Ethyl's NAFTA lawsuit was finished, the AIT panel decided in favour of Alberta. Basically, the panel's majority objected to how the ban was designed—it limited trade in MMT instead of banning use of the chemical outright—and called for the federal government to withdraw the ban. The dissenting member of the panel would have allowed the ban to go ahead on environmental grounds. Indirectly, the case pointed to weaknesses in Canada's environmental regulations when a product's health or environmental risks are uncertain.

Having lost the AIT case, and still facing Ethyl's NAFTA lawsuit, the federal government pulled the proposed ban in 1998. It also issued a public statement that MMT was not a health or environmental threat and paid Ethyl about CDN$19.5 million in compensation. This amount of compensation was more than the budget (CDN$16.9 million) for Environment Canada's enforcement and compliance programs at the time. In exchange, Ethyl withdrew its NAFTA lawsuit.

Personally, I think the *Ethyl* settlement was an unfortunate cave-in by the federal government, and a good example of regulatory chill. After taking a stand in support of the ban, the government allowed trade deals to trump health, the environment, and the pocketbooks of car owners. Yet, in the debate about regulatory chill, promoters of investor-state arbitration often deny that this case is even an example of a regulatory change due to an investment treaty. They point to the role of the AIT to deny that Ethyl's NAFTA lawsuit contributed to the settlement.

It is more credible to say that the Ethyl settlement was linked both to the AIT and to NAFTA. Clearly, the federal government's public statement and payment of compensation were directly tied to Ethyl's NAFTA lawsuit, since Ethyl was not a party to the AIT case. Even the government's withdrawal of the ban is hard to attribute only to the AIT case, since the AIT panel could only make a non-binding recommendation and, even then, its decision was limited to the internal—not international—trade of MMT.

More broadly, it is revealing that Ethyl failed in its efforts to keep lead in gasoline, despite the uncertain science at the time about the dangers of leaded gasoline, but that Ethyl later succeeded in opposing the MMT ban. A key difference in Ethyl's successful MMT campaign was its right to use NAFTA arbitration, supported by the AIT.

MMT was phased out of Canadian gasoline on a voluntary basis in 2004. On the other hand, MMT was never used widely in the United States, where other additives replaced lead. So, one can say reasonably that, for about six years, NAFTA contributed to Canadians' exposure to MMT, and to emissions of other pollutants from cars when automobile emissions control systems failed because of MMT. It also contributed to innumerable trips by Canadians to the auto repair shop, after a car's engine light came on because MMT gummed up the catalytic converter.

These are unstudied costs linked to the ability of U.S. investors to sue Canada under NAFTA. They are hard to track, but still real for those who were affected.

With the China FIPA in mind, I would sum up the regulatory chill issue in this way, based mostly on several dozen interviews with government insiders about how investor-state arbitration has affected government decision-making:

- Chinese investors clearly have new powers to pressure governments in Canada by threatening FIPA lawsuits. This institutional change is important in itself.

- Under pressure from foreign investors, governments may change their decisions. The pressure on governments rises as more public money is at stake. Even a non-negligible risk of large financial liability would be a significant—and sometimes a determining—factor in government decision-making.

- Evidence of governments in Canada changing their decisions on a widespread basis, due to the risk of foreign investor lawsuits, has not emerged to date. Related to this, there appears to be a general lack of awareness among government officials about the risk of such lawsuits. That said, in some cases, governments clearly have changed course due to an actual or threatened foreign investor lawsuit. In each case, the change elevated the position of foreign investors in government decision-making, compared to other government priorities.

- In some cases, a government may go ahead with a planned decision, despite the risk of a foreign investor lawsuit. Such perseverance appears to be especially likely if the government has competing legal advice, and a strong political commitment, to support its original plan. The choice to persevere may lead to a foreign investor lawsuit, or it may not.

- There is clearly a learning curve for governments. They appear more likely to change their decisions if they have been involved in past foreign investor lawsuits. It seems to be a bit like getting slapped in the face: the memory fades but it rarely goes away completely.

Thus, the FIPA has shifted decision-making in Canada to the benefit of Chinese companies, though it's hard to say how much. The key questions are how often changes will be made as a result of the FIPA, what the changes will mean for others, and where the institutional shift of power will ultimately lead. These questions can be answered reliably only with government support for a thorough, independent, and public review. Having watched the FIPA get pushed through, I'm not holding my breath for a proper investigation of the risk of regulatory chill.

CHAPTER 19.

OUTCOMES OF LAWSUITS

What might happen in actual FIPA lawsuits against Canada, if they are not settled before an award is issued?

One can only answer this question by taking an anticipatory approach, informed by the experience of investor-state arbitration so far under other investment treaties. There is a lot of evidence to work with. There have been more than six hundred foreign investor lawsuits worldwide, about three hundred of which have been resolved, according to the UN Conference on Trade and Development. From this, researchers have gathered information about how the system is being used, though much more could have been gathered in a thorough review of the FIPA before it was ratified.

For example, what have been the outcomes in cases that have been resolved? It appears that about a third of the cases have led to an award for the foreign investor, and about a third have not. The remaining third were apparently settled, usually on unknown terms. Thus, foreign investors do not always get compensation when they sue under an investment treaty. There are various reasons for this. For example, the investor may not pay its arbitration fees on time. The arbitrators may decide that they lack authority over the claim. More typically, the arbitrators decide in the end that the country did not violate the treaty's protections for foreign investors.

On the other hand, no foreign investor has ever been ordered to compensate a country—or anyone in a country—after being found to have violated an investment treaty. The treaties are written to allow investors to sue countries, not vice versa. Thus, no country really ever "wins" in investment treaty arbitration—it avoids losing. Even when it avoids losing, a country may face extremely high costs for its lawyers and the arbitrators—in the worst cases, tens of millions of dollars—which the foreign investor usually does not have to cover.

This is one way in which investor-state arbitration is skewed in favour of foreign investors. One side, typically a very large company or a very wealthy individual, has actionable rights; the other side, the people of a country, has actionable responsibilities.

Promoters of investor-state arbitration sometimes respond to this observation by saying that countries can bring "counterclaims" under the treaties. This is a fancy way of avoiding the obvious. The right to bring a counterclaim—which is not laid out in investment treaties, but usually said by promoters to be implicit in them—is at best a very limited right. It depends on the foreign investor deciding to bring a claim in the first place, and on the foreign investor then framing that claim in a way that makes it vulnerable to a counterclaim. There have been a handful of attempts by countries to bring counterclaims. None have been allowed to proceed fully and none have led to compensation for a country. Meanwhile, there are hundreds of foreign investor claims and, together, they have led to orders of compensation for foreign investors in the billions of dollars.

Basically, this point about counterclaims hammers home that the treaties are one-way. They help foreign investors, especially those from the country with more economic power under the treaty. They are at the expense of anyone who has a conflicting interest. That can be awkward for promoters of the treaties, but it's really not complicated.

What about the third of cases that have apparently settled?

Because the terms of settlements are usually not public, it is hard to know whether a settlement favoured the foreign investor or the country. However, presumably most or all of the settlements involved some change to a country's decisions—in exchange for withdrawal of the lawsuit—such as a decision to change a proposed regulation or pay off the company. In that sense, settlements are a win for the foreign investor if they created an outcome that would not have been possible for the investor, or would have been a lot more difficult to get, by other means. Likewise, each settlement reflects a cost to the people of a country, tracking back to the country's original decision to accept an investment treaty.

Beyond that observation, it is next to impossible to evaluate what is happening in settlements. Even if we know that a settlement exists, its terms are rarely public. The terms should be public, at least in a democratic country like Canada, because they involve public money and public policies. But in nearly all cases they aren't.

Promoters of investor-state arbitration sometimes emphasize that foreign investors, even when they win a case, usually do not get the full amount they sought. That is true. Usually, an award is for only part of that amount, sometimes a very small part. What should we make of that fact?

First, it would be silly to expect all litigants in any adjudicative system to get everything they want whenever they win. Second, foreign investors have sometimes claimed inflated amounts of compensation, possibly as a bargaining tactic, and this skews the numbers.

For example, when Ethyl Corporation sued Canada under NAFTA, as I discussed in the previous chapter, it initially sought "not less than" USD$251 million because the federal government had proposed to ban MMT in gasoline. Ethyl said this would cover the loss in value of its subsidiary in Canada, the cost of reduced operations in Canada, and lost sales in other countries that might follow Canada's example. That was a big ask. Not surprisingly, the case was settled for far less than what was originally sought. Yet, this was still a big win for Ethyl, considering that the odds of a Canadian court awarding compensation to a company for business loss caused by the introduction of a general law were basically nil.

On the other hand, it is also wrong to say that foreign investors always win under investment treaties, or that they always get the compensation they want. Arbitrators in general should be assumed to have good sense and integrity, and investor-state arbitration is not so flawed that it only delivers show trials against countries.

I think the real issue is, do treaties like the FIPA give foreign investors special access to public compensation or to government favours that would not otherwise be available? Clearly, the answer to that question is yes. All kinds of things in investor-state arbitration privilege foreign investors, compared to how individuals and companies are treated in judicial processes that would otherwise decide anyone's complaint against a country's legislature, government, or courts. For example:

- Foreign investors get to make their claims and arguments in the absence of other parties whose interests are affected by the dispute.

- Foreign investors have a major role in deciding the makeup of the tribunal, by appointing one of the arbitrators and negotiating with the country about the presiding arbitrator.

- Where the foreign investor and the country cannot agree on the presiding arbitrator, he or she is in some cases chosen by an outside business organization (such as the

International Chamber of Commerce) that is accountable directly to foreign investors, not to the public in any country.

- All of the arbitrators lack institutional safeguards of independence that would otherwise insulate them from financial dependence on foreign investors, who are the ones that can bring claims and trigger the payment of all the arbitrators.

- The arbitrators' orders of compensation for foreign investors are much easier to enforce than the decisions of domestic or international courts.

Other examples of the privileging of foreign investors are even more technical. Indeed, they become clear only after detailed study of how arbitrators have interpreted the treaties in ways that help foreign investors even more:

- Arbitrators have allowed foreign investor lawsuits to go ahead, on a broad basis, against general laws and regulations.

- They have almost never applied the deferential approaches used by courts to show respect for elected legislatures or expert regulators.

- They have usually avoided any overall, explicit balancing of a foreign investor's interests against those of others or against the public interest.

- They have allowed foreign investors, on a widespread basis, to sidestep their commitments on dispute settlement in a separate contract.

- They have intensified the treaties' constraints on countries by interpreting foreign investor rights more broadly than comparable rights in domestic law and customary international law.

I hope these examples give some sense of how the FIPA can benefit Chinese investors in their relations with Canadian decision-makers. Essentially, the FIPA marks a structural shift in Canada's sovereign priorities toward Chinese investors and away from everyone else.

CHAPTER 20.

WHAT IF IT WAS A JUDICIAL PROCESS?

One of the key flaws in investor-state arbitration is that it leads to final decisions about issues of great importance for countries (and foreign investors too), but does not use a judicial process. As a result, treaties like the FIPA have removed basic safeguards of independence and fairness in the final resolution of public law and policy.

This flaw raises an interesting question. To what extent does the makeup of investor-state arbitration—the lack of safeguards of independence, the lack of representation for other parties, and the confidential process—actually benefit foreign investors or powerful countries? How many cases would go ahead and how much would be awarded, if the treaties used a judicial process instead? These questions cannot be answered conclusively; there is no way to verify how a foreign investor in any case would have fared, if the same case was brought to a court. But there are some clues.

For example, arbitrators under investment treaties have allowed most cases to go ahead even though, in many cases, the dispute related to a separate contract in which the foreign investor agreed to resolve any disputes under that contract in some other forum. Would judges have allowed such cases to go ahead? It is credible to think they would not. In practice, judges usually don't allow parallel court proceedings when a claimant has agreed to use another forum instead. On this basis, it seems reasonable to expect that judges would be more inclined to hold foreign investors to their contractual commitments, not least because the judge's income would not depend on letting the parallel treaty case go ahead.

In contrast, the widespread tendency of the investor-state arbitrators has been to green-light parallel treaty cases. This tendency provides support for the concern that the arbitrators' unique incentives do affect how they decide cases. At least, it is an example of how arbitrators have taken a flexible approach when it comes to protecting foreign investors, thus expanding the arbitrators' own role.

In a systematic study of how arbitrators interpreted investment treaties, I found that they tended to resolve a range of legal issues in ways that encouraged more foreign investor lawsuits. The story was not all one-way; however, there was statistically significant evidence of a tendency for the arbitrators to interpret the treaties—when they were unclear—in ways that favoured foreign investors.

Numerous examples of this expansive tendency emerged upon investigation of how arbitrators ruled on a series of disputed legal issues under investment treaties. One example was the arbitrators' expansive approach to the issue of whether a foreign investor should be allowed to bring a claim when its ownership of an investment wound through holding companies in other countries. Overwhelmingly, arbitrators allowed such claims to go ahead. Similarly expansive approaches were found on the issues of whether foreign investors should be able to "import" arbitration provisions from another treaty, on whether a country's decision should be classified as an "indirect expropriation" of the foreign investor's assets instead of legitimate regulation, and on whether the concept of "fair and equitable treatment" should be limited to specific situations of abuse of a foreign investor or used much more broadly to protect foreign investors from risks that are inherent to democracy and politics. Overall, arbitrators were found to have favoured expansive approaches to these and other ambiguous issues—thus favouring the foreign investors that brought the lawsuits over the countries that defended them—by a ratio of about 3 to 1.

Surprisingly, in this study, I also found that the arbitrators were more likely to take an expansive approach to ambiguous issues if the foreign investor was from the United States, the United Kingdom, or France. On the other hand, they tended to take a restrictive approach that favoured the sued country when the lawsuit was against the United States (although this finding was less robust because there was less data to support it). Even under NAFTA—where all foreign investor lawsuits were based on the essentially same treaty terms—Canada and Mexico were less likely than the United States to benefit from a restrictive approach by the arbitrators. All of these findings on the tendencies of the arbitrators were statistically significant, meaning simply that they were unlikely to be explained by chance.

I stress that there are important limitations in this research on arbitrators' decision-making. The findings are systemic and do not establish actual bias on the part of any individual or in any specific case. They always rely on some degree of trust in the researchers involved and in the quality of a project's design. There are broad limitations to the methods available to analyze these kinds of questions. Basically, the research offers tentative support—not more than that—for expectations of systemic bias due to the absence of judicial safeguards in investor-state arbitration.

I think the most important conclusion to draw from this research is that judicial safeguards are important because they reassure the public that disputes have been resolved independently and fairly. That is the essential issue. And, compared to a judicial process, it seems to me impossible to say that investor-state arbitration passes the test. A judicial process is much preferable to for-profit arbitration under the FIPA or any other investment treaty.

As an aside, it emerged from this research on arbitrator decision-making that one of the most active repeat players among the arbitrators was a Canadian, Yves Fortier. Before he became an important figure in investor-state arbitration, Fortier was a lawyer in a large Canadian firm, Canada's ambassador to the United Nations (appointed by the Progressive Conservative government of Brian Mulroney), and a commercial arbitrator.

The research also indicated that Fortier played a prominent role in expanding the scope of investment treaties. For example, he was the presiding arbitrator for at least three tribunals whose decisions blew open the system in a big way.

The first was a World Bank "annulment" panel that, in 2002, struck down an earlier investor-state tribunal's decision. The earlier tribunal had dismissed an investor's claim against Argentina because the dispute related to a contract and the foreign investor had not gone first to the agreed forum under the contract. In striking down the earlier tribunal's decision, the annulment panel in this case, with Fortier presiding, essentially created the arbitrators' policy of letting parallel treaty cases go ahead in such situations. In doing so, this annulment decision downplayed the principle of sanctity of contract, and helped to fuel the explosion of investor-state litigation. Personally, I think the decision was questionable, especially because an annulment panel is supposed to defer to an earlier tribunal and, in this case, the earlier tribunal dismissed the parallel treaty case for a very good reason. However, for our purposes, the importance of the annulment panel was its role in opening the system to far more litigation, by helping foreign investors to avoid their contractual commitments on dispute settlement.

The second of Fortier's significant decisions came when he was the presiding arbitrator in a case called *Occidental Petroleum v. Ecuador*. In 2012, the tribunal in this case gave an award of USD$2 billion against Ecuador. That was by far the largest known award to that point under any investment treaty. I jokingly referred to it as a big flashing sign that investor-state arbitration is open for business, meaning simply that the arbitrators were able to award vast sums to foreign investors.

The dispute in the *Occidental* case involved a major oil contract that had been breached by the U.S. oil giant Oxy and then terminated by Ecuador. The tribunal awarded compensation primarily on the basis that Ecuador's termination of the contract, even though allowed under the contract, was not "proportionate." In my view, the tribunal's decision was based on several questionable rulings. For example, the tribunal let the case go ahead in spite of a contractual provision in which Oxy, for disputes about the contract, arguably waived its right to resort to any other forum. The tribunal did not give effect to the waiver, taking the Oxy-friendly approach that any exception to the availability of arbitration under the treaty required "clear language to this effect." Also, the tribunal expanded dramatically the notion of fair and equitable treatment in an investment treaty. Its ruling that Ecuador had to act "proportionately" manufactured a new and open-ended obligation for countries. Thus, the tribunal interpreted the treaty creatively and expanded a country's obligations in its contractual dealings with oil companies, without putting a similar obligation on the oil companies themselves.

The third example came when Fortier presided over the tribunal in a case called *Yukos v. Russia*. Without getting into the details, this tribunal made several expansive rulings that let the case go ahead and then awarded an astounding USD$50 billion against Russia (in favour of the former shareholders of the oil company Yukos). As a rough comparison, the European Court of Human Rights decided a similar complaint brought by the former Yukos shareholders against Russia and ordered a comparatively meagre USD$2.5 billion in compensation. Even that amount of compensation was the largest ever ordered by the European Court of Human Rights.

This third example of a case involving Fortier also showed just how high the fees in investor-state arbitration can go. Fortier alone billed just over USD$2.3 million for his services as an arbitrator, which is equivalent to seven years' salary for a judge on the Supreme Court of Canada. His co-arbitrators each billed about the same amount. The tribunal's assistant, Montreal-based investor-state lawyer Martin J. Valasek, billed over USD$1.3 million. The tribunal also ordered Russia to pay 75 per cent of the foreign investors' legal and arbitration costs, the bulk of which were USD$40 million in fees billed by numerous lawyers at the global law firm Shearman & Sterling. The lawyers' rates topped out at USD$1,065 per hour. Reflecting the overlapping roles of investor-state lawyers and arbitrators, the foreign investor's lead lawyer, Emmanuel Gaillard, also works as an investor-state arbitrator.

All of this sloshing around of money in investor-state arbitration doesn't mean that anyone in the system is biased or that anyone acted wrongly. Moreover, in the *Yukos* case, there were presumably good reasons to deliver some remedy for the former owners of Yukos, even if USD$50 billion looks extremely excessive.

No, the key point is simply that the *Yukos* award—like other awards under investment treaties—lacks credibility because it did not come from a judicial process. When a process of adjudication is tainted by a lack of basic safeguards of independence and fairness, then the outcomes of that process are also tainted, no matter who ends up with the money.

CHAPTER 21.

THE ROLLER COASTER CONTINUES

Watching the explosion of lawsuits under investment treaties has been like riding a roller coaster. Every year or so, a new award comes along that blows open the system even more.

The ride doesn't seem likely to end soon. Awards of compensation for foreign investors have risen to billions of dollars, and now tens of billions. Lawyers have developed new and creative arguments for compensating foreign investors, helped by the arbitrators' expansive interpretations. Hundreds of cases are ongoing.

Among the most controversial ongoing cases are two lawsuits brought by the tobacco giant Philip Morris against Australia and against Uruguay. Each country made the mistake (from the perspective of Big Tobacco) of adopting new rules on cigarette packaging. Uruguay was reportedly ready to settle the case by withdrawing the new rules, until former New York mayor Michael Bloomberg's foundation stepped in to help pay the legal defence costs.

In the 1990s, Canada withdrew its own proposed plain packaging law. Ostensibly, this was done for reasons other than NAFTA. However, decision-makers were clearly aware of the threat of a NAFTA lawsuit by R.J. Reynolds Tobacco Company when they withdrew the proposed law. More recently, other countries have apparently also delayed plain packaging proposals, watching especially for the outcome of the cases against Australia and Uruguay. In other words, governments may be waiting for investor-state arbitrators to decide if the public must compensate tobacco companies for their lost profits, before the governments go ahead with a public health measure to limit cigarette addiction.

In the meantime, how many children will take up smoking who otherwise would not? Philip Morris' goal is presumably to maintain the profit stream. Investment treaties have helped it to achieve that goal.

Personally, I expect Philip Morris will lose these cases. I say so partly because the cases create a political embarrassment for investor-state arbitration, and the arbitrators might want to avoid killing the goose that lays the golden eggs. Yet, even if one company loses a creative or repugnant case, there is no system of appeal in investor-state arbitration to stabilize the rules. Countries always face a risk that companies will bring similar claims in the future and that new arbitrators will see things differently. This setup makes for a never-ending risk of pressure on countries to shy away from desirable policies when the policies are opposed by big multinationals or tycoons.

Another reason to expect the roller coaster of lawsuits to keep rolling along is that the existing treaties cover only a small share of global foreign investment flows. That is especially true for investment flows among developed countries. Indeed, just one proposed trade deal—the Europe-U.S. Transatlantic Trade and Investment Partnership (TTIP)—would approximately triple the scope of arbitrator power based on thousands of existing investment treaties.

Also, as arbitrator power expands further into investment relations among developed countries, there is a risk that the arbitrators will become even bolder. That is, they may be even more willing to downgrade the interests of countries—compared to foreign investors—after the biggest sovereign fish are on the hook long-term.

Promoters of investor-state arbitration often present the treaties in a different light. To support new deals like the FIPA, they point to the roughly 2,500 investment treaties now in force. What's the difference if one or two new treaties are added?

Well, first of all, the figure of 2,500 treaties is not as big as it seems. Almost all of these treaties involve two countries, meaning that it would take about 19,000 such treaties to match a global investment treaty. On this rough measure, existing treaties cover less than 15 per cent of world investment flows.

Second, if we use the United States as a proxy for the world, one can estimate the scope of arbitrator power by looking at how much of the investment that flows in and out of the United States is covered by existing U.S. treaties. As it happens, that coverage is also quite small: 15 to 20 per cent. About half of the U.S. flows are with Europe. Very little of those flows are covered by an existing treaty. Most of the rest are with Japan, China, and a few other countries with which the United States does not have an investment treaty.

Third, the vast majority of the 2,500 existing treaties simply do not cover significant investment flows. They are unlikely ever to lead to lawsuits. Indeed, about half of the 395 known lawsuits (that had public documentation up to the spring of 2014) came under just 29 treaties. These treaties were NAFTA; an energy treaty among European and former Eastern bloc countries, called the Energy Charter Treaty; a U.S. trade deal with Central American countries and the Dominican Republic, called CAFTA; and twenty-six U.S. bilateral investment treaties. Thus, nearly half of all lawsuits were brought under just one per cent of the treaties.

Canada's experience with investor lawsuits follows a similar pattern. Before the FIPA, Canada had twenty-nine treaties that allowed investor-state arbitration, and has now faced over thirty lawsuits. All of the lawsuits come under one treaty, NAFTA, and all but one minor case were brought by a U.S. investor.

So it was misleading when promoters of the China FIPA referred to thousands of inconsequential treaties, as if one more deal wouldn't make much difference. Because of the sheer size of Chinese-owned assets in Canada, that new FIPA has expanded arbitrator power over decision-makers in Canada to a far greater extent than had all of Canada's other FIPAs put together.

The Harper Government is now pursuing two other new trade deals that would include investor-state arbitration: the Canada-Europe CETA and the U.S.-led Trans-Pacific Partnership. If they go ahead, the power of the arbitrators will extend to almost all parts of Canada's far-flung foreign-owned economy. I have often wondered why Canada is a world leader in conceding its sovereignty in this way.

PART 3.

THE COURTS AND THE CONSTITUTION

CHAPTER 22.

THE FIPA AND THE COURTS

I mentioned in the preface of this book that investor-state arbitration plays the role of a supreme pseudo-court for the world, albeit protecting only property rights of foreigners and using for-profit arbitrators instead of judges.

To be "supreme," this arbitration system would need to trump a country's courts. It does so in treaties like the FIPA by allowing the arbitrators to review all decisions of a country, including the decisions of its courts. In this way, the FIPA gives arbitrators a final power to condemn Canada's courts and impose financial penalties on Canada for court decisions.

For example, in one foreign investor lawsuit against the Czech Republic, the arbitrators ordered the Czechs to pay about USD$35 million in compensation to a European multinational called Eastern Sugar. The company launched its lawsuit after the Czech legislature and government made changes to an agricultural law. Among other things, the changes responded to earlier decisions of the Czech constitutional court, which had struck down the agricultural law twice, before upholding the version that was then attacked by Eastern Sugar.

As usual under an investment treaty, Eastern Sugar sued the country as a whole, not the Czech legislature or the constitutional court by itself. More remarkably, the investor-state arbitrators took for themselves a very broad role in supervising decisions of the Czech legislature and courts at the highest level. They did not decide, for example, that a degree of deference might be in order because of the greater independence and legitimacy of a country's highest court. Rather, they went ahead with a categorical review of the different versions of the law and the constitutional court decisions. And, in an investor-friendly ruling, the arbitrators essentially read into the treaty a requirement for the Czech Republic to give an explanation—beyond the legislative process that exists for everyone else—for changes made to the agricultural law that had created problems for Eastern Sugar, and then they ordered compensation for Eastern Sugar on the basis that the government's explanations in the arbitration were good enough. The arbitrators also said it made no difference whether the changes were caused by the Czech government or the Czech constitutional court—either way, they were attributable to the Czechs as a country.

This example shows how investor-state arbitrators can review a country's highest courts, and order its people to pay for whatever the arbitrators order as a protection for foreign investors. Thus, it shows how the arbitrators are supreme.

More recently, a U.S. pharmaceutical company called Eli Lilly brought a NAFTA lawsuit against Canada. The lawsuit attacked decisions by Canada's federal courts dealing with patent law. Eli Lilly complained that the courts had approached patent law more restrictively than in the United States and Europe, and argued that this violated NAFTA's guarantees of fair and equitable treatment and compensation for indirect expropriation. According to Eli Lilly:

> In a series of decisions issued since 2005, the Federal Court of Canada and the Federal Court of Appeal have created a new

judicial doctrine whereby utility is assessed not by reference to the requirement in the *Patent Act* that an invention be "useful," but rather against the "promise" that the courts derive from the patent specification. This non-statutory "promise doctrine" is not applied in any other jurisdiction in the world. . . .

The "promise doctrine" not only contravenes Canada's treaty obligations, it is also discriminatory, arbitrary, unpredictable, and remarkably subjective. A patentee cannot know how the promise will be construed by the Federal Courts.

For the sake of argument, let's accept all of this as true. It sounds dire. Why shouldn't Eli Lilly be compensated? The answer is straightforward. Court decisions are final, including on the issue of compensation for whoever lost. If all losers in the courts could seek compensation, court decisions would not be final. Probably, we couldn't afford to have courts.

Lots of people dislike court decisions. Usually, it's because they lose money. Some have their reputations sullied. Some lose their liberty. Some people have been wrongly convicted of terrible crimes and imprisoned for years. The question is, if the courts are okay to decide the personal freedom of Canadians, why aren't they good enough to protect the patents of foreign investors?

Eli Lilly is a giant company. In 2013, its revenues hit about USD$23 billion. The company is represented by big law firms in the NAFTA case: Gowlings in Ottawa and Covington & Burling in Washington, D.C. Even so, I would wager that Eli Lilly will lose the case, and that its main purpose may have been to draw attention to aspects of Canadian patent law that it doesn't like, for whatever reason.

First, Eli Lilly's argument is quite creative, though I admit that this has not stopped foreign investors from winning surprising awards in other cases. Second, like the Philip Morris lawsuits against Australia and Uruguay, Eli Lilly's lawsuit is an awkward case for investor-state arbitrators because of how it attacks a series of decisions by domestic courts. The arbitrators may prefer to dismiss it, to lessen the chance of countries pulling out of the treaties.

Even so, it is still remarkable that court decisions are no longer supreme in Canada and that they can trigger massive liability that would not exist in Canadian law or in other areas of international law.

This trumping of a country's courts highlights another way in which treaties like the FIPA favour foreign investors. The treaties give foreign investors a right to sue a country under international law, without going to the country's courts first. Promoters of investor-state arbitration justify this special waiver by saying that some countries' courts are unreliable. But the waiver is given to all foreign investors, regardless of the reliability of the courts in a particular country or the foreign investor's circumstances.

The special waiver for foreign investors is a radical departure from how international law usually works. Usually, an international claim cannot be brought against a country on a private person's behalf, unless the person has exhausted reasonably available "local remedies" in the host country. Only foreign investors have been relieved of this customary rule. That is, no one—not victims of torture, rape, false imprisonment, or any other mistreatment at the hands of a country—has the right to bring an international claim, with a waiver from the duty to go to the country's courts first. Indeed, only a handful of treaties worldwide (none signed by Canada) allow private parties other than foreign investors to challenge a country's decisions *at all* at an international tribunal with binding and enforceable powers. Meanwhile, there are now thousands of investment treaties that allow foreign investors to do so and, as a bonus, the treaties throw in a waiver from a country's domestic courts.

It's an extremely skewed situation, made worse by the FIPA. If one doubts the reliability of any country's courts, it might make sense to allow for further review by an international court, for everyone who suffers from the lack of protection. Yet, treaties like the FIPA do not give this power of further review to international judges. They give it to for-profit arbitrators who do not have judicial safeguards. As I discussed in chapter 12 of this book, a key difference between a judge and an investor-state arbitrator is that the latter depends financially on those foreign companies that bring claims and on the executive officials who appoint arbitrators. Because the FIPA allows foreign investors to replace Canadian judges with arbitrators in this way, the FIPA is a big step backward for judicial independence.

In effect, the FIPA gives foreign investors an enclave legal status in a country. Only they can opt out of a country's courts and go to an international tribunal whose role is to protect their rights.

Yet, in reply to this observation, the FIPA promoter John Manley claimed in an opinion article in 2012 that it was a "myth" to say that Chinese investors would get an enclave legal status under the FIPA. As I explain in a moment, Manley's claim only worked because he skewed the original observation. Before turning to that flaw in his claim, however, I will highlight a few things about Manley's own connection to investor-state arbitration.

Manley was a minister in the Liberal government in the 1990s and early 2000s. He is now the president of the Canadian Council of Chief Executives (CCCE), which represents chief executives of big companies in Canada. Many of the companies represented by the CCCE are themselves foreign investors in Canada. Some are affiliates of U.S. multinationals—including Chevron and Cargill—that have used investment treaties to pursue awards for hundreds of millions of dollars. Incidentally, in his article promoting the FIPA, Manley did not mention that parent companies of CCCE members have benefited from investor-state arbitration in this way.

To illustrate further, another CCCE member, Dow Chemical, used NAFTA to sue Canada through one of its affiliates, after the Quebec legislature banned the use of a chemical pesticide called 2,4-D. Dow eventually withdrew the lawsuit and received, in exchange, a public statement by Quebec that 2,4-D, if used according to instructions, does not pose an unacceptable health or environmental risk. This settlement was heralded by the federal government as a win for Canada on the basis that Dow did not get any compensation. However, it seemed an unfortunate ending to a case that should not have been possible to begin with. Among other things, the settlement gave Dow a way to say that 2,4-D was safe in other countries, where governments may be less able to regulate a company like Dow.

Returning to his article promoting the FIPA, Manley claimed it was a myth to say that Chinese investors in Canada will have an enclave legal status under the FIPA. However, he interpreted this idea of an enclave status narrowly to mean only a status "allowing them to bypass Canadian laws." Then he replied with this "reality": "All foreign investors in Canada, from China or anywhere else, are subject to the same laws and regulations as Canadian firms. A FIPA does not exempt a foreign investor from Canadian laws."

Well, yes, except Manley's definition missed the key problem. The enclave status of Chinese investors comes from their new FIPA right to challenge Canadian laws in an exceptionally powerful way, outside of Canada's courts and constitution. It is not about bypassing the law completely. It is about having a special power to attack and undermine the law when it applies to them, even though the law applies to everyone else in Canada in the same way. By skipping that bit, Manley did not deal with how the FIPA changes the role of Canada's courts in relation to Chinese investors.

In any country, it is a profoundly important role of the courts to make final decisions about what can be done using sovereign power. Now, when there is a FIPA lawsuit, arbitrators have this final authority in Canada, backed by an unprecedented power to order compensation for Chinese investors.

Some judges have noticed the impact of investment treaties on the role of courts.

For example, an early NAFTA lawsuit against the United States involved a challenge to court decisions in Massachusetts. The state's Supreme Court chief justice at the time, Margaret H. Marshall, reportedly heard of the NAFTA lawsuit at a dinner party. Her reaction: "To say I was surprised to hear that a judgment of this court was being subjected to further review would be an understatement." Similarly, the California Supreme Court chief justice at the time, Ronald M. George, commented on the NAFTA lawsuit: "It's rather shocking that the highest courts of the state and federal governments could have their judgments circumvented by these tribunals." The Canadian investor who brought this NAFTA lawsuit lost. (Canadian investors have lost all of their NAFTA lawsuits against the United States.) Even so, the fact that the arbitrators had a final power of review over U.S. courts was obviously a significant concern for the judges.

Another example comes from South Korea. When the United States-Korea trade agreement was being negotiated, South Korea's Supreme Court reportedly warned government officials that the deal's provisions on investor-state arbitration "could give rise to extreme legal chaos," by subjecting court decisions to review by arbitrators. Later, a group of sitting South Korean judges issued a public statement that expressed concerns about the implications of investor-state arbitration for judicial sovereignty.

A further example returns us to the United States. In a recent decision that involved a foreign investor lawsuit against

Argentina, the Supreme Court of the United States decided to limit its role in reviewing the arbitrators' decisions (for complicated reasons, the arbitration against Argentina was subject to limited review in U.S. courts, not Argentine courts), even on the issue of whether a country had agreed to arbitration in the first place. Members of the investor-state legal industry intervened in force to support the foreign investor—energy multinational BG Group—and were evidently successful in urging the Supreme Court not to interfere with the arbitrators' power. On the other hand, in a dissenting opinion, Supreme Court Chief Justice John Roberts said:

> It is no trifling matter for a sovereign nation to subject itself to suit by private parties; we do not presume that any country—including our own—takes that step lightly. . . . But even where a sovereign nation has subjected itself to suit in its own courts, it is quite another thing for it to subject itself to international arbitration. . . .
>
> [B]y acquiescing to arbitration, a state permits private adjudicators to review its public policies and effectively annul the authoritative acts of its legislature, executive, and judiciary. . . .
>
> Under [the investment treaty], [Argentina or the United Kingdom] grants to private adjudicators not necessarily of its own choosing, who can meet literally anywhere in the world, a power it typically reserves to its own courts, if it grants it at all: the power to sit in judgment on its sovereign acts.

Thus, there was recognition by the U.S. Supreme Court chief justice that investor-state arbitration changes a country's sovereignty in important ways.

A final example of judicial awareness about investor-state arbitration is this statement in 2014 by the chief justice of the High Court of Australia, Robert French, in a speech about investor-state arbitration:

> Arbitral tribunals set up under ISDS [investor-state dispute settlement] provisions are not courts. Nor are they required to act like courts. Yet their decisions may include awards which signif-

icantly impact on national economies and on regulatory systems within nation states.

Later in the speech, Chief Justice French called for greater involvement by the courts in the debate about investor-state arbitration:

> So far as I am aware the judiciary, as the third branch of government in Australia, has not had any significant collective input into the formulation of ISDS clauses in relation to their possible effects upon the authority and finality of decisions of Australian domestic courts. This is an issue which presently is of small compass. It has the potential to become larger and it is desirable that it be addressed earlier rather than later.

Based on these examples, there has been recognition by some judges of how investment treaties change the role of the courts and anyone else who acts for a sovereign country. Meanwhile, in Canada, judicial reaction has been muted and, in a few cases, defensive of the federal government's position. In a few NAFTA-related cases that have come before them, courts in Canada have usually approached investor-state arbitration as if it was just another form of commercial arbitration. This led them to understate the impact of using arbitration to review legislative or court decisions and to re-direct public money.

As well, to my knowledge, no Canadian judge has spoken publicly about how investor-state arbitration affects the role of courts. That may be a little surprising, since Canada has been sued more often than almost any other country. I expect the main explanation is that most judges, like most Canadians, are not really aware of the details of investment treaties. I expect another factor is that the courts are highly deferential to the federal government's treaty-making power.

I don't want to be too hard on judges. Investor-state arbitration is very complex. To understand it properly, one has to review hundreds of cases under the treaties. Lawyers from the federal government or a large company may run interference in any actual case about investor-state arbitration that comes before the courts, by spinning the record of arbitrations and the treaties.

Ultimately, it is up to governments to make good decisions about investment treaties. If a government fails to do so, the most obvious option is to respond in the political domain, not in the courts. Even so, judges in Canada could do more to learn about the issue, and consider the perspectives that differ from those of federal trade officials and the investor-state legal industry.

Because of the FIPA, today and for years to come, a Canadian court decision that displeases a Chinese investor will not be final until the investor runs out of time to bring a FIPA lawsuit. In the FIPA, that cut-off is three years.

For example, the Supreme Court of Canada recently tightened the constitutional requirement for governments to consult with aboriginal peoples about projects that affect their rights. Where the duty is not met, a court may annul permits for the project. If that happened to a Chinese investor, could the investor sue under the FIPA?

Certainly it could. For instance, the investor could allege that the court decision was an indirect expropriation of its permit or an unfair change in the rules. It is hard to predict how this would turn out (partly because a lot would depend on who the arbitrators were). However, in this situation, the investor appears to me to have a decent case. And, if the case were to involve a major project, the court decision could end up costing Canadians hundreds of millions of dollars. That potential cost to Canadians would be impossible in Canadian law, which respects the finality of the courts' decisions and does not allow one who loses money because of a court decision to receive public compensation for the loss.

Simply, under the FIPA, Canada's courts are no longer

supreme, even at the highest level, and the new supreme decision-makers are not courts.

CHAPTER 23.

THE LEGAL CHALLENGE TO THE FIPA, PART ONE

The public opposition to the China FIPA included thousands of people who took steps to support an effort by the Hupacasath First Nation, an aboriginal community on Vancouver Island in British Columbia, to bring a legal challenge against the FIPA. Basically, the First Nation argued that the FIPA should not be ratified because of the deal's impact on their aboriginal rights under Canada's constitution.

As an aside, a First Nation could bring a legal challenge to the FIPA more directly than other Canadians because it had an automatic right of standing, due to its constitutional rights as an aboriginal people. Other Canadians usually can challenge something a government is planning to do only if they can show that the decision affects them more intensively than Canadians in general, or if they can make a case for public interest standing, which can be challenging.

Many people in Canada hoped the courts—in hearing the Hupacasath First Nation's legal challenge—would review the FIPA's implications carefully and step in to protect Canadian interests. No doubt many were disappointed when the legal challenge was dismissed by the Federal Court of Canada in

August 2013, and again when an appeal was denied by the Federal Court of Appeal in January 2015.

Why was the legal challenge dismissed? Mainly, it was for reasons of Canadian aboriginal law. The courts basically accepted the federal government's argument that concerns about the FIPA's potential adverse impacts for the Hupacasath First Nation were not sufficiently "possible," as the legal test required, and were too "speculative" to require any consultation with that First Nation before the deal was ratified. This area of law is outside of my expertise, so I am not in a good position to evaluate whether the courts were more stringent in the Hupacasath First Nation's case than in other cases in refusing to recognize any duty to consult with aboriginal peoples.

However, I do have a few things to say about the case, as it relates to my expertise in investment treaties. I also respond, in the next few chapters, to the decision of the original Federal Court judge, who was dismissive of my opinion as an expert in investment treaties, given on behalf of the Hupacasath First Nation.

Part of the background for the First Nation's legal challenge was that the Harper Government had not done a serious review of the FIPA, alongside its plan to lock in the deal for decades. As a result, there was no thorough and reliable record to resolve what the FIPA actually said and meant. A promising thing about the First Nation's legal challenge was that it enabled a review to take place, in this case by a Federal Court judge.

Unfortunately, the review ended up telling us little about what the FIPA means for Canadians. At the government's urging, the judge focused narrowly on the FIPA's implications for the Hupacasath First Nation only, and did not consider how the FIPA would affect other First Nations or Canadians broadly. According to the judge's decision:

The Respondents [the federal government] also submitted that any declaration that this Court may issue should be confined to addressing the asserted duty to consult with HFN [Hupacasath First Nation], and should not address whether a duty to consult is owed to other First Nations. I agree. . . . the only issue to be determined in this application is whether, prior to ratifying the [FIPA] . . . Canada has a duty to consult with HFN.

This approach was not surprising, in a case brought by a single First Nation. Courts typically focus only on the point of view of the parties before them. Even so, it is important to show the narrow focus because, after the decision was released, the case was presented differently by the federal government.

According to a spokesman for International Trade Minister Ed Fast: "The decision [by the Federal Court judge] supports Canada's position that the Canada-China Foreign Investment Promotion and Protection Agreement (FIPA) respects its obligations and does not adversely impact the rights of aboriginal peoples." Thus, the government drew a link between the court decision and the rights of other aboriginal peoples, which was inaccurate. The decision really only supported the government's position that the FIPA would not adversely impact the Hupacasath First Nation alone, based on the evidence before the court.

Also at the government's urging, the Federal Court judge adopted a demanding standard of proof in scrutinizing the First Nation's claims about how the FIPA could impact them. The First Nation's claims were based on predictions, of course, because the FIPA was not yet in force and, if it was put into force, its impacts would be felt for decades.

For example, the judge accepted the government's point of view that the First Nation, before establishing any right to be consulted about the FIPA, needed to give enough evidence to show, "irrespective of Canada's experience to date under the NAFTA and the 24 other FIPAs to which [Canada] is a party," that:

(i) [Chinese] investment in [the First Nation's] territory may occur in the future,

(ii) a measure may one day be adopted in relation to that investment,

(iii) a claim may be brought against Canada by the hypothetical investor,

(iv) an award will be made against Canada in respect of the measure in question . . ., *and*

(v) Canada's ability to protect and accommodate [the Hupacasath First Nation's] asserted Aboriginal interests will be diminished, either as a result of that award, or because Canada would be chilled by the prospect of such an award (emphasis his).

Thus, the judge required evidence of a series of detailed expectations about what would happen in the future under the FIPA. He put a heavy burden on the First Nation to show that there may be Chinese investors in their territory, that a decision may be taken that the investors don't like, that the investor may sue under the FIPA, that Canada will lose the case, and that legislatures, governments, or courts in Canada will be less able to protect the First Nation's interests as a result.

I don't wish to question this approach to the law; again, I am not well-positioned to do that because I am not a specialist in Canadian aboriginal law. But I think it fair to observe that—on this approach to what is "possible" under the FIPA—it seems practically impossible to show an adverse impact of the FIPA on anyone in Canada, until after the FIPA has been in force for some time. Only then would it be realistic to get reliable, non-speculative evidence of how the FIPA had been used by investors and interpreted by arbitrators, whether relevant awards had been made against Canada, and how the deal had affected governments. Even then, one is assuming that information about behind-the-scenes discussions or settlements under the FIPA could be uncovered.

On the other hand, in evaluating the Hupacasath First Nation's legal challenge *before* the FIPA was ratified, one could only make an informed guess about these things. The informed guesses would have to be based mostly on the experience of investor-state arbitration under similar treaties. In this respect, as noted above, the Federal Court judge referred to the relevance of Canada's experience "under the NAFTA and the 24 other FIPAs to which [Canada] is a party." However, he did not refer to the experience of other countries under similar investment treaties. This selective approach to the record limited the evidence that could be used to anticipate what may happen under the China FIPA.

Also, as I discussed in chapter 4 of this book, Canada's other FIPAs are not a very useful comparison to the China FIPA because, even taken altogether, they do not cover substantial investment in Canada and so are unlikely to lead to foreign investor lawsuits against Canada. NAFTA is useful for comparison; it has led to numerous lawsuits that could be analyzed systematically. However, as I discuss a bit later, the record of NAFTA cases was examined only selectively and rosily by the federal government, by the government's expert in investment treaties, and, most importantly, by the judge.

What was missing from the judge's examination of the evidence was an assessment of foreign investor lawsuits under investment treaties other than NAFTA.

This matter was put before the judge because of the expert evidence that the Hupacasath First Nation submitted, from me (in writing; experts did not testify in person before the judge). Below, I reproduce parts of my opinion in case readers want to reflect on whether they think it was "possible" to say that the China FIPA would have an adverse impact on the First Nation or, out of interest, anyone else in Canada.

In my written opinion to the court, I said:

> It is realistic to expect that disputes will arise with Chinese investors, that claims will be brought, and that orders for compensation will be issued in situations involving land or resources subject to aboriginal or treaty rights claims.

I explained,

> *Under other investment treaties*, claims by foreign investors have most commonly involved decision-making about natural resources; major utilities or infrastructure; health or environmental regulation; administration of justice; taxation, financial regulation, or the monetary system; or planning permitting decisions (emphasis added).

I also offered examples of the kinds of disputes and specific cases that had led to investor lawsuits under other investment treaties, noting that some had been won and some lost by the foreign investor, with many cases ongoing:

- Moratoriums on drilling or mining activities and the corresponding non-approval or freezing of permits (here, I cited *Lone Pine Resources v. Canada; Pac Rim v. El Salvador*).

- Refusals of a proposed project such as a quarry or power project following an environmental assessment, public opposition, or the election of a new government (*Clayton/ Bilcon v. Canada; St. Marys v. Canada; Vattenfall v. Germany No 1*).

- Local opposition to a major project such as a pipeline or waste disposal site (*Saipem v. Bangladesh; Metalclad v. Mexico; Tecmed v. Mexico; Aguas del Tunari v. Bolivia*).

- Local opposition, including by indigenous peoples, to resource exploration/ exploitation activities (*Burlington Resources v. Ecuador*).

- New laws or regulations on the content of gasoline, exports of hazardous wastes, pesticide use, or anti-tobacco measures (*Ethyl v. Canada; SD Myers v. Canada; Dow AgroSciences v. Canada; Chemtura v. Canada; Philip Morris v. Australia*).

- New mining remediation requirements to protect environmental or Native sites (*Glamis v. United States*).

- Implementation or revision of rules on power generation, such as under the Ontario Green Energy Act (*Mesa Power v. Canada*; *Windstream Energy v. Canada*; *Mercer v. Canada*).

- Hunting and fishing restrictions such as the re-issuance of Caribou tags. On this topic, I noted in my opinion that three relevant NAFTA claims had been brought by U.S. investors against Canada (*Andre v. Canada*; *Bishop v. Canada*; *Greiner v. Canada*), that none of them had led to the establishment of a tribunal, and that all were described by the federal government as withdrawn or inactive. I highlighted the open question in these and some other NAFTA cases of how the claims were resolved; for example, did the claimant run out of funds or was the claim settled off the public record?

- Reversal of a privatization decision (*Eureko v. Poland*; *Parkerings v. Lithuania*).

- Expropriation of properties (*AbitibiBowater v. Canada*; *Gallo v. Canada*).

- New taxes or royalties, such as in the resource sector (*Occidental v. Ecuador No 1*; *Paushok v. Mongolia*; *Gottlieb v. Canada*).

After laying out these examples, I added that they were "intended to provide an indication of areas of decision-making that may lead to claims or awards against Canada under the FIPA, where a decision affects Chinese-owned assets as well as land and resources subject to aboriginal or treaty rights claims."

Later in my opinion, I highlighted for the court a few "potential scenarios that may lead to a dispute under the FIPA if Chinese-owned assets were affected," and said the scenarios were "based on the factual background of arbitrations *under other treaties* (emphasis added)":

- A significant oil, gas, mining, or logging activity involving Chinese investors, especially if the activity was subject to a significant change—such as a moratorium; new conservation measures; or a court order cancelling or suspending a permit pending consultation with Aboriginal peoples—after the issuance of a permit or licence.

- A new or reinvigorated health or environmental law that applied to Chinese investors, such as a requirement to use local workers or suppliers or to satisfy added environmental requirements, especially where the investment was made in connection with government commitments, linked to the existing regulatory framework.

- A controversial major project with Chinese ownership in the project, such as the Northern Gateway pipeline, especially if it was approved at the federal level and then subject to new or revised rules at the provincial level, or frustrated by serious public opposition.

Finally, I qualified the scenarios in this way: "These are intended as illustrations based on known cases under other investment treaties. Closer assessment would be required to assess the risk of liability in any specific case. That said, in all cases, there would be significant uncertainty due to the variable interpretations adopted by tribunals acting under other investment treaties."

This was some of the evidence that was available to the court, which seemed relevant to whether it was "possible" for the FIPA's ratification to have an adverse impact on the Hupacasath First Nation's aboriginal rights. Speaking for myself, I am not sure if this evidence established that an adverse impact was possible, and stress that I do not want to question the judge's overall view that the line between possibility and mere speculation was not crossed in the First Nation's circumstances.

However, as it turned out, none of this evidence really mattered. The judge chose not to rely on my evidence—virtually entirely—for reasons I discuss in chapters 25 and 26. As a result, it proved much harder for the Hupacasath First Nation to show that it was possible for the FIPA to have an adverse impact.

CHAPTER 24.

THE LEGAL CHALLENGE TO THE FIPA, PART TWO

What evidence did the judge in the First Nation's legal challenge rely on, instead of mine? Well, on all of the relevant issues, he chose to accept the federal government's expert in investment treaties. That expert was J. Christopher Thomas, an investor-state lawyer and arbitrator.

What was the thrust of Thomas's opinion? He and I agreed on many issues. And, I should say that I thought his overall opinion was reasonable, even if he spent a lot of time on topics that seemed irrelevant, such as the desirability of investor-state arbitration in general. However, Thomas's opinion was also misleading in a few important respects, especially on the record under other investment treaties.

Among my top concerns, Thomas described Canada's FIPA obligation to give "fair and equitable treatment" to Chinese investors as a standard that was "considered to be *a basic standard of treatment* that all members of the international community are capable of meeting (emphasis mine)." Frankly, this statement swept under the rug the history of many investor-state arbitrators who have taken the concept of fair and equitable treatment far beyond its clearest comparator, the so-called minimum standard of treatment for foreigners in international law.

To explain briefly, when the explosion of investor-state arbitration began in the 1990s, there was an accepted notion of the "basic standard of treatment" for foreigners, including foreign investors, that was expected by the international community. It is called the "minimum standard of treatment" in customary international law.

Since that time, a substantial majority of investor-state arbitrators have interpreted the concept of fair and equitable treatment in ways that go well beyond the minimum standard in customary international law. This has ratcheted up the entitlements of foreign investors to compensation in situations when, on the basic customary standard, they would not have a credible case.

Moreover, this expansion of foreign investor protections under the treaties has been widely discussed among specialists. Indeed, for years, it has been perhaps the most controversial issue of substantive interpretation in the field. So, it's really not possible for a serious expert to have missed the issue. Most importantly, although this record of arbitrator decision-making clearly contradicts Thomas's description of fair and equitable treatment as "a basic standard of treatment," the Federal Court judge relied on Thomas's description when he evaluated the risk of FIPA lawsuits against Canada.

Another of my top concerns about Thomas's opinion is how he chose to present the record of arbitrator decision-making under investment treaties. Thomas's choice in this respect was important because it led to a selective and very rosy portrayal of what had happened in other foreign investor lawsuits.

To backtrack, my own approach to the record—as highlighted in the previous chapter—was to look at all cases in aggregate and then to summarize the disputes that had arisen across the cases. On the other hand, Thomas's opinion highlighted a small number of cases that appeared to support his view, for example, that the China FIPA's obligations were not onerous for Canada.

In particular, Thomas focused on a few cases that were exceptionally country-friendly (usually U.S.-friendly). He put special emphasis on a NAFTA case called *Glamis Gold v. United States*, which is one of the most country-friendly cases under any investment treaty and which, presumably for this reason, is often criticized by lawyers who represent foreign investors. Yet, Thomas described it as "*a typical approach* taken by a tribunal when considering a country's domestic law in an investment treaty arbitration (emphasis mine)."

In turn, the judge relied on Thomas's evidence—and the *Glamis* decision in particular—to conclude that foreign investors' FIPA rights to fair and equitable treatment and to compensation for indirect expropriation were merely "basic" or "very basic" obligations for Canada to meet. Unfortunately, this conclusion flies in the face of many other cases under investment treaties, including NAFTA, that expand "fair and equitable treatment" or "indirect expropriation" beyond the notion of a basic obligation.

To be fair, these criticisms in reply to Thomas's opinion were not before the judge at the time because my opinion was filed before Thomas's. The point I want to make here is that the judge's decision turned on his choices about what evidence to accept and what to discard. Those choices are the judge's bailiwick. My role as an academic is to say where I think the judge's choices led to questionable conclusions. His characterization of Canada's obligations under the FIPA as "basic" stands out like a sore thumb when viewed against the full record of arbitrators' decisions under investment treaties.

However, even if the judge had preferred my evidence over Thomas's, I still doubt that the Hupacasath First Nation could have won, due to the judge's approach to weighing the possibility that the FIPA would have an adverse impact. For example, it seems practically impossible—based on what has happened under other treaties—to show, as the judge required, that a FIPA award "will be made" in the circumstances of future Chinese investment in the First Nation's territory and that Canada's ability to protect the First Nation's aboriginal interests "will be diminished, either as a result of that award, or because Canada would be chilled by the prospect of such an award."

The Hupacasath First Nation appealed to the Federal Court of Appeal. They lost. The appeals court deferred to the original judge's factual findings, as is usual in judicial appeals. The appeals court also agreed with the original judge that the First Nation did not show that adverse impacts of the FIPA on their rights were possible. It concluded that the case was too speculative to require any consultation before the FIPA was ratified. The appeals court also declined to revisit the original judge's discounting of my expert evidence for the First Nation.

On the other hand, the appeals court did say that if evidence of an adverse impact on aboriginal rights came about in the future, then at that point a Canadian court could require a decision-maker in Canada to prioritize aboriginal rights over Canada's FIPA obligations. This was positive for First Nations, but it pointed to new complications.

For example, some First Nations have modern treaties with the federal government that subject all the First Nation's rights under the modern treaty to Canada's *international* obligations as interpreted by international tribunals, which would include Canada's FIPA obligations as interpreted by FIPA tribunals. With that in mind, wasn't it important to consult with First Nations about the FIPA—as the Hupacasath First Nation had argued—before the deal was ratified and became part of Canada's international obligations?

Also, the appeals court's decision seemed to avoid the complication that, if a future Canadian court decision affirming aboriginal rights is later reviewed by FIPA arbitrators, then the FIPA arbitrators would be bound to apply Canada's obligations under the FIPA, not Canadian law. As a matter of international law, the arbitrators could not prioritize the constitutional rights of a First Nation, or of anyone else in Canada. In turn, it seems to be implicit in the appeals court's decision that a future court's defence of constitutional rights in Canada may wind up costing Canadian taxpayers a whole lot of money.

At any rate, the Hupacasath First Nation's legal challenge was basically moot by the time the appeals court issued its decision. In the meantime, the Harper Government had gone ahead and ratified the FIPA, while the appeal was pending. Thus, by the time of the appeals court's decision, it was simply impossible for the First Nation to get what they asked for: an opportunity for consultation on the FIPA *before* it was locked in.

The appeals court glossed over this troubling development in the case. It said simply: "While this matter was under reserve [i.e., under consideration by the court], the parties advised us that Canada has now taken the above steps and the Agreement is now in effect. This development does not affect our analysis of the issues in this appeal."

To which I say respectfully: regardless of whether the development affected the appeals court's analysis, it most certainly affected the case itself. The government's pre-emptive ratification completely prevented the appeals court from granting the most obvious remedy for a failure to consult with First Nations, which was to delay the FIPA's ratification until consultation took place.

In other words, before the FIPA was ratified, the legal challenge could have stopped the FIPA from having any adverse impact on the Hupacasath First Nation. But after the FIPA was ratified, the legal challenge could not lead to this outcome at all, regardless of what the appeals court decided. At that point, it was impossible for the courts, the federal government, or anyone else to pull Canada out of the FIPA, without China's consent. As I discuss in Chapter 43 of this book, and as was on the record before the judges who decided the legal challenge, Canada's obligations had been locked in for at least thirty-one years.

Thus, the real ending of the legal challenge did not come in January 2015 when the appeals court issued its decision, but rather in September 2014 when the FIPA was ratified. Considering the constitutional rights at stake, it was not a reassuring ending to the case.

Overall, the legal challenge to the FIPA did not lead to a thorough review of the deal that could support an informed public debate. In important ways, it made things worse.

In fairness to the courts, they are best suited to scrutinizing past events, not making predictions about the future. That is especially so when it comes to complex questions like the impact of a FIPA on Canada or even a small First Nation. The federal government's lawyers exploited this weakness of the legal challenge very well, by pushing the court not to question the government's decisions about the FIPA even though the deal had a very long lock-in period.

The outcome to the legal challenge also hammered home the huge power of the federal Cabinet to conclude treaties that lock in all future governments in Canada, for the long term. Thanks to this power, it is legally easy for the federal government to change the institutions of the country in fundamental ways. Other countries take a more careful approach to their sovereignty. For example, they require approval of new treaties by the country's legislature or highest court, or by a national referendum.

I repeat that I am not criticizing the courts' conclusion that the Hupacasath First Nation's evidence was not sufficient to establish a duty to consult with them before the federal government ratified the FIPA. The courts were much more able to make that call than me. My main criticism relates to the courts' handling of the evidence about investment treaties and of the government's hasty ratification of the deal.

And, regardless of the legal challenge, the FIPA called for consultation with Canadians, based on a review of what the deal means for the country. We all deserved this, before the FIPA was locked in. We did not get it. We did not get it from the courts, thanks largely to the federal government. We did not get it any other way, thanks almost entirely to the federal government. The blame for the FIPA lies, above all, with the government.

CHAPTER 25.

A REPLY TO THE CHARGES OF BIAS, PART ONE

I have a little more to say about the court's response to the legal challenge to the FIPA, focusing on the Federal Court judge who ruled on it. As I have mentioned, one reason the legal challenge failed was that the government successfully attacked the Hupacasath First Nation's expert in international investment law. I know, because that expert was me. The government's strategy on this point was a diversion from the FIPA, but needs to be surveyed to support what I say elsewhere in this book.

After the FIPA's text was released in September 2012, I criticized the deal, including in an open letter to Prime Minister Harper. This evidently did not go down well with some Conservatives, at least one of whom chose to smear the messenger. For example, a few months after I went public, I appeared as a witness before the House of Commons trade committee in Ottawa. The purpose of the hearing was to discuss a Canada-India trade agreement, not the China FIPA. (The Conservatives previously cut short the committee's hearing on the China FIPA.) The hearing was rescheduled twice and, when it finally went ahead in March 2013, I didn't have time to travel to Ottawa, so I appeared by video link.

A Conservative member of parliament who was on the trade committee, Ron Cannan, soon ambushed me with a question about having given money to the federal NDP. He said that he had "a list of [my] donating to the NDP about eleven times in the last couple of years." That was probably true—I didn't see much point in checking afterward—since I give small amounts by monthly withdrawals to charities and political parties. And, as I told Cannan, it was certainly true that I'd given to the NDP, partly because I respect their longstanding opposition to investor-state arbitration.

However, it was also true that I'd given to other political parties too: the Liberals, Greens, and Progressive Conservatives. I am not sure if Cannan uncovered these additional facts when he or others dug into my history of political donations. The interesting thing is that Cannan didn't mention any of the other parties when he asked about the NDP. Evidently, it didn't fit the box he wanted to put me in. I flagged to Cannan at the time that I'd given to other political parties besides the NDP. If he'd asked, I would have elaborated on which ones and explained that I sometimes change my mind about which party to support.

What should one make of such questioning about a person's history of political donations? The questioning arguably had some relevance for those assessing my opinion about the Canada-India trade agreement or the China FIPA. Yet, the usefulness of such questioning seems to me to be outweighed by the intrusiveness of asking those who come before a House of Commons committee, out of the blue, to disclose details of their political affiliations and personal lives.

If I'd had more of an opportunity to address the issue at the committee, I would have elaborated on how, after I went public on the FIPA, I was conscious of the need to be neutral when dealing with different political parties. For example, I tried to answer all the questions put to me, whether in private communications or public hearings, no matter who was asking. Though it's a fine distinction, I tried to focus my FIPA-related criticisms on the federal government, not the Conservatives, since it was the government that did the deal. I was also keen to work with concerned Canadians of all political stripes, knowing it would take support from a lot of people to change the government's mind about the FIPA. Above all, I felt it was my responsibility in the circumstances to be open and truthful, certainly not partisan.

Not surprisingly, after Ron Cannan delved into my history of political donations at the House of Commons trade committee, the hearing went downhill. The NDP and Liberal members objected to his approach, and countered by asking about other witnesses' past donations. On the next day in the House of Commons, NDP and Liberal members rightly denounced Cannan's tactic as prying and McCarthyist. As they pointed out, one of the problems with Cannan's approach is this: Who wants to volunteer his or her time to testify in the House of Commons, at the risk of having the minutiae of his or her life picked apart? More broadly, it's just wrong for Cannan or anyone in government to keep files on the personal lives of critics. Canadians should not be tracked because they are against a FIPA.

As it turned out, this whole episode was a prelude to what came next, in the legal challenge brought by the Hupacasath First Nation.

I became involved in the Hupacasath First Nation's legal challenge in late 2012, when the First Nation's lawyers asked me to give an opinion on investment treaties for the case.

It was a fairly straightforward task. I had to answer the lawyers' questions about the FIPA and investor-state arbitration, which is what I'd been doing for lots of other people—journalists, politicians, concerned citizens, students, and so on—for several months.

I considered that the First Nation was being supported by many Canadians whom I'd warned about the FIPA in October 2012. With that in mind, it seemed appropriate to give my opinion for free, which I did (later, my travel costs of about CDN$900 for a flight and hotel in Vancouver for my cross-examination were paid by the First Nation's lawyers). It occurred to me that, if I was paid for my opinion, I might be painted by Conservatives or the government as trying to profit from an alarm that I'd helped to raise.

Alas, the judge who decided the First Nation's legal challenge—Federal Court of Canada Chief Justice Paul Crampton—dismissed my expert evidence, at the urging of the federal government, on the basis that (1) I was biased as an expert and (2) my opinion was unsubstantiated. In this chapter and the next one, I reply to Chief Justice Crampton's decision on these points, arguing that it was troubling in its background assumptions and reasoning, inaccurate in a key respect, and less substantiated than my own opinion.

I take no pleasure in giving this critical reply, having worked previously in the courts and developed a great deal of respect for judges. However, as mentioned earlier, I think it necessary to defend what I say about investor-state arbitration and the FIPA, and considering the government's past attacks on my credibility. I note also that I did not have a chance to reply to the government's claim that I was biased in the course of the legal challenge itself, before or after Chief Justice Crampton's decision. That is part of the usual role and jeopardy of an expert witness.

Here is the full extent of how Chief Justice Crampton discounted my expert evidence:

The Respondents [i.e., the federal government] submitted that

Mr. Van Harten's evidence should be accorded reduced weight because he has been a vocal critic of the type of investor state arbitration provisions that are included in the [FIPA] and because he has frequently and publicly voiced his opposition to ratification of the [FIPA].

Given that HFN [the Hupacasath First Nation] acknowledged and did not dispute these allegations, I am inclined to agree with the Respondents' position, primarily on the basis that Mr. Van Harten's ability "to assist the Court impartially," as required by the Court's *Code of Conduct for Expert Witnesses*, SOR/2010-176, would appear to be somewhat compromised. . . .

Given Mr. Van Harten's acknowledged partiality, and given that I generally found Mr. Thomas to be more neutral, factually rigorous and persuasive, I generally accepted his evidence over Mr. Van Harten's when they did not agree. In any event, I found that Mr. Van Harten's evidence did not materially assist HFN to demonstrate that the potential impact of the [FIPA] on its Aboriginal interests is appreciable and non-speculative, as required to trigger a duty to consult. To a large extent, this was due to the fact that his assertions on key issues were baldly stated and unsubstantiated.

Thus, according to Chief Justice Crampton, my opinion on the FIPA was tainted by a lack of impartiality and was unsubstantiated on key issues. I will address each of these claims in turn.

Why was I biased—that is, lacking impartiality—in the chief justice's eyes? It is not easy to tell from his decision. Beyond the paragraphs that I quoted above, Chief Justice Crampton provided no explanation for why he thought my impartiality was "somewhat compromised" or why my evidence was tainted by "partiality." However, from the evidence put before him by the federal government, it seems that he had two reasons for saying this about me.

First, the government argued that I was partial because, before I became an expert in the case, I wrote opinion articles that had criticized investor-state arbitration and the FIPA. Second, Chief Justice Crampton said that the Hupacasath First Nation "acknowledged and did not dispute" the government's claim that I was biased.

On this second point, Chief Justice Crampton appears to have been mistaken. In fact, when the First Nation's lawyers dealt with the government's claim that I was biased, they pointed to my "decision to maintain academic objectivity by refusing paid work in the arbitration field" which was contrasted with "the background and work" of the government's expert, J. Christopher Thomas, who—unlike me—had earned a lot of income in investor-state arbitration. If my opinion was to be discounted, they implied, presumably it was also important to consider Thomas' apparent financial interest in defending investor-state arbitration. I return to this error in the chief justice's decision in the next chapter of this book.

What about the opinion articles I wrote before becoming an expert? Here is an outline of the views I expressed, drawn from the evidence cited by the government to support its claim that I was biased. (I have posted the relevant parts of my cross-examination in full on my blog, gusvanharten.wordpress.com.)

- Investor-state arbitration should be made into a judicial process to ensure its legitimacy.

- Canada should follow Australia by not including investor-state arbitration in future trade agreements.

- The FIPA with China should have further public study before it is ratified.

- The lack of safeguards of judicial independence in investor-state arbitration may operate to Canada's disadvantage in actual arbitrations.

- Investor-state arbitration should be reformed to resemble other international courts and tribunals.

- I opposed the FIPA publicly because I was concerned about investor-state arbitration and that Canada should not commit to investor-state arbitration when in the capital-importing position under a treaty.

- I felt obliged to speak out publicly on the FIPA so decision-makers were informed about the concerns and because I was one of few specialized researchers, outside of government and large law firms, who was in a position to understand the treaty and go on record about it.

How did these opinions make me inappropriately biased as an expert? I confess, I am not really sure. It could not be surprising that I have opinions. I am an academic who works in a controversial field. Part of my role is to say what I think, based on my expertise. If I think a government has made a mistake, shouldn't I say so?

Indeed, it seems odd to expect that an expert in investment treaties would not have expressed views on investor-state arbitration, since that system has been put into use only in the last fifteen years and has prompted a lot of debate. Ironically, the government's own expert, J. Christopher Thomas, had also expressed public views on the subject—as was noted in the evidence in the case before Chief Justice Crampton—by taking a position modestly similar to mine on the need for judicial review of investor-state arbitrators.

I also doubt that I am less able than others (such as a judge) to distinguish the role of expressing candid views from the role of giving of objective advice to a court. I highlight this point because Chief Justice Crampton had also expressed views on controversial aspects of Canadian foreign investment law, before he was appointed as a judge. Those views are discussed in the next chapter.

In addition, when I filed my opinion with the court, I certified—as all expert witnesses must do—that I agreed to be bound by the code of conduct for expert witnesses in the Federal Courts. I swore to uphold precisely my duty "to assist the Court impartially on matters relevant to [my] area of expertise." At the time, I recall reflecting on the need to give a fair assessment to the court, and was familiar with that role partly because I had worked previously for judges on an appeals court in Ontario and as a legal advisor to a senior judge.

Yet, my opinion was apparently doomed from the start because I had previously expressed views about investor-state arbitration and the FIPA.

CHAPTER 26.

A REPLY TO THE CHARGES OF BIAS, PART TWO

I knew nothing of Chief Justice Crampton when I gave my expert opinion. Indeed, I had very little to do with the legal challenge except for my role as an expert. This seemed the right approach to take because of my duties to the court. However, after Chief Justice Crampton dismissed my opinion in his judgment, I took more of an interest in him. I lay out aspects of his background here, not to suggest that Chief Justice Crampton was himself biased, but rather to defend myself against the charge of inappropriate bias.

The Harper Cabinet appointed Mr. Paul Crampton, as he then was, to the Federal Court of Canada in 2009. Two years later, he was promoted to the role of chief justice. This made him the chief justice of the first of the three levels of courts in Canada, at the federal level.

Before he was appointed as a judge, Mr. Crampton worked for a large law firm in Toronto called Osler, Hoskin & Harcourt. For our purposes, this aspect of his background is not significant. Lots of judges used to work at big law firms.

Also before he was appointed, according to the *Ottawa Cit-*

izen, Mr. Crampton donated to the Conservative Party. That detail is about as relevant as was my history of political donations when it was raised by Ron Cannan at the House of Commons trade committee. That is to say, it is not significant, if thought relevant at all. Many judges have a history of partisan support before their appointments to the bench.

More revealing is what Mr. Crampton did during his roughly fifteen-year career on Bay Street. He was a Canadian competition and foreign investment lawyer. Thus, among other things, he gave advice to companies that were involved in foreign takeovers of Canadian firms. This connects in general to the FIPA because a key effect of investment treaties is to give special rights to foreign companies involved in such takeovers. I doubt that Mr. Crampton had much exposure to FIPAs which, before the China FIPA, did not apply to significant takeovers in Canada. However, he would have worked on specific deals under the Investment Canada Act, which is now part of the FIPA's legal framework for Chinese investors in Canada.

Even so, this aspect of Chief Justice Crampton's background is also not a significant issue. It is only distantly connected to the Hupacasath First Nation's legal challenge. It is not as if Mr. Crampton, like I did, expressed views about Canada's laws and policies related to foreign investment. Except that he did, which leads to my next point.

In 2008, not long before he was appointed as a judge, Mr. Crampton wrote an opinion article in the *Globe and Mail*. In the article, he discussed a government panel's proposed reforms of the Investment Canada Act and expressed the following provocative views:

- Canada's foreign investment law was part of an "outdated" and "protectionist" domestic economy.

- Governments should not erect "fences that shield local market participants from global competitors."

- The federal government should adopt competition law reforms undertaken in Australia.

- Canadian investment law should be reformed to reduce the federal government's role in reviewing foreign takeovers of Canadian companies.

- The federal government should be encouraged to make it more difficult for Industry Canada "to extract undertakings" from foreign companies that take over Canadian firms.

- Industry Canada's requirements for foreign investors to give undertakings associated with a foreign takeover are "embarrassing" for Canadian lawyers who advise foreign investors.

These criticisms differ from mine in that they did not involve the FIPA (which had not been concluded at the time) or investor-state arbitration. Even so, they were strongly-worded criticisms of Canada's law and policy on foreign investment. In that respect, they were at least broadly comparable to views I had expressed about the federal government's approach to investment treaties, which were the evidentiary basis for Chief Justice Crampton's conclusion that I was biased in the Hupacasath First Nation's legal challenge. (My own views were summarized in the previous chapter.)

In a few ways, Mr. Crampton's opinions were similar to mine. Both related to the position of foreign companies in Canada, both advised the government that its policies should change, both even pointed to Australia for guidance. Finally, both were given before our respective appointments as judge and expert.

However, there is a key difference between our points of view. The difference is, we took roughly opposite positions.

Mr. Crampton called for reforms that would make it easier for foreign companies to take over Canadian firms. I called for reforms that would stop foreign investors from being given special rights that are not available to Canadians.

Some might think that Chief Justice Crampton's past opinions might make him less open to criticizing a treaty like the FIPA, which helps foreign investors wanting to buy into Canada's economy. Personally, I don't think his past opinions establish that the chief justice lacked impartiality. At least, judges (and experts) should not be considered biased merely because they wrote an article expressing views about topics in their field, before they were appointed. It's too unrealistic a standard and too remote from the possible bias.

That said, this last aspect of Chief Justice Crampton's background also caused me to have greater concern about his role in the First Nation's legal challenge. Chief Justice Crampton was (and is) the chief justice of his court, the Federal Court of Canada. Thus, he has the ultimate authority over which judges get assigned to which cases at the court. Normally, an individual judge does not control his or her own case assignments, to preserve judicial independence. However, the situation is apparently different for a chief justice. For this reason, a chief justice needs to take extra care not to assign a sensitive case to himself or herself, if there is a reasonable basis to doubt his or her own objectivity in deciding that case.

When the legal challenge came before the Federal Court, both the case and the FIPA were politically sensitive for the Harper Government. Both touched on the explosive issue of Chinese ownership of natural resources in Canada, for example. As a result, it was important that the public not be given reason to think that the court challenge was somehow kept in safe hands.

To be clear, I am not suggesting that Chief Justice Crampton did this in fact; that is, use his powers over case assignment to keep the case in safe hands. However, the essential question is not whether he did it in fact. The question is whether there is a basis for a reasonable and fair-minded belief that the chief justice acted inappropriately by taking or keeping the case for himself. This higher standard—meant to preserve public confidence—reflects the reality that no one can enter the mind of a judge in order to verify his or her motivations.

And, if we consider his later decision to deem me biased because of my pre-appointment opinions, it also seemed fair to ask whether Chief Justice Crampton—in light of his own pre-appointment opinions and his evident view that such opinions give rise to individual bias—should have assigned the First Nation's legal challenge to someone other than himself, or recused himself, when he first learned that the case involved sensitive issues about foreign investment in Canada. Alternatively, it would seem that Chief Justice Crampton may have been too exacting in the standard of impartiality he applied to me, as an expert, in the course of dismissing the legal challenge.

Because of this question about case assignment, I filed a formal complaint with the Canadian Judicial Council, arguing essentially that it was inappropriate for Chief Justice Crampton to have assigned the case to himself or to have not disqualified himself in the circumstances. Shortly before this book went to press, I received notice from the council that my complaint had been dismissed. Rather than attempt to summarize the council's detailed reasons here, I plan to post my formal complaint and the council's decision on my blog, gusvanharten.wordpress.com, and urge readers to examine the council's decision before drawing any conclusions based on what I have said or written.

Having decided I was biased, Chief Justice Crampton went on to say that the "assertions" (as he called them) in my opinion on international investment law "were baldly stated and unsubstantiated." He gave no explanation of what parts of my opinion were inadequate in this way. This lack of an explanation makes it practically impossible for me to respond to his claim, other than by elaborating on everything I already said. In other words, Chief Justice Crampton's conclusion that my opinion was "baldly stated and unsubstantiated" could itself be described as baldly stated and unsubstantiated.

In his decision, Chief Justice Crampton did not identify a single error in my opinion. This was after the government's experts had their run at my opinion, which was filed before theirs was. It was also after the government's lawyers cross-examined me about what I had said. Despite this close scrutiny of my opinion, nothing was put in evidence and cited by Chief Justice Crampton that revealed any errors in what I wrote. To me, this was not surprising: my opinion was accurate, with the exception of a few minor corrections, mostly typos, that I had identified myself at the start of my cross-examination by the government's lawyers.

The closest Chief Justice Crampton came to identifying a possible error in my opinion was to say that I did not give examples of investment treaties to support my view on a loophole in the China FIPA, arising from its rule that Canada and China must provide "most-favoured-nation treatment" to foreign investors. Without getting bogged down in the details here, Chief Justice Crampton's purpose in requesting these examples was to verify my opinion that there were post-1994 investment treaties concluded by Canada that do not contain certain moderating language found in the China FIPA. However, as any well-informed expert in the field would know, there are many such treaties (by my count, fourteen of them), for the straightforward reason that the relevant moderating language was developed in the early 2000s and Canada has lots of FIPAs pre-dating that period.

For our purposes, the important point is that, if I made any mistake on this issue, it seems to have been in thinking that it was enough for me to swear the truth of my opinion and give references to support it (including a series of arbitration cases from which my examples and aggregate data were drawn), without supplying a long series of treaty or case excerpts to prove each point in detail. On the present issue involving Canada's investment treaties, the opinion I expressed was not contradicted by the government's experts. If Chief Justice Crampton had asked for examples of relevant treaties to support my opinion on any issue, then I or the First Nation's lawyers could easily have supplied them. That the chief justice did not ask for examples on this issue suggests that it was not essential to his decision.

For me, the most disquieting thing is how Chief Justice Crampton handled the Hupacasath First Nation's reaction to the federal government's claim that I was biased. In his judgment, Chief Justice Crampton said that the First Nation had "acknowledged" my partiality.

Here is what the Hupacasath First Nation actually said on this issue in their written submission to the court:

> The expert opinion of Professor Van Harten is provided in order to assist the Court in understanding how the [FIPA] operates and what actions or legislative measures may be subject to its provisions. The fact that Professor Van Harten has been a critic of investor-state arbitration in his academic work *should properly have no bearing on the weight to be given to his opinion* in this case, particularly when his decision to maintain academic objectivity by refusing paid work in the arbitration field is contrasted with the background and work of Canada's expert (emphasis mine).

This statement—the most direct submission made by the First Nation on the issue—makes clear that the First Nation did not acknowledge that its own expert was partial. On the contrary, the First Nation objected to the government's claim, and countered it by questioning the impartiality of the government's expert.

In particular, the First Nation highlighted that the government's expert, unlike me, earned income as an investor-state lawyer or arbitrator. In his cross-examination, J. Christopher Thomas had testified that there were times in the previous five years when more than half of his income came from work as an investor-state arbitrator. On this basis, he could credibly be said to have a financial stake in the expansion of investor-state arbitration and, by implication, even in the outcome of the First Nation's legal challenge.

Yet, in his judgment, Chief Justice Crampton did not even mention the First Nation's submission on this point. Instead, he said that the First Nation had "acknowledged and did not dispute [the government's] allegations" that I was partial. I find it hard to make sense of this statement. In fact, any acknowledgement of my past opinions—though certainly not an admission of partiality—came from me, not the Hupacasath First Nation. In my opinion to the court, I disclosed from the beginning that I had criticized investor-state arbitration and the FIPA, before being appointed as an expert. I gave this summary of my views:

> I should disclose that, although I support the use of international adjudication to resolve major or sensitive disputes involving the treatment and activities of foreign investors, I have criticized publicly and actively the Canada-China investment treaty (or FIPA) due to what I see as its problems relative to other investment treaties concluded by Canada and due to my broader concerns about the lack of institutional safeguards of independence in international investor-state arbitration.

I then summarized my concerns about the FIPA, including on market access, discrimination, secrecy in the arbitrations, Canada's vulnerable economic position, and the risks and constraints assumed by Canada, and added:

> I am conscious that a wider set of costs and benefits arising from the FIPA must be weighed by government decision-makers and thus have focused my own criticism on the need for a thor-

ough, public, and independent review of claims about the FIPA to inform decision-makers at all levels before a decision is taken on whether the FIPA should be finalized long-term by Canada.

I said these things to be open about my opinions and the reasons for my criticism. I thought that a judge would accept that an academic is capable of playing more than one role, like a lawyer or judge often does, including that of an objective advisor alongside that of a critic. Borrowing from the Canadian Judicial Council's *Ethical Principles for Judges*, I would put it this way: an academic, to be considered impartial, should remain "free to entertain and act upon different points of view with an open mind" rather than the unrealistic standard that he or she should "have no sympathies or opinions."

Chief Justice Crampton also did not mention in his judgment that I disclosed my past criticisms at the outset of my expert opinion. Perhaps when he referred to my "acknowledged" partiality, he simply mistook my own disclosure for an acknowledgement by the Hupacasath First Nation? That is possible, but also puzzling, especially because, when I filed my opinion, I certified that I would uphold my duty to assist the court impartially. It doesn't seem to make sense to interpret a person's disclosure of past criticism as an admission that the person cannot act impartially when, at the same time, the person has sworn to do just that.

Having looked at this background, it struck me that Chief Justice Crampton's dismissal of me as biased was reminiscent of the strategy used by Ron Cannan. It was a label that made it easier to avoid the substance of what I said based on my expertise, derived from many years of study of the subject. Indeed, one of my first reactions to this part of Chief Justice Crampton's judgment was that it made it easy for promoters of investor-state arbitration to cut and paste the section about me, in order to discredit me as an academic in the field. In at least one circumstance I'm aware of, this is exactly what happened.

Shortly after Chief Justice Crampton's decision came out, a U.S. lawyer and arbitrator who promotes investment treaties posted the precise excerpt dismissing me as an expert on a listserv that is followed by hundreds of specialists in the field. The evident purpose was to attack my credibility. Ironically, on the listserv at the time, I had among other things been defending Canada's courts from the allegation that they do not reliably protect foreign investors in Canada, making investor-state arbitration necessary in the proposed Canada-Europe CETA.

To repeat, I do not wish to suggest that Chief Justice Crampton was biased in fact, and even perceptions of bias are very much in the eye of the beholder. One must keep in mind that judges have a difficult job to do, and give them the benefit of the doubt that they carry out their duties with integrity. Chief Justice Crampton is restricted in his ability to respond to criticism because of his judicial office, and the Canadian Judicial Council dismissed my complaint about his choices on case assignment.

Most importantly, putting aside any questions about the chief justice's background or opinions, the simple fact is that his judgment did not address the FIPA's impacts on Canadians in general. The Federal Court of Appeal's decision was also narrowly focused on the FIPA's impacts for the Hupacasath First Nation alone, and it deferred to Chief Justice Crampton's factual findings and characterization of the evidence. Thus, despite the legal challenge, it remains the case that there was no thorough review of how the FIPA would affect the country before the deal was ratified.

That's the saddest truth, for Canada.

PART 4.

PROMOTERS OF THE FIPA,
UP CLOSE

CHAPTER 27.

THE FIPA MEDIA BLITZ

When Prime Minister Harper announced the FIPA in early 2012, he told Canadians, not surprisingly, that his government had done a great job in getting the deal.

Some commentators quickly parroted the government's line. For example, the *Globe and Mail's* editors trumpeted the FIPA as "a leap forward by Canada." They said:

> The foreign investment promotion and protection agreement with China is a significant accomplishment, in this respect putting Canada ahead of the United States and Europe....
>
> *China is remarkably cautious about trade relationships*. . . . As for the species of treaty to which Canada and China have now agreed—known in Ottawa dialect by the acronym FIPAs, but elsewhere as BITs (bilateral investment treaties), *Beijing has one of these with ASEAN*, a group of 10 Southeast Asian countries, but not with the United States or the European Union, in spite of China's huge amount of trade with both (emphasis mine).

Much in these statements about the FIPA was misleading, especially the portions I italicized in the above excerpt. At the time, China had well over one hundred bilateral investment treaties (BITs) with other countries, not one as the *Globe* implied. China was actually the second-most-active country in the world when it came to signing BITs! The deal was hardly a case of "cautious" China getting reeled in by the Harper Government. If anything, it was the opposite, based on the deal's then-secret terms.

The *Globe*'s editors continued:

> Since 1989, Canada has been trying to obtain as many FIPAs as possible. . . . Such an agreement with China has been sought for 18 years. This is not the work of the present government alone, but Mr. Harper and his colleagues have achieved this favourable outcome; their rocky start with China seems to be a thing of the past.

This too was blind cheerleading. The *Globe*'s editors did not ask and had no way to verify what the Harper Government gave up to "achieve" the deal after eighteen years of others' trying. One obvious point, not flagged by the *Globe*'s editors, was that the Harper Government might have given up more to China than what other governments had been prepared to do. As I explained in earlier chapters of this book, major concessions were made to China on market access, discrimination, investment screening, and secrecy in the arbitration process.

At the time, the *Globe*'s editors must have known that there was no way to verify the government's claims about the FIPA. Its text was not public. Worse, the *Globe*'s editors did not make this basic fact clear. Instead, readers were left to think the *Globe*'s endorsement of the FIPA was rooted in something more than government spin.

With any investment treaty, the devil is in the details. One cannot evaluate a FIPA's value without reviewing the text, comparing it to other treaties, and evaluating it against the record of investor-state arbitration. Months later, when the text was finally released, it became clear that the government's description of the FIPA when it was announced was misleading.

I do not blame journalists for reporting what a government says about a complex agreement. Journalism has been hit by the loss of readers and advertisers, cuts to investigative resources, and the relentless concentration of media owner-ship. Journalists face a lot of pressure to deliver stories quickly. It's not surprising that stories feed off of spin by governments, large companies, or other organizations with hired spokes-people and public relations teams. Personally, after the FIPA was released, I found it hard to explain the details to journalists in a short time. Overall, I would say most journalists did their best, often very well, to come to terms with a complicated subject.

Even so, in February 2012, it should have been reported that the government was making self-serving claims about the FIPA without anyone being able to evaluate their accuracy. That was a key part of the story. Would the *Globe's* editors celebrate someone buying a house without seeing the terms of sale? This was a newspaper helping to pump out the government's propaganda.

My favourite example of poorly informed spin about the FIPA was an interview on TVO's show called *The Agenda* in December 2012. This was after the FIPA had become controversial. The host, Steve Paikin, spoke with former Conservative Member of Parliament and Canadian Alliance Leader Stockwell Day about the deal.

I happened to be watching and immediately wondered how Day came to have knowledge about the subject. Quickly it was clear that he came, but without basic knowledge.

For example, Day told the story of his sister-in-law, who had a candle-making business that used imported wax from China. He said the FIPA would help people like her:

Whether you're talking huge companies: oil and gas, financial institutions. Or, I think of a sister-in-law of mine, who is in the candle-making business and ordered a container of a certain type of high-quality wax to obviously make candles. It came out that entire container was defective.

With rules in place in another country, let's say the U.S., there are ways you can follow up on that, ways you can bring people to account. There is still some difficulty with that, dealing with China, though it's improving, but there's still difficulty.

So, an agreement like this goes a long way to protecting Canadians and also to give them ways to follow up: arbitration, ways to pursue people who they think have not lived up to their side of the agreement.

I take my hat off to entrepreneurs like Day's sister-in-law. I respect their drive and hard work. But this example was absurd. The FIPA does not go "a long way" to helping people like Day's sister-in-law. She would not be able to use the FIPA at all to chase a wax supplier in China. Why not?

Investment treaties give rights to *foreign* owners of assets. Judging from Day's story, his sister-in-law owned assets in Canada, not in China. As a result, she would not qualify as a foreign investor under the treaty. Even if she did qualify as a foreign investor, it typically costs millions of dollars to arbitrate a dispute under an investment treaty. How many Canadian candle-makers have that kind of money? If anything, small businesses in Canada seem worse off under the FIPA. This is because Chinese companies who compete with them in Canada end up with new FIPA rights that Canadian companies don't have, in their own country.

Day was wrong about other things too. He claimed ignorance of the FIPA's minimum thirty-one-year lifespan and said misleadingly that "deals can be cancelled for a variety of reasons." He portrayed the FIPA as a means "to allow business between companies or between individuals or investors," though the deal governs relationships between foreign investors and a country, not relationships among private parties. Actually, just about everything Day said about the FIPA was inaccurate or misleading. Worse, there was no one to answer Day, and the host did little to challenge or correct him. Anyone who watched the interview and trusted in Day and TVO was badly misled.

Soon after watching the interview, I emailed TVO to explain

errors in Day's account. I suggested that the network should air another point of view. I got no reply. Maybe TVO aired a correction and I missed it, or maybe my email was not received. Usually, TVO and Steve Paikin do a very good job. Any host, producer, or former politician can have a bad day. Whatever the explanation, this guest spot on the FIPA was a charade.

TVO was not alone in giving a boost to the Harper Government's push for the FIPA. Other media commentators joined the blitz to sell the deal after it became controversial. How did this blitz begin and proceed? Here is what I saw.

When the FIPA was released publicly in September 2012, a few news stories were written about it. They were descriptive and informative. There was also an early and thoughtful opinion article by Paul Wells in *Maclean's*. Beyond that, there was very little scrutiny of the deal in the mainstream media.

Personally, I learned that the FIPA was being released from a good *Globe and Mail* story by journalists Bill Curry and Shawn McCarthy. A few days later, I read the deal. It was clear that the federal government had given up on important goals for Canada. However, it seemed that few members of the public, and few decision-makers, would be able to see the concessions even if they read the text.

Worse, the government had announced that it would ratify the FIPA twenty-one sitting days after the FIPA was put before Parliament. That suggested that the FIPA would be finalized in late October or early November 2012. There were no plans to hold a vote or even a debate in Parliament, let alone to launch a proper review of the deal before it was locked in.

Toward the end of September, I decided to write some opinion articles on the FIPA. Usually, I sent them to the *Globe and Mail*, the *National Post*, and the *Toronto Star*. If an article was not accepted by any of these newspapers, I sent it to Troy Media (a great online clearing house of opinion articles). The *Toronto Star* picked up one of the opinion articles, as did newspapers across the country, via Troy Media. Yet, the *Globe and Mail* and *National Post* repeatedly did not.

By mid-October, with the clock ticking to ratification, I was worried that many decision-makers were not informed about the problems with the FIPA. If they did ratify the FIPA, I did not want them to be able to say down the road that they didn't know about the FIPA's risks. I recall thinking, what if Canada is one day ordered to pay a billion dollars to a Chinese company? What if the order comes from a province's decision, and the province justifiably balks at paying because it was the federal government that concluded the treaty? It was not hard to imagine viable scenarios that would cause serious problems under the FIPA. If that happened, I wanted the concerns to be on the public record while it was still possible to avoid the FIPA.

So, I put some concerns about the FIPA in an open letter to the prime minister. I also wrote to the federal trade minister and various premiers. There was nothing slick about the letters. I recall sending them by email from the couch in my basement, while watching Dora the Explorer with my five-year-old daughter. None of the federal ministers replied. Some premiers and provincial ministers did, saying mostly that they deferred to the federal government on treaties like the FIPA.

However, by this point, a public response was brewing from the bottom up, via online and regional newspapers, local radio stations, and social media. Within a few weeks, thousands of Canadians wrote to the government and members of parliament. This impressive response was encouraging to see. Word about the FIPA's flaws appeared to have spread outside of Canada's two major newspapers, and many, many people responded.

As this public response was getting going, other commentators also aired insightful criticisms of the FIPA: Lawrence

Martin in the *Globe and Mail*, Michael Den Tandt in the *National Post*, Diane Francis in the *Financial Post*, and (in a comic rant) Rick Mercer on the CBC, for example. Also, other media—especially, from what I saw, the CBC and the Business News Network—began to give serious attention to criticisms of the FIPA. Serendipitously, I managed to get an opinion article about the FIPA's uncertain constitutional implications in the *Globe*. This greater scrutiny came in late October and early November 2012, as the FIPA appeared to be on the brink of ratification.

Then, quite suddenly, a media blitz to sell the FIPA began. Various FIPA promoters emerged. The most active seemed to be Andrew Coyne, John Ivison, John Manley, Matthew Kronby, Milos Barutciski, Lawrence Herman, Laura Dawson, and eventually Stephen Gordon. In this part of the book, I debunk much of what they said, line by line. This makes for some repetition. However, it seems better to shine a wide and bright light on their claims, for posterity.

Before I start, I should acknowledge that critics of the FIPA also made inaccurate claims. I don't think this was surprising in the mad rush to learn about the deal, while the narrow window before expected ratification remained open. For example, critics sometimes said the FIPA could "prevent" (not simply deter) Canada from passing new laws for Chinese investors. Technically, this claim was accurate, since investor-state arbitrators can use their power to issue interim orders to block a country from passing or enforcing a law. However, it was also misleading because the arbitrators usually order compensation rather than striking down laws.

Even so, the inaccuracies from FIPA critics are not as deserving of scrutiny as those spread by FIPA promoters. First, in my estimation, there were far more inaccuracies or exaggerations from the FIPA promoters. Second, one of the key promoters was the federal government, which was the most able to disseminate accurate information. Third, the spin by promoters encouraged the finalization of an essentially irre-versible deal.

That is, FIPA promoters helped lock Canada into a lopsided, risk-laden pact for decades. If the critics got things wrong in the debate, it could have been addressed through a review of the FIPA before the deal was locked in. And, if the full story had emerged, it might have saved Canada from a lopsided treaty.

For these reasons, I focus on how promoters sold the FIPA after it became controversial in October 2012. In the end, the promoters got their way, and should be remembered for what they got wrong.

CHAPTER 28.

ANDREW COYNE, PART ONE

My scrutiny of the FIPA's promoters begins with *National Post* columnist Andrew Coyne.

Coyne has defended investor-state arbitration since the early days of its explosion under NAFTA, about fifteen years ago. After early U.S. investor lawsuits against Canada, he defended both the NAFTA investment chapter and an even bigger proposed deal called the Multilateral Agreement on Investment (MAI), which fell apart in the late 1990s due to public opposition in many countries.

In this early defence of investor-state arbitration, Coyne downplayed the significance of U.S. investor lawsuits against Canada. Much later, he repeated the same line to defend the FIPA. Then and now, Coyne also resorted to name-calling. In the late 1990s, he singled out then-Liberal trade minister Sergio Marchi because Marchi had flagged the possibility of reforming investor-state arbitration:

> Maybe Mr. Marchi, once a stalwart of the Liberal left, never really was converted to free trade. Maybe all that born-again blather about "open markets" is a bluff. Maybe he's a mole, a double agent working to sabotage trade liberalization efforts from within.
>
> It wasn't long ago, after all, that Mr. Marchi, by much foot-dragging and demands for exclusion, helped to deep-six the Mul-

tilateral Agreement on Investment. Now he's threatening to do the same to NAFTA, or at least one of its signal provisions: Chapter 11, a set of rules, like the MAI, requiring fair treatment of foreign investors.

So clearly, Coyne was not a newcomer to the cause of investor-state arbitration.

I first learned of Coyne's concern about public opposition to the FIPA on October 31, 2012, when he appeared on the CBC's political panel on *The National*.

The panel's host, Peter Mansbridge, asked Coyne and *Toronto Star* columnist Chantal Hébert two fair and open-ended questions about the FIPA: "Is [the FIPA] something that's not getting enough light shone on it? Is it something that should be studied a lot harder by people in general?" These questions tracked the calls of critics for a public review of the FIPA. They went to a key issue: why not sort out what was true and untrue about the FIPA before locking it in?

Coyne and Hébert responded dismissively. They characterized public concerns about the FIPA as overblown or irrational. They did not discuss any specific criticisms, instead urging the Harper Government to do a better job of promoting the deal. That is, they took the role of public relations advisors for the government on how to sell the FIPA.

Hébert said:

[The FIPA] should be debated in the House of Commons *for the good of the government that is actually promoting it*. . . . In the absence of a government voice to explain and defend it, in that vacuum, it is becoming a bogeyman. . . . The fears may be overblown, but there is not a voice from the government to say, here is what it is and what it isn't and, in that absence, it's getting ripped apart in public opinion (emphasis mine).

I ask, is that why we should have debates in the House of Commons, for "the good of the government"? No, I suggest that a debate in Parliament is supposed to hold the government to account for its decisions. Hébert's choice of language suggested which side of the FIPA debate she wanted to be on.

Coyne went much further than Hébert did. He began: "This is a foreign investment agreement to treat each other, you know, in mutual ways and not expropriate each other's investments." That statement was misleading from the outset. In important ways, the FIPA is not mutual. As we have seen, it lets China keep its protectionist and discriminatory measures. Coyne continued:

> A lot of these fears that are being raised are very similar to the types of fears that were raised back during the original Free Trade Agreement [with the U.S.] and NAFTA. That, you know, the Americans were going to be able to come in and buy up our health care and, you know, put nuclear missiles in Baffin Island.

Thus, Coyne avoided talking about any specific criticisms of the FIPA, which had been on the public record for weeks. Rather, he invoked a crazy line, attributed it to the critics, and then dismissed them for doing what he made up about them.

Finally, Coyne advised the Harper Government on its public relations strategy for the FIPA:

> If nobody counters these things, the charges and the accusations and the fears that are raised get more and more extreme. So, yes, I agree that once again the government's got to get out and actually pitch this thing.

Again, Coyne's dismissal of concerns about the FIPA as mere accusations and fears came after specific aspects of the FIPA had been criticized in detail and on the public record; yet, Coyne did not mention any of these specific criticisms.

Soon after his appearance on *The National*, Coyne used another of his media platforms, as a Postmedia columnist, to release two opinion articles that I debunk below. It seems he was not satisfied to leave it to the federal government to "pitch this thing." However, in leading the media blitz for the

FIPA, Coyne was beaten to the punch by his fellow Postmedia columnist, John Ivison.

CHAPTER 29.

JOHN IVISON

What was John Ivison's foray into the FIPA debate, at the eve of the deal's expected ratification on November 1, 2012?

He began by attacking NDP Leader Thomas Mulcair, without noting any of the specific issues that motivated Mulcair's concern about the FIPA. Instead, Ivison accused Mulcair of having "outsourced his trade policy to Maude Barlow and the Council of Canadians," and then denounced FIPA critics as "hysterical." In addressing the supposed hysteria, however, Ivison had a lot of trouble making accurate claims in the FIPA's defence.

For example, Ivison said that Green Party Leader Elizabeth May had suggested "Chinese companies could sue provincial or municipal governments who enact any legislation that hits their profits." He also presented May's view in this way: "Both countries are bound to the potentially dangerous terms of the deal, which include China's right to sue Canada for damages relating to decisions made by any level of government for an initial 15 years."

Yet, even if we accept Ivison's summary of her criticisms, May was right, and right to warn Canadians on each of these points. Without a doubt, the FIPA lets Chinese companies that own assets in Canada "sue provincial or municipal governments"—as part of sovereign Canada—for any provincial or municipal law that diminishes the value of their assets, which includes, in a measure of the assets' value, "their profits." In international law, Canada is a unified entity. It consists of all the country's legislatures, governments, and courts, and the FIPA obligations attach to Canada as a whole.

Likewise, when a foreign investor lawsuit succeeds under an investment treaty, the arbitrators usually award compensation that includes lost profits. In itself, this right to sue is a profound change in the status of Chinese investors in Canada, some owned directly by the Chinese government. Finally, the deal clearly has a minimum term of fifteen years and, if one includes its one-year notice period and fifteen-year "survival clause" for the rights of established Chinese investors, the FIPA will have a lifespan of at least thirty-one years.

Why shouldn't May and other Canadians be deeply concerned about these things? Indeed, without May's early and forceful criticism of the FIPA, many others might never have learned of it.

Digging his hole deeper, Ivison also claimed: "But the action has to clearly discriminate against the company." He got that badly wrong. Without question, the FIPA does not require discrimination by Canada to establish a violation of the deal. Some foreign investor rights in the FIPA require this, but the most widely invoked ones do not. In addition, Canada would violate the FIPA if any decision-maker in the country was found to have violated even a single right of a Chinese investor in the FIPA. This is Investment Treaties 101.

To elaborate, perhaps the most obvious rights of foreign investors that do *not* require any evidence of discrimination are "fair and equitable treatment" and "full protection and security." These two rights are particularly "dangerous," to use Ivison's language, because most awards by arbitrators have relied on one or both of them to order compensation against countries. Also, when interpreting these rights, many arbitrators have used them to introduce new entitlements of compensation for foreign investors.

Indeed, a leading criticism of the arbitrators has been that they too often condemn countries for decisions that are not discriminatory. Simon Lester, a trade analyst for the Cato Institute in the United States, responded to the error made by Ivison and other FIPA promoters:

> As every reader of this blog knows, discriminatory treatment is *one* basis for a complaint, but it's not the only one. Importantly, it's not the one people generally criticize. There may be someone, somewhere who objects to national treatment obligations in investment treaties, but for the most part, that's not what critics focus on. The biggest problem area is "fair and equitable treatment" (emphasis his).

Even worse for Ivison—given his erroneous claim about the need for a government to clearly discriminate in order to violate the FIPA—the China FIPA actually lets China and Canada keep in place all existing discriminatory laws, regulations, practices, and so on. As I discussed in chapter 3 of this book, this works to China's advantage.

Ivison's article had many other problems. Basically, it was a checklist of dubious claims about the FIPA and investor-state arbitration. For example, Ivison stressed that the FIPA has exceptions:

> And even Ms. May admits there are exemptions to cover health, safety, and environment measures.

He explained that a lawyer told him the FIPA was okay:

> As trade lawyer Lawrence Herman, senior counsel at Cassels Brock, points out, many of these criticisms are overblown.

He called for Canadians to trust in the Investment Canada Act:

This is not about Chinese companies buying into Canada—the Investment Canada Act still applies and the debate about whether it should be amended will come soon enough, when the government releases its ruling on state-owned China National Offshore Oil Corp's CDN$15-billion bid to buy Calgary-based Nexen.

And, once again, Ivison was wrong. As we saw in chapters 6 and 7, the FIPA is very much about Chinese companies buying into Canada, and it denies Canadian investors the same right in China. Even with the Investment Canada Act, there is a lot of room for takeovers of major assets in Canada, without any right of review by the federal government except on national security grounds.

Ivison also said the FIPA critics had it backwards:

Don Davies, the NDP's trade critic, put forward perhaps the weakest assault on the [FIPA] . . . when he suggested on CBC's *The House* that the deal is flawed because there is triple the amount of Chinese investment in Canada as there is Canadian investment in China. But that's the reason to support the deal, not oppose it. The aim is to change that ratio in Canada's favour by growing investment in the world's second-largest economy.

Here, Ivison's pitch for the FIPA was undermined by the terms of the deal. If the Harper Government's aim was to increase Canadian investment in China, relative to Chinese investment in Canada, why would the deal require Canada to open its economy, but not China? It is safe to assume that changing the lopsided ratio of investment flows was not a deal breaker for the Harper Government.

Ivison continued:

Mr. Davies is a smart man—his point was that the [FIPA] will freeze restrictions on investment for Canadian companies, even though he must know that the successful passage of the [FIPA] will likely lead to free trade talks that would ease those trade irritants.

Yet again, Ivison leapt over many facts to reach his preferred conclusion.

For example, if the Harper Government's aim really was to get a trade agreement with China, then by doing the FIPA first it gave up an important bargaining chip. I would have thought it was fairly obvious that an investment deal—which protects foreign investors—operates more to the benefit of the country whose investors own more in the other country. On this measure, as I discussed in chapter 4, China clearly benefits more from the FIPA than Canada. In turn, Canada's thirty-one-year agreement to investor-state arbitration, for Chinese owners of assets in Canada, was a bargaining chip that could have been traded for an agreement by China to "ease those trade irritants," as Ivison put it. If Ivison really wanted to see a good trade deal with China, he should have criticized the Harper Government's sequencing of negotiations.

Ivison concluded his article with another swipe at the NDP, Maude Barlow, and the Council of Canadians for opposing the FIPA, saying that the NDP's Official Opposition Critic on International Trade, Don Davies, had been "energetic in trying to liberalize NDP trade policy but those attempts have fallen at the first hurdle" and "Ms. Barlow and her supporters are back and they're driving the New Democratic trade bus."

In essence, Ivison's claim was (1) the NDP is wrong because (2) the NDP has taken a position shared broadly by others whom (3) Ivison thinks are wrong. That was a sad attempt at a reasoned argument, if Ivison intended to make one. Where Ivison highlighted any specific criticisms of the FIPA, his primary answer was to make inaccurate or exaggerated counterclaims.

The next day, it was Andrew Coyne's turn.

CHAPTER 30.

ANDREW COYNE, PART TWO

Andrew Coyne weighed in, on November 2, 2012, with the first of his two *National Post* columns in defence of the FIPA. The column ran in many Postmedia newspapers across the country.

The structure of Coyne's article mimicked Ivison's. FIPA critics were accused of "near-hysterical wailing." Coyne dismissed them as "anti-globalization activists" and "online petitioners." He cherry-picked a few quotes from Green Party Leader Elizabeth May and complained that not enough organizations had joined critics in openly opposing the deal. Like Ivison, he dismissed the NDP's opposition, calling it perfunctory. In other words, Coyne began by smearing a few bogeymen, real or imagined, on the other side.

Next, Coyne reassured readers about the FIPA. He described it as "a treaty that has ample precedent in international law; that enjoins us to do no more than we are doing already; and all with respect to a relatively minor investor in this country." On all three points, Coyne was wrong or misleading.

Coyne's first point would require another whole chapter of this book to debunk thoroughly. In summary, there is no precedent—let alone an "ample" one—for investor-state arbitration, beyond investment treaties themselves. Treaties like the FIPA mark a major transformation in international law because of how they allow a select group of investors to bring arbitration claims directly against countries. I laid out the significance of this transformation in 2007 in the first of my academic books in the field, *Investment Treaty Arbitration and Public Law*, published by Oxford University Press.

Coyne's second point was plainly wrong; the FIPA clearly requires Canada to do more than Canada is "doing already." Simply, it gives Chinese investors a new right to sue Canada based on legal standards that would not apply if it weren't for the FIPA.

Coyne's third point was merely misleading. He called China a "relatively minor" investor in Canada, which only works, on a country-by-country comparison, for the United States. Obviously, U.S. companies are collectively the largest foreign owners of assets in Canada. However, Chinese ownership is far from "minor," relative to other countries', especially considering that China only began to open up its outbound investment in 1999.

Coyne continued in his reassurances about the FIPA:

[T]he agreement is not hugely different from the investor protection chapters of NAFTA, or from the two dozen other [FIPAs]. Canada has signed with other countries around the world; where it does differ, as in the provision for closed-door arbitration hearings, it is in line with treaties China has signed with other countries.

This too was misleading. The FIPA is significantly different from other FIPAs of Canada, as we saw in earlier chapters of this book. As for Coyne's comparison of the FIPA to China's other investment treaties, it would require a study of more than one hundred treaty texts—and of aspects of the treaties of China's many treaty partners—to test Coyne's claim properly. However, even without such a study, it is safe to say that the vast majority, and perhaps all, of China's investment treaties with more than one hundred countries do not provide for non-reciprocal market access in the manner of the FIPA with Canada, to China's advantage. They do not provide for non-reciprocal investment screening in the manner of the FIPA, to China's advantage. They do not diminish protection for aboriginal peoples in the manner of the FIPA, to China's advantage. They do not say explicitly that each government can keep arbitration claims confidential "in the public interest," to the disadvantage of Canadians.

Thus, Coyne's sweeping claim—that the FIPA is "in line with" other Chinese treaties—was unsupported by evidence from him, and was contradicted by evidence known to specialists in the field. I wonder, on what basis does a non-expert like Coyne make such a claim without some reference to support it?

Coyne soldiered on, claiming the FIPA's "major undertakings" were "standard boilerplate in most international trade agreements, including the World Trade Organization." Again, he was wrong. The World Trade Organization's investment agreement—called the Agreement on Trade-Related Investment Measures (TRIMs)—is far more limited than a FIPA. For example, the TRIMs Agreement (like all other WTO agreements) does not have any provisions on the controversial FIPA standards of fair and equitable treatment and indirect expropriation. Most importantly, investor-state arbitration does not even exist at the WTO. Disputes are resolved through litigation between countries, which is typical in international law. The WTO does not let a select group of private actors bring claims against countries, unlike the FIPA.

Coyne then reported:

What does the deal commit us to? In broad terms, both parties agree not to discriminate against or otherwise mistreat each other's investors. Each agrees to apply no restrictions that it would not apply to investors from other countries (most-favoured-nation treatment) or, for the most part, to its own (national treatment).

Thus, like Ivison, Coyne focused on the non-discrimination rules in the FIPA, but did not mention the FIPA's carve-out for all existing discriminatory measures. He added:

> And each promises to provide fair compensation in the event it expropriates the other's assets—which is not only a standard of international agreements, but of our own common and statutory law. It's one of the things that until now distinguished us from countries like China.

There are three problems with this statement about the FIPA's provision on compensation for expropriation.

The first is that the FIPA does not provide for "fair" compensation. Rather, it incorporates the so-called Hull standard of compensation, named after the U.S. Secretary of State from 1933 to 1944, Cordell Hull. This standard of compensation has its own history in debates about expropriation in international law, dating from the Mexican government's nationalization of U.S. oil interests in Mexico in the 1930s. The notion of "fair" compensation is arguably more akin to another historical standard, called "appropriate" compensation, which is not reproduced in the FIPA.

The second problem with Coyne's statement is that Canadian law actually does allow for expropriation without compensation. This reflects the well-established principle of parliamentary supremacy, which ultimately affirms Canadian democracy. The FIPA supersedes this bit of Canada's constitution.

I am guessing Coyne was aware of this last point, since he massaged it. He spoke of "common law and statutory law" in Canada, but didn't mention the Canadian constitution. The common law and a range of statutes (i.e. laws) in Canada do create a presumption that compensation must be paid if a government expropriates property—to build a pipeline, dam, or highway, for example—and the law authorizing the expropriation is unclear about compensation. Also, the long-standing legislative practice in Canada has been to require compensation for any direct expropriation. Basically, in Canada, compensation is required for what most people think of as expropriation: a taking of title that benefits the state.

This leads to the third problem with Coyne's statement. He avoided the difficult but critical question of what qualifies as "indirect" expropriation under Article 10 of the FIPA (i.e. "measures having an effect equivalent to expropriation"). Should a general law in Canada that reduces the value of Chinese assets require public compensation of Chinese owners? In Canadian law, the answer is basically no. Under the FIPA, it is generally yes. And, this creates other risky uncertainties for governments: does the reduction of value have to be "near-complete" or, as many arbitrators have decided, merely "substantial" or "significant," to trigger a foreign investor's entitlement to compensation?

The issue of compensation for indirect expropriation is a big question for voters and taxpayers. Indeed, it is important for Canada's whole democratic makeup. The FIPA gives the power over this key question to investor-state arbitrators, instead of legislatures and courts. Coyne treated the issue far too simplistically.

Returning to Coyne's claims about the FIPA and discrimination, he noted later in his article that the FIPA excludes existing discriminatory measures. However, he actually tried to spin this as a plus:

> If anything, the deal is rather less sweeping than some others. It applies only to new laws—*existing measures are grandfathered*—and new investments, all of whom are still subject to the Investment Canada Act (emphasis mine).

So, Coyne appears to have been aware of the important carve-out from the FIPA's rules against discrimination. Yet, he avoided the concern, stressed by critics, that this carve-out works in China's favour. Also, when he pointed to the Investment Canada Act, he did not mention the concern that the

FIPA's carve-out of investment screening was also unequal, in favour of China.

Eventually, Coyne touched on the profound transfer of sovereignty from Canadian institutions to FIPA arbitrators, but downplayed this transfer as old news:

> Yes, it allows investors to take governments to binding arbitration if they feel these promises have not been kept. That, too, is nothing new. It is part of NAFTA, it is a part of the other [FIPAs], and while the attempt to extend these generally through the Multilateral Agreement on Investment failed, *governments* may take each other to the WTO under the same rules. Sometimes, not often, these decisions go against Canada. News flash: sometimes they should (emphasis his).

Thus, like many other FIPA promoters, Coyne skirted the first-order question of the FIPA's impact on the powers of Canadian legislatures and courts. Instead, he jumped to the questions of whether Chinese investors will or should win FIPA lawsuits. As we saw in various chapters in part 2 of this book, no one can answer these second-order questions with confidence.

Personally, I think there is a much more serious risk of FIPA lawsuits than Coyne claimed. That is partly why I called for a review of the deal before it was locked in. Evidently, Coyne was more prepared to take risks with public money over the next few decades. I sincerely hope he's right.

At this point, Coyne took another swipe at FIPA critics:

> That's true of many of the critics' complaints. Provisions of the agreement are breathlessly unearthed as if they were some strange and threatening new idea, in apparent ignorance of our existing obligations under international law—the prohibition on local performance requirements, for example, simply copies in the corresponding provision from the WTO.

But once again, Coyne's reference (here to the WTO) was misleading. It is true that the FIPA incorporates one of the few substantive provisions on investment in the WTO TRIMs

Agreement. However, even for this provision, the FIPA goes well beyond the TRIMs Agreement and Canada's other existing international obligations. As I discuss further in chapter 38 of this book, the FIPA exposes Canada to Chinese investor lawsuits and backward-looking orders of compensation, whereas the WTO does not. Coyne's example actually confirmed how the FIPA goes beyond "our existing obligations under international law," though it requires a long explanation to show why.

A few days after his first opinion article, Coyne released another one, also in the *National Post* and several other newspapers owned by Postmedia. It was called "What does Canada's investment deal with China actually say?"

In the second article, Coyne surveyed a few provisions in the FIPA, and then pronounced the deal safe for Canada. Not surprisingly, he jumped to a lot of simplistic conclusions. Mostly, this was because he missed key elements of the FIPA, failed to compare it to other investment treaties, and failed to appreciate the record of investor-state arbitration.

I responded to Coyne's assessment of the FIPA in an opinion article that I posted soon after on Troy Media. I pointed out some of the problems in his assessment, and called for an independent and public review of the deal.

For example, I pointed out how, on market access, the FIPA gave China far more flexibility to block Canadian investments than vice versa. I explained how Coyne missed the FIPA's carve-out for existing discriminatory measures. I noted that federal officials had not been able to produce a list of China's existing discriminatory measures and that, without such a list, it would be hard to hold China to its commitment to non-discrimination in the future.

I agreed with Coyne that the FIPA protects foreign investors. However, I noted catches, and explained that awards under similar treaties had taken the concept of indirect expropriation beyond analogous rules in Canadian law, thus giving an advantage to Chinese investors over their Canadian competitors in Canada. I warned that the apparently benign concepts of fair and equitable treatment and full protection and security had been used by arbitrators more often than other provisions to order compensation, and had often been taken in expansive directions. I noted how the arbitrators are for-profit adjudicators, not tenured judges, and how this factor gives rise to a reasonable suspicion that the arbitrators will favour foreign investors and powerful governments in order to expand business for the "arbitration club," as it is called in the literature.

Without "breathless hysteria," I explained these and other provisions in the treaty, drawing on my expertise. By this point, most of my criticisms were already on the public record, but I thought it worthwhile to reply directly to Coyne. I urged him not to dismiss so quickly the need for a study of the FIPA, since the treaty could lead to billion-dollar awards against Canada and, if finalized, would be beyond any Canadian legislature or court's authority for decades.

To my knowledge, Coyne never corrected any of the errors in his own articles.

Coyne was right to ask what the FIPA meant, but he should have been more humble. The decision to ratify the FIPA was important for our country. Coyne claimed to have reliable answers, but he was reassuring Canadians based on bad information. He led a blind rush to ratify a long-term deal.

Personally, I found most of this spin troubling but also boring. Ivison and Coyne followed a simple template. They smeared critics. They peddled inaccuracies while avoiding specific concerns. It was important to debunk their spin, but a distracting chore.

However, one point in Coyne's first opinion article was interesting to me for what it suggested about his thinking.

Basically, as I discussed in chapter 3, Coyne claimed that a non-reciprocal FIPA would actually be good for Canada; even if Canadian companies did not get the same rights in China, he said the FIPA would stop Canadians from putting protectionist restrictions on Chinese firms in Canada. Also, in contradiction to Ivison, Coyne thought it was "the point of the agreement to bring in more" Chinese investment to Canada.

Thus, Coyne appeared to endorse giving Chinese companies a one-way right to enter Canada's economy and buy its natural resources and infrastructure. As he said on *The National*, "[i]t wouldn't bother somebody like me, but it would bother the public if you saw a large section of the oil patch falling under foreign control all in a hurry."

Okay, let's break that down:

- Coyne said on October 29, 2012, that he expected most Canadians would disagree with him about foreign control of the oil patch.

- The next week, Coyne used his Postmedia platform to defend the FIPA at the time of its expected ratification, while others were calling for a public review.

- Coyne pushed for ratification, even though the treaty would require Canadians to do something that he did not think they wanted: open Canada's resources to more foreign control.

- In pushing for ratification, Coyne was also extremely dismissive of others who were trying to warn Canadians that they should be concerned about the FIPA.

As one who believes in letting Canadians make up their own minds based on accurate information, I think this record of events reflects poorly on Coyne. I hope he won't think me near-hysterical for saying so.

CHAPTER 31.

MILOS BARUTCISKI AND MATTHEW KRONBY, PART ONE

Another group that emerged to defend the FIPA after it became controversial was lawyers who work in investor-state arbitration.

Two such lawyers who joined the media blitz in early November 2012 were Milos Barutciski and Matthew Kronby. The same day on which Coyne's first column in the *National Post* appeared, the *Globe and Mail* ran an opinion article by Barutciski and Kronby, which I discuss later in this chapter. Before doing so, I would like to stress the importance of lawyers disclosing their financial interests, especially when they engage in a public debate.

Barutciski and Kronby were identified in their article as partners in the international trade and investment practice of a Toronto law firm called Bennett Jones. Kronby was also identified as the former head of the federal government's trade law office. This conveyed that both of these lawyers, unlike Ivison and Coyne, had relevant expertise in the field. Certainly, they do.

However, a related point was not mentioned explicitly in the opinion article. Barutciski and Kronby appear to have had a financial stake in treaties like the FIPA. In particular, they and their firm were in a position to profit if foreign investors obtained new rights to sue Canada and China in investor-state arbitration. Obviously, the prospect of FIPA lawsuits benefits investor-state lawyers.

Lawyers can contribute to public understanding of complex issues. However, they should also disclose if they stand to benefit financially from a position they are advocating publicly. Shortly after Barutciski and Kronby wrote their article, University of Toronto professor David Schneiderman—who also has expertise in investment treaties—and I emphasized this issue of disclosure in an article in the *Toronto Star* (the article was declined by the *Globe and Mail*, where Barutciski and Kronby's article was published).

Schneiderman and I highlighted the dilemma for the public. Who should the public believe, we asked, when FIPA critics expressed concern about accepting long-term commitments to protect Chinese state-owned investors from governments in Canada, while proponents of the deal, often lawyers, replied that the critics' concerns were overblown? Schneiderman and I also emphasized the intricacies of evaluating the FIPA:

> One challenge in debating investment treaties is that the treaty text is not the whole story. There is an ever-expanding body of international investment law—arising from disputes between investors and states and decided by arbitrators who operate outside of national or international courts—providing authoritative interpretations of the treaties. Systematic research of these interpretations indicates that they often expand the arbitrators' own authority and are highly protective of foreign investors, especially where the investor is from an economically powerful state.

We then highlighted the role of lawyers in the debate:

> The Canadian public should know that many, perhaps all, of the legal experts who have come forward in recent weeks to defend the Canada-China treaty are lawyers who have, or whose law firms have, a financial stake in expanding investor-state arbitration. Alongside the recent spread of the arbitrations, a lucrative new legal industry has emerged. Lawyers in the field provide ser-

vices as experts, as counsel, or as arbitrators in disputes between investors and states. Even scholars in the Canadian legal academy often provide services as lawyers, arbitrators, or experts in these arbitrations.

Finally, we stressed that lawyers and academics alike, when they take part in the debate over the FIPA, need to disclose their financial interest in the expansion of investor-state arbitration to help the public to weigh the evidence. We added that "[n]ew treaties that further the interests of international investment lawyers may not necessarily benefit Canada as a whole," especially when the deal "exposes Canadian taxpayers to significant risks and Canadian voters to powerful legal constraints that preclude changes to Canadian public policy."

Barutciski and Kronby's article in the *Globe and Mail* was called "Investment agreement with China will benefit Canada." How did they support this statement? As a word of warning, their explanations get a bit wordy.

Barutciski and Kronby began by connecting the FIPA debate to the issue of state companies in Canada, which they downplayed as a concern. Eventually, they segued to technical aspects of the FIPA by invoking the "rule of law" and, as they put it, "decisions based on principle,"

> Canadians believe in the rule of law—at home as well as abroad. It is therefore important that we make decisions based on principle. The Canada-China investment agreement includes a most-favoured-nation (MFN) commitment that will not allow discrimination against Chinese investors relative to other foreign investors. Nor would we want to discriminate, given China's importance as a source of foreign investment for the foreseeable future.

Thus, readers were assured that the FIPA would limit discrimination against foreign investors. As usual (for FIPA promoters), there was no mention of the FIPA's extensive carve-out for China's existing discriminatory measures. Keep in mind, these are lawyers who specialize in the field.

Barutciski and Kronby looped back to Chinese state companies, saying for example that concerns about political interference by the Chinese government may be "imagined" and that political interference can happen with other countries' companies too. Then they returned to technical aspects of the FIPA, starting with the complex standard of most-favoured-nation treatment:

> Apart from the most-favoured-nation obligation, which applies to both prospective and existing investments, the [FIPA] focuses on the treatment of investments that have already been made. It offers protections to investors against such risks as discrimination, expropriation without compensation, and arbitrary decisions by governments, once they are established in the other country.

It was fair to highlight these FIPA protections as the most useful ones in the deal, for Canadian investors. But Barutciski and Kronby should also have mentioned China's ability to keep all of its existing discriminatory measures and, using those measures, damage Canadian companies by other means. They also should have mentioned that foreign investors have never been known to sue China and win, while Canada has been sued many times under NAFTA and lost important cases. Their version of the FIPA had heavy makeup, to stress only a benefit for Canada.

Barutciski and Kronby's article was also mired in technical detail, as the next excerpt shows:

> This distinction [between prospective and existing investments] highlights an important point: that the [FIPA] will not change the ability of either country to review or reject investments from the other when it determines that they are not in the national interest. "Net benefit" decisions under the Investment Canada Act (ICA) are expressly excluded from the [FIPA]. Prime Minister Stephen Harper has announced the federal government's intention to add further clarity to the "net benefit" test and the review

of investments by state-owned enterprises. The [FIPA] will not change anything in this regard, and Canada will retain the power to approve, impose conditions or block state-owned enterprises or private investments when they are not of benefit to Canada.

This lawyerly shout-out for the Investment Canada Act is familiar by now. Like others, Barutciski and Kronby stressed that the FIPA lets Canada keep the Investment Canada Act, but neglected to add that the FIPA gives China a much broader right to screen Canadian investments. If they had time to introduce details like the "net benefit" test under the act, Barutciski and Kronby could also have noted the act's high thresholds for review, its non-application to investments that don't involve takeovers of Canadian companies, and its exemptions for foreign companies with existing operations in Canada.

Once again, it was a highly selective portrayal.

Having to this point passed over the FIPA's features that favour China, Barutciski and Kronby finally noted that "some critics have nevertheless criticized the [FIPA] because it is not 'reciprocal.'" They put the term "reciprocal" in quotes, suggesting they might have thought it wrong even to use this word to criticize the FIPA.

To be clear, the FIPA is non-reciprocal because important aspects of the deal are not equally binding on Canada and China; China simply has fewer or less intense obligations, or more rights, than Canada. Barutciski and Kronby were skeptical of this description because, according to them, "[q]uite apart from the fact that the obligations in the [FIPA] apply to both China and Canada, the reciprocity argument ignores two obvious realities."

Take a moment to digest that last nugget. Barutciski and Kronby did not mention *any* of the specific examples of inequality in the FIPA. Instead, they implied that the FIPA was actually reciprocal because its obligations, as a whole, "apply to both China and Canada."

This response to the criticism was a complete dodge. All treaties obviously apply, as a whole, to both sides. That is the essence of any agreement! Simply, both sides agree to something. On Barutciski and Kronby's approach, a deal in which a person sells his or her child into slavery for $1 can be called reciprocal.

However, as any lawyer should be able to grasp, the criticism of the FIPA was more specific: in key ways, the FIPA's obligations did not apply to both sides equally. Instead, they applied more broadly or intensively to Canada than to China. What did Barutciski and Kronby have to say about that issue? They responded by asserting two "obvious realities," as they put it:

> One is that the benefits of a predictable, rules-based environment for investment under the [FIPA] are far more likely to accrue to Canadian investors in China than to Chinese investors operating in Canada, who already take a predictable, rules-based environment for granted.

Thus, it was apparently obvious that Canada was not likely to be sued under the FIPA. So, according to Barutciski and Kronby, the deal was actually non-reciprocal in Canada's favour. However, as we saw in chapter 10 of this book, Canada has been sued far more often in investor-state arbitration than China, even though Canada has far fewer investment treaties than China.

What about Barutciski and Kronby's second "obvious reality" to explain the FIPA's non-reciprocity? According to them, "the other is that growing Chinese investment in Canada is virtually certain (and desirable) with or without the [FIPA]."

At this point, the lawyers were transforming themselves into economists, even utopians. Without serious review of the FIPA by anyone on this question, Barutciski and Kronby were content to reassure the public that Chinese investment in Canada will be "desirable." Quick question: will it be desirable for Canada, or will it be desirable merely for the law firms that work on Chinese takeovers of Canadian companies and FIPA lawsuits?

To highlight how flippantly these claims about Chinese investment were being made, let's backtrack to another FIPA promoter, Andrew Coyne. Like Coyne, Barutciski and Kronby said that more Chinese investment in Canada would be desirable, without explaining why. Unlike Coyne, they predicted that more Chinese investment is "virtually certain" to come, regardless of the FIPA. Hold on there. Why should Canada give Chinese investors a special right to sue Canadians, in a lopsided FIPA, if all that desirable Chinese investment is going to come anyway?

Barutciski and Kronby identified another criticism of the FIPA:

> Others have asserted that its investor-state dispute procedure will open the door to Chinese investor claims that will overrule the decisions of democratically elected governments or expose Canadian governments to ruinous liability awards.

In response, they explained that Chinese investors could not "ask dispute tribunals to strike down government decisions." Instead, "all they can ask for is monetary damages for breaches of the agreement."

Thus, Barutciski and Kronby used some choice words—"overrule" and "strike down," instead of "deter" or "frustrate"—to re-frame the criticism so it became untenable. They also did not mention how Chinese investors' FIPA right to sue gives them special bargaining power in negotiations with governments in Canada. Barutciski and Kronby added:

> The critics ignore Canadian experience with investment disputes under the NAFTA where, over 18 years, claims against Canada have resulted in awards totalling only about CDN$8-million. Canada did choose to settle two other cases for about CDN$150-million, mostly relating to Newfoundland's expropri-

ation of AbitibiBowater's assets, but investment rules exist precisely to provide redress in such cases.

Once again, like other promoters, Barutciski and Kronby skipped quickly to the second-order question about the FIPA: whether Chinese lawsuits are likely to sue and win. They passed over how the FIPA gives new rights to Chinese investors and how this changes the role of Canadian legislatures and courts. And, to answer the second-order question in a reassuring way, they offered an extremely brief summary of Canada's record under NAFTA, highlighting the federal government's settlement of a NAFTA lawsuit by AbitibiBowater.

Obviously, Canada's NAFTA record is a long story. Different people will have different views about it, and about any particular case. It is not possible to back up sweeping claims about such things in an opinion article. Even in a book, it's easy to get lost in the cases. We need not belabour the details here, but since Barutciski and Kronby raised the *AbitibiBowater* case as an example, I have included additional information about that case on my blog, gusvanharten.wordpress.com. I have done so partly because investor-state lawyers in the United States and Europe have used the *AbitibiBowater* case for another purpose, treating it as a poster child for the need for investor-state arbitration to protect foreign investors in Canada. Meanwhile, Barutciski and Kronby pointed to the case as a reason for Canadians not to worry about getting sued by Chinese investors.

Do you see any contradiction there?

In my experience, there is one message from investor-state lawyers about the NAFTA record that is constant: whether Canada wins or loses a NAFTA case, it's because investor-state arbitration worked. Whatever happened, we need investor-state arbitration.

CHAPTER 32.

MILOS BARUTCISKI AND MATTHEW KRONBY, PART TWO

The key claim in Barutciski and Kronby's *Globe and Mail* article was that the FIPA would benefit Canada.

When they made this claim, I suggest that Barutciski and Kronby should have identified and addressed criticisms of the deal: its lopsidedness, its allowances of secrecy, its transfer of powers from judges to arbitrators, its risks for voters and taxpayers. I say this because Barutciski and Kronby had expertise in the area, but also because they did not join the call for a proper review of the FIPA before it was ratified. Instead, they exploited a vacuum of reliable information about the deal to soft-pedal its risks for Canada.

Remarkably, less than a week after the *Globe* article was published, Barutciski himself was listed as the lead lawyer for a U.S. company that filed notice for a NAFTA lawsuit against Canada. The lawsuit attacked Quebec's restrictions on oil and gas drilling in the St. Lawrence River basin. Thus, as Barutciski and his partner Kronby were telling Canadians that concerns about foreign investor lawsuits against Canada were misguided, he was about to launch—and did not mention—a foreign investor lawsuit against Canada. To me, that really crossed the line for when and how lawyers should participate in a public debate.

Personally, I do not expect an immediate rush of Chinese lawsuits against Canada, now that the FIPA has been ratified. Among other things, Chinese investors may prefer to limit their use of the FIPA to behind-the-scenes lobbying.

Even so, there is a real prospect of major Chinese lawsuits, with hundreds of millions or even billions of dollars at stake. The prospect is real because it has happened to other countries unexpectedly under similar treaties. It has also happened to Canada under NAFTA. Based on the NAFTA record, we can also expect the FIPA to deter governments in Canada from making decisions that Chinese investors oppose. Unfortunately, we now have decades to wait and see how hard it rains under the deal—assuming that what happens becomes public—and to consider whether Barutciski and Kronby's hasty assessment was wise.

Barutciski and Kronby wrapped up their opinion article by saying "Canada has the tools under the Investment Canada Act to determine whether investments *beyond the statutory financial threshold* are in its economic interest (emphasis mine)." Thus, they repeated the usual line about the Investment Canada Act, but added the legalistic phrase "beyond the statutory financial threshold." This phrase reveals—albeit indirectly and inaccessibly—that the FIPA in fact *limits* Canada's ability "to determine whether [Chinese] investments . . . are in its economic interest," in cases where a Chinese buy-up of natural resources or infrastructure falls below the "statutory financial threshold."

Barutciski and Kronby continued:

> Canada has the tools under the Investment Canada Act to determine whether investments beyond the statutory financial threshold are in its economic interest. To the extent that Canadians

believe additional clarity and transparency in the investment review process is beneficial, the Canada-China investment agreement does not preclude that.

Thus, Barutciski and Kronby flagged a point—usually raised by supporters of foreign investors in Canada, not critics of the FIPA—that the FIPA does not prevent Canadians from putting "additional clarity and transparency" into the Investment Canada Act's review process. However, they left out the much more pertinent criticisms of the FIPA's lack of transparency. They also did not mention that any changes to the Investment Canada Act will only be reliable under the FIPA if they don't tighten the review process for Chinese investors.

Lastly, Barutciski and Kronby said that Canada should not have held out for market access commitments from China, because of the FIPA's trade-off for Canadian investors in China after they are let in:

> [T]he fact that China has chosen to protect some of its markets from foreign investment is not a cogent reason for denying Canadian businesses the protections that the [FIPA] will provide when they make investments in China. In our view, the [FIPA] is clearly of benefit to Canada and Canadian investors in China.

Remarkably, the interests of Canadians were not mentioned at all in this final tally. The FIPA might as well have ceded Vancouver Island to China for thirty-one years. It could still be said to be "of benefit to Canada."

Barutciski and Kronby were not alone in misleading the public about the FIPA. On the other hand, there were other investor-state lawyers who provided a more descriptive and fair account of the FIPA, usually in articles aimed at a business clientele.

For example, after the FIPA was released in September 2012, John W. Boscariol and other lawyers at the firm McCarthy Tétrault wrote a less overtly promotional article about the deal. Unlike Barutciski and Kronby, they managed to catch that the FIPA's provisions on non-discrimination did not apply to "all existing non-conforming measures."

They also highlighted that the FIPA's rules on indirect expropriation were controversial, "as scholars and arbitral tribunals continue to struggle to distinguish between measures that are confiscatory or equivalent to expropriation and measures that constitute bona fide or legitimate regulation."

They appeared even to criticize the FIPA, saying that its approach to openness in arbitration was "more restricted" and that this marked "a significant reduction in transparency compared to an open Tribunal process" and "a significant deviation" from Canada's usual approach.

Alongside the FIPA's carve-out of the Investment Canada Act, they highlighted the broader exception for any "Law, Regulations and Rules relating to foreign investment" in China. And, they had no trouble acknowledging that the FIPA was "likely to become one of Canada's most significant investor protection treaties."

This analysis by the McCarthy Tétrault lawyers still fixated on foreign investors' interests, rather than others' who were affected by the FIPA. As the lawyers said, the FIPA would be "of interest to foreign investors seeking to bring a damages claim against a State" and noted that they could give advice "on remedies available to foreign investors under bilateral investment treaties." But lawyers are entitled to promote themselves to clients, and this article was a marked improvement compared to Barutciski and Kronby's.

Two years later, when the FIPA was ratified, other lawyers also wrote reasonable assessments of it, again for business clients. They did not talk about the FIPA's lack of reciprocity, but they also did not dismiss the criticisms or claim to have evaluated the deal's costs and benefits for Canada.

For example, the law firm Goodmans published an update that lauded the FIPA for foreign investors, while acknowledging some of its downsides. The update noted that the FIPA did not apply to existing discriminatory laws and alerted readers that "for inbound investment, the FIPA may make it riskier for the Canadian government to take steps that displease Chinese investors." The update also acknowledged that "unlike many FIPAs with other countries, there are many Chinese investors with significant stakes in Canadian companies, and they will likely not hesitate to use investor/ state procedures."

The update also included an important caution for Canadian investors:

> Ironically, while the FIPA should be a significant help to Canadian companies doing business in China, it may result in the Canadian government being less likely to itself intervene to assist a particular company in China. In our experience, when investor/ state procedures are available, the government tends to advise the Canadian investor to pursue the remedies available to it and to not seek assistance from Canada.

Thus, the update suggested that Canadian investors could actually be worse off under the FIPA, if the deal were to cause the federal government to reduce its diplomatic support.

These examples show that lawyers could be more responsible in their portrayal of the FIPA.

Here's a parting thought. If Canada ever has to pay Chinese investors under the FIPA, perhaps those lawyers who downplayed that risk, before the deal was ratified, could chip in with any fees they earn from the FIPA?

CHAPTER 33.

THE TRADE SPECIALISTS

There are not many people in Canada who have specialized expertise in investment treaties and the arbitrations under them. Outside of governments and private law firms, I'd say there are about ten who have detailed knowledge in the field. Most are academics at law schools, some of whom work on the side as investor-state lawyers or arbitrators.

I am pointing this out because individuals cited by FIPA promoters as authorities in the subject were usually not in this small group. To my knowledge, their expertise—as reflected primarily by their record of publications—was in trade law and policy, less so (if at all) in investor-state arbitration. These other areas were relevant to the FIPA, but they are different branches of expertise from the directly relevant area: international investment law and arbitration. To have thorough knowledge in this area, one has to keep track of numerous treaties and hundreds of arbitration awards. My general impression in debates over the FIPA was that some of the "trade specialists" who championed the deal were not well-informed about how investment treaties have been used, especially in arbitrations under treaties besides NAFTA.

On the other hand, by widening one's measure of expertise in the field, it was possible to paint the FIPA's critics as loners

among the experts. Some FIPA promoters did just that in my case; for example, Andrew Coyne asked:

> How can it be that so few people should have discovered its treacherous potential—apart from [Elizabeth] May, there's Maude Barlow, and an associate professor at Osgoode Hall, Gus Van Harten—while trade specialists such as Michael Hart, director of the Centre for Trade Policy and Law at Carleton University, or Daniel Schwanen of the C.D. Howe Institute, give it a pass?
>
> Maybe because it's not that big a deal.

Well, if Hart or Schwanen, or anyone else Coyne may have spoken with, thought—and I must say I find it hard to believe—that the FIPA was "not that big a deal," they were wrong. That is, they were wrong if one compared the significance of the China FIPA to all of Canada's other investment treaties since NAFTA in the early 1990s.

Consider it this way. A twenty-year storm is a big deal for those who live in its path. It is an even bigger deal when the storm twenty years earlier was the first one of such force in the country's history.

As it happens, critics of investor-state arbitration are far from loners among the disinterested experts in international investment law. To demonstrate the extent of the criticism, I will highlight two academic statements, both of which I helped to draft and joined.

The first statement is from 2010 and was signed by over seventy academics from universities in many different countries who have knowledge in investment law or policy. Among other things, the statement noted the harm caused by investment treaties and the arbitrators' record of going too far:

> We have a shared concern for the harm done to the public welfare by the international investment regime, as currently structured, especially its hampering of the ability of governments to

act for their people in response to the concerns of human development and environmental sustainability. . . .

Awards issued by international arbitrators against states have in numerous cases incorporated overly expansive interpretations of language in investment treaties. These interpretations have prioritized the protection of the property and economic interests of transnational corporations over the right to regulate of states and the right to self-determination of peoples. . . . This has constituted a major reorientation of the balance between investor protection and public regulation in international law.

The award of damages as a remedy of first resort in investment arbitration poses a serious threat to democratic choice and the capacity of governments to act in the public interest by way of innovative policy-making in response to changing social, economic, and environmental conditions.

The second statement is from 2014, and is more detailed in its concerns. It was signed by over 120 academics, mostly at universities in Europe, and cast doubt on the controversial plan of the European Commission—to which the statement was submitted—to include investor-state arbitration in a proposed Europe-U.S. trade deal called the Transatlantic Trade and Investment Partnership (TTIP).

On the one hand, this second statement commended the commission for recognizing, in a public document about the TTIP, some of the flaws in investor-state arbitration:

The [commission's] document . . . implicitly condemns the investment arbitration community for its failure to police itself adequately in matters of ethics, independence, competence, impartiality, and conflicts of interest. By implication, the document acknowledges that the institutional design of investment arbitration has given rise to reasonable perceptions that the decision-making process is biased against some states and investors as well as various interests of the general public.

On the other hand, the statement criticized the commission for proposing to give so much more power to investor-state arbitrators:

... the Commission seems content to entrust to these same actors the vital constitutional task of weighing and balancing the right to regulate of sovereign states and the property rights of foreign investors. This task is one of the most profound roles that can be assigned to any national or international judicial body.

Unlike many promoters of investor-state arbitration, the academics who supported these statements did not have a financial stake in what they were recommending. If anything, some stood to lose potential income if investor-state arbitration was nixed, or replaced by a judicial process.

Of course, no one is right merely because he or she follows closely the record of arbitrations and publishes detailed studies about it. My point is that the federal government should have put the competing claims about the FIPA to the test, in public, by organizing a thorough and independent review. It should have brought in experts from inside and outside of Canada to assess the deal from different perspectives. Because that didn't happen, and there was no baseline of accurate information, it was easier for promoters of the deal to spin the FIPA.

CHAPTER 34.

LAWRENCE HERMAN

I turn to another prominent FIPA promoter: Lawrence Herman.

Herman worked for many years at a Bay Street law firm called Cassels Brock, where his practice focused on international trade and business law. He left the firm in 2014 but, as I understand, still works in private practice.

When Prime Minister Harper announced the FIPA in Beijing in February 2012, the *Globe and Mail* celebrated the deal in an editorial that I discussed in chapter 27 of this book. In the editorial, which came out long before the FIPA's text was made public, Lawrence Herman was cited as saying the Chinese are "pragmatic and skeptical of international entanglements . . . . So this is a good, indeed very good, first step for Canada." I ask, assuming that Herman was not misquoted, what lawyer would say that a treaty is "good" or "very good" for a country, even as a first step, when the treaty's text is not public?

The *Globe*'s editorial then identified two essential ingredients in a FIPA: "each country 'shall accord to investors of the other [country] treatment no less favourable than that it accords . . . to its own investors,' and. . . there will be a dispute settlement mechanism." It was not clear whether the *Globe*'s editors relied on Herman for these further points but, whatever their source, they indicate a lack of knowledge about what investment treaties do. That is, the treaties do much more than protect against "less favourable" treatment. Unfortunately, the same error was later repeated by other FIPA promoters, including John Ivison and Stephen Gordon.

More importantly, when the FIPA's text was at last made public in September 2012, it became clear that the deal was exceptionally weak in its protection of Canadian investors against discrimination in China (i.e. "less favourable" treatment, compared to China's own investors). To my knowledge, neither the *Globe* nor Herman highlighted in response that the deal lacked one of its two supposedly essential ingredients.

Herman's support for the FIPA appeared to intensify after the deal became controversial in the fall of 2012.

Indeed, he was one of the first promoters out of the blocks in the blitz to suppress public angst about the FIPA. Two days before Andrew Coyne's appearance on *The National*, Herman wrote an article in the *Financial Post* with Daniel Schwanen, a C.D. Howe trade analyst. The article was relatively mild in its tarring of FIPA critics. It said only that they "vastly overstate [the FIPA's] potential downside while overlooking its concrete benefits" and that the debate initiated by the critics was "characterized by more heat than light." Why?

Many of the reasons given by Herman and Schwanen were similar to what we have seen from Ivison, Coyne, Barutciski, and Kronby. They mentioned that "two and a half thousand such agreements" existed, without saying that most investment treaties were concluded before investor-state arbitration exploded, or that the vast majority of them are unlikely ever to trigger an investor lawsuit.

They got right that China has concluded "well over one hundred" investment treaties, but neglected the fact that China—unlike Canada—has never been ordered to pay damages in a known case. This fact seemed especially important, since Herman and Schwanen claimed that Canadian investors would be "better off investing in China within a rules-based framework." That is, it suggested that all of China's existing FIPA-like treaties—and the rules-based framework they supposedly delivered—had made little verifiable difference, on the record of investor-state arbitration.

True to form, Herman and Schwanen flagged the role of the Investment Canada Act, without highlighting the FIPA's lopsidedness on this point. They also erroneously implied that the FIPA was reciprocal on market access: "In any event, both Canada and China retain under this agreement their existing capabilities to screen for foreign investment—an investor is protected by the agreement only once it is allowed in."

The second part of this sentence was wrong, as we saw in chapter 6 of this book. An investor from China, though not from Canada, "is protected" under the FIPA *before* "it is allowed in." This is because Chinese investors alone have a general right of market access under the FIPA. For some of those Chinese investors, this general right is subject to the Investment Canada Act, but due to the act's limitations, other Chinese investors clearly do have a FIPA right to be "allowed in."

I accept that this point about the FIPA's inequality on market access was hard to garner from the treaty's text. It required several steps of analysis, based on good knowledge of the relationship between the FIPA's provision for (pre-establishment) most-favoured-nation treatment and other investment treaties of Canada and China. Even so, when Herman and Schwanen weighed in at this critical stage in the budding controversy over the FIPA, they claimed to know better. Instead, they led the pack in getting it wrong.

Like other FIPA promoters, Herman and Schwanen also gave a brief, whitewashed account of Canada's experience in investor-state arbitration under NAFTA. Like other promoters, they selected the *AbitibiBowater* case as their example, saying wrongly that the federal government's CDN$130 million settlement in that case "was required" under NAFTA and international law. They also did not mention that NAFTA gave AbitibiBowater a special right to opt out of Canadian legislative and court processes, in order to seek compensation under NAFTA's more favourable rules.

These themes in the FIPA sales pitch are by now familiar even if, at the time, they paved the way for other FIPA promoters. However, three of Herman and Schwanen's other arguments are new to our story. I will examine them more closely.

First, Herman and Schwanen responded to the observation that Canada is the capital-importer under the China FIPA, and therefore takes on more risks. They said:

> Much has been made of the fact that Canada is a net recipient of Chinese investments, suggesting that somehow this makes Canada particularly vulnerable to future investor-state arbitration rulings in favour of Chinese investors. But this view disregards the fact that Canada is now a net exporter of direct investment overall—Canadian businesses have grown by expanding globally, and this is a key reason why Canada seeks such agreements.

Thus, Herman and Schwanen downplayed—but did not dispute—that Canada was more vulnerable to FIPA lawsuits because Chinese investors owned more assets in Canada than Canadian investors owned in China. Instead, they implied that this disparity was okay because Canadian investors in China would still benefit (even if Canadian voters and taxpayers back home lost out).

They continued: "[i]t would be disingenuous of Canada to say it wants protection against discrimination and uncompensated expropriation for our investments in other countries without being willing to afford the same standard of treatment to foreign investors in Canada."

Let's get that straight. Even if the FIPA costs Canadians far more than it benefits us, we must above all not be *disingenuous* when negotiating investment treaties. Put differently, it seems we must not stand up for our interests when another country is more powerful because we have used investment treaties to exploit other countries when they faced more of the risks. There's a guilt trip for you.

I also dislike hypocrisy. But the principled approach for Canada would be to do what we can to fix the problems with investor-state arbitration, for everyone. That principle holds, regardless of whether Canada is in the stronger or the weaker position in a particular treaty. Instead, the Harper Government—supported by commentators like Herman and Schwanen—is expanding investor-state arbitration by leaps and bounds, for strong and weak countries alike. In this way, the government is sacrificing voters and taxpayers worldwide in order to privilege foreign investors.

It is also a bizarre argument to say that Canadians should accept a lopsided deal with China merely because Canada has done lopsided deals with other countries. That is, Herman and Schwanen seem to be saying that Canadians should accept getting fleeced by China because the federal government has fleeced other countries, usually to provide lopsided protections for Canadian investors—especially resource companies—in Africa and Latin America. If only China showed such benevolence to us. Likewise, if other countries can say no to investor-state arbitration in a treaty with Canada—as some have done—why shouldn't Canada do the same with China?

The second of Herman and Schwanen's points that I want to address is their misrepresentation of what investment treaties actually do. Herman and Schwanen declared that it was false for FIPA critics to say that "any measure by a government that may impose costs on a foreign investor, such as a tax or an environmental regulation, can give rise to compensation claims under these types of agreement."

But this criticism is not false. Under the FIPA, any government measure clearly "can" give rise to compensation claims. It might be that Herman and Schwanen meant to say they don't think many of these claims *will* give rise to compensation. That's a very different point. Even assuming they mistakenly said "can" instead of "will," Herman and Schwanen—like so many other promoters—skipped quickly from how the FIPA gives new powers to arbitrators to the uncertain question of how the arbitrators will use their powers in the future.

Herman and Schwanen went on by highlighting the FIPA's exceptions, with a notable sleight of hand:

> These agreements explicitly exclude such [tax or environmental] measures taken for a public-policy purpose and that do not discriminate against the foreign investor. The [FIPA] states that a government really has to have acted in bad faith and the impact on the investor or investment must have been really severe, for a measure to be construed by a tribunal as constituting expropriation.

Let's look closely at this statement.

The first sentence says that investment treaties exclude tax and environmental measures if they are for a public purpose and not discriminatory. That is never completely true, and rarely true at all. For example, in Article 14 of the China FIPA, Canadian tax measures are mostly excluded, but the arbitrators can still order compensation for a tax measure on grounds of direct or indirect expropriation, unless China agrees within six months of the Chinese investor's claim that the measure is not an expropriation and does not have "an effect equivalent to expropriation." Whoops, Herman and Schwanen didn't allude to that part.

For environmental measures, FIPA arbitrators can order compensation even more easily. Such measures are subject to an exception in Article 33(2) of the FIPA. But that exception has key limitations, and, to my knowledge, it has never been used by arbitrators to block compensation under any investment treaty.

Herman and Schwanen's second sentence played a different game. It focused on the FIPA's moderating language for one of the FIPA's provisions: indirect expropriation. However, that moderating language doesn't apply to other investor rights in the FIPA, including the one used most often to order compensation: fair and equitable treatment. Even for the FIPA's indirect expropriation provision, the moderating language has important limitations and is vulnerable to a complicated loophole created by the FIPA's most-favoured-nation treatment rule. (The loophole is very involved so, instead of bogging us down here, I discuss it on my blog, gusvan-harten.wordpress.com.)

Thus, Herman and Schwanen put a shiny gloss on the FIPA. They left a false impression that the FIPA could not lead to compensation for Chinese investors for any Canadian tax and environmental measure, if the measure is introduced for a public purpose and kept non-discriminatory. Though it takes a lot of time to explain, they also exaggerated the reliability of the FIPA's exceptions and moderating language. Basically, their pitch for the FIPA exploited the limited ability of most Canadians to do a research project to find out what the deal really meant.

The last of Herman and Schwanen's points that I want to discuss is how they responded to criticisms of the FIPA's thirty-one-year minimum lifespan, based on its minimum term of fifteen years, its requirement for one year's notice of termination once the initial fifteen-year term is up, and then a "survival clause" that preserves the rights of existing foreign investors for another fifteen years after termination. In defence of this long lifespan, Herman and Schwanen said:

But if the agreement is meant to encourage long-term investments, it is apparent that a treaty which can be denounced on very short notice will not do the trick. That is why long-term notice provisions are fairly standard.

Further, they pointed to a China–Germany investment treaty as an example of a comparably long lifespan, due to that treaty's ten-year minimum term and twenty-year survival clause.

There were several problems with this defence of the China FIPA. One was that many criticisms of the FIPA focused on its flaws that are not shared by other treaties, and that would be impossible for future governments to fix because of the FIPA's long lifespan. For example, the China–Germany investment treaty—unlike the FIPA—does not give Chinese investors a non-reciprocal right of market access because Germany's practice (like China's, but not Canada's) is to not give up market access rights in its investment treaties. Germany is not stuck in a lopsided deal—at least not nearly so much as Canada.

A second problem with Herman's and Schwanen's defence was that, for those concerned about safeguarding democracy, no investment treaty should have such a long lock-in period. That is, democratic accountability should trump investor security, even if there is compelling evidence (there is not) that prioritizing democracy in this way makes Canada less attractive to foreign investors.

A third problem with Herman and Schwanen's defence was that they sidestepped the best marker for evaluating the China FIPA's long lifespan: Canada's other FIPAs. These were the best marker because they pointed to Canada's past practice in compromising Canadian democracy to protect foreign investors.

Why did Herman and Schwanen not discuss this marker? Perhaps it was because the great majority of Canada's FIPAs have *no* minimum term; typically, they have only a one-year notice requirement and a lengthy survival clause. Arguably, even this structure in other FIPAs is much too long-lasting. But at least it gives some flexibility to future governments to terminate the deal, while still delivering long-term security for foreign investments made prior to termination. It's a much better compromise for voters and taxpayers than the China FIPA.

In fact, other than the China FIPA, just four of Canada's FIPAs have any minimum term at all. They are Canada's FIPAs with Hungary, Poland, and Tanzania (each of which has a minimum term of ten years) and with Egypt (which has a minimum term of fifteen years). Chinese investors in Canada own far more assets in Canada than do investors from these smaller countries, making the China FIPA by far the greatest compromise of Canadian democracy in the history of Canada's investment treaties.

The long lifespan of the China FIPA looks even more irresponsible if one considers that only one of the four comparable FIPAs—the one with Tanzania, in 2013—was concluded after investor-state arbitration exploded in the 1990s. And, the risks and constraints of the Tanzania FIPA for Canada are practically non-existent compared to the China FIPA. As such, the Tanzania FIPA is a very good example of the Harper Government being "disingenuous," to use Herman and Schwanen's term, by locking a weaker country into an anti-democratic, lopsided deal for the benefit of Canadian investors, mostly resource companies, in Tanzania. Canada's FIPA with Tanzania undermined democracy in that country, while the China FIPA has undermined democracy in Canada.

Incidentally, one of Canada's big investors in Tanzania is the mining company Barrick Gold, which owns a controversial gold mine that has been the site of deadly clashes between local villagers and police. It is not heartening to think of the new tools that the Tanzania FIPA has delivered to Canadian investors to pressure the Tanzanian government for "stronger" protection in that context. Coincidentally, Canada's foreign affairs minister at the time that the Tanzania and China FIPAs were brought into force was John Baird, who recently left politics and was soon after hired by Barrick Gold as a member of its international advisory board.

The fourth and biggest problem with Herman and Schwanen's defence of the FIPA was that it put foreign investors' interests ahead of everyone else's, by prioritizing long-term security for foreign investors only. No one else is protected by treaties that can be enforced nearly as powerfully as a FIPA, with its long lifespan. I ask, does a potential victim of torture have less of an interest in stable protection than a foreign investor in relation to its assets? Does a possible victim of pollution have less of an interest in safeguarding his or her country's ability to regulate polluters? The long lock-in period in the China FIPA is just another example of how investment treaties favour foreign investors over everyone else.

After the FIPA was ratified in September 2014, Herman popped up to sell it again.

In an opinion article in the *Financial Post*, Herman repeated the opinion that he apparently formed when the FIPA was announced in February 2012, six months before the text was made public. Surprise! He still thought the FIPA was a good step for Canada, and his reasons still tracked those of other FIPA promoters.

In this post-ratification article, Herman zeroed in on a straw man, what he called a "sky-is-falling attack" on the FIPA; unspecified criticisms were "wide of the mark," he said. More straw flew as Herman dismissed the claim that the FIPA would "unleash a litany of arbitration claims by aggressive Chinese companies." Herman pinned FIPA opponents as "interests groups, mostly on the left of the political spectrum." And, once again, he offered a whitewashed summary of Canada's experience in NAFTA investor-state arbitration, while ignoring the experience of other countries under similar treaties.

As usual, Herman did not mention any of the specific examples of non-reciprocity in the FIPA. He did not mention any criticisms of the lack of independence in investor-state arbitration, which by that time had been acknowledged by the Organization on Economic Cooperation and Development and the European Commission—not exactly radical leftists. He repeated the familiar refrain that the FIPA was "merely the last in line of almost 3,000 bilateral investment protection agreements around the world," without acknowledging its obvious exceptionality for Canada. He said critics had suggested that "dozens of governments from countries . . don't know what they're doing and have unwittingly signed away their rights to regulate." I read many critics' simply as saying that governments can get their priorities wrong, including in a FIPA with China, and note that this can happen partly because of bad information from commentators like Herman.

Herman said that, overall, the opposition's arguments were "highly overblown." He backed this up by referring to investment treaties concluded by China, again without mention that China has rarely been sued and never lost in a known case. On the other hand, Herman found room to say that there are only a few cases brought by Chinese investors (though even on this point his numbers were wrong).

Herman added that China's investment treaties with countries like Switzerland, Austria, Germany, and the U.K. have an investor-state arbitration mechanism similar to the Canada-China FIPA. He did not say, and may not have been aware, that these other treaties do not have lopsided parts of the FIPA. Herman claimed that the FIPA "simply follows a 20-year-plus history" of Chinese investment treaties with other Western countries, and just left out the important ways in which it doesn't.

After reading this post-ratification article by Herman, I wondered what one has to do to educate an outspoken trade specialist about a FIPA. I wondered because, months earlier, I had sent Herman a sixty-page technical study I wrote that explained how the FIPA was unique and non-reciprocal in favour of China. Herman was kind enough to thank me and compliment my analysis. Yet, he did not acknowledge any of the specific concerns—on market access, discrimination, investment screening, secrecy, and so on—when he championed the FIPA publicly, once again, after it was ratified.

Near the end of his post-ratification article, Herman praised the FIPA's "symbolic—let alone the legal—value" as being of "immense importance." In doing so, he implicitly supported doing a lopsided FIPA in exchange for symbolism.

I really hope Chinese investors will accept "symbolic" value, instead of hard currency, to pay awards against Canada under the FIPA.

CHAPTER 35.

A LEFT-WING HOBBY HORSE?

FIPA promoters sometimes portray critics of investor-state arbitration as left-wing. This presumably signals to people elsewhere on the political spectrum that they should feel comfortable supporting investor-state arbitration.

Personally, I see the tactic as an insult to anyone who is not familiar with the subject and the debate. It suggests that anyone who is not left-wing will not care—or will not have time—to look at the arguments. It treats them like bulls, easily distracted by a red flag. Join the charge, just don't scrutinize.

To show that this promotional line is also based on misinformation, I highlight in this short chapter some perspectives on investor-state arbitration that are critical and decidedly not left-wing.

Here is how investor-state arbitration—also known as investor-state dispute settlement—was described in the magazine *The Economist*:

> If you wanted to convince the public that international trade agreements are a way to let multinational companies get rich at the expense of ordinary people, this is what you would do: give foreign firms a special right to apply to a secretive tribunal of highly paid corporate lawyers for compensation whenever a

government passes a law to, say, discourage smoking, protect the environment or prevent a nuclear catastrophe. Yet that is precisely what thousands of trade and investment treaties over the past half century have done, through a process known as "investor-state dispute settlement," or ISDS.

Here is what a researcher for the Cato Institute concluded in a study of investor-state arbitration in U.S. trade agreements:

> For practical, economic, legal, and political reasons, ISDS [investor-state dispute settlement] subverts prospects for U.S. trade liberalization. Yet it is tangential, at best, to the task of freeing trade. Any benefits to availing MNCs [multinational corporations] to third-party adjudication are all but totally overwhelmed by the additional costs. In the proverbial airplane that is down one engine and losing altitude, throwing ISDS out of the cargo hold to reduce unnecessary weight is the best solution.

Here is how Marine Le Pen, the leader of the French National Front, responded to plans for investor-state arbitration in the Canada-Europe CETA:

> The text that we have will put in place private justice for the disputes between investors and states. . . . I am fundamentally against this set-up for multinationals and justice has to be fair and transparent.

Here is what the Productivity Commission of the Australian government thought about investor-state arbitration, in a study of Australia's trade policies:

> It is the Commission's assessment that although some of the risks and problems associated with ISDS [investor-state dispute settlement] can be ameliorated through the design of relevant provisions, significant risks would remain. Meanwhile, it seems doubtful that the inclusion of ISDS provisions within IIAs [international investment agreements]. . . affords material benefits to Australia or partner countries.
>
> Against this backdrop, the Commission considers that Australia should seek to avoid accepting investor-state dispute settlement (ISDS) provisions in trade agreements that confer addi-

tional substantive or procedural rights on foreign investors over and above those already provided by the Australian legal system. Nor, in the commission's assessment, is it advisable in trade negotiations for Australia to expend bargaining coin to seek such rights over foreign governments, as a means of managing investment risks inherent in investing in foreign countries. Other options are available to investors.

Objections to investor-state arbitration come from across the political spectrum, and they come from non-partisan sources too. In my experience, a person's politics are not the best indicator of what the person will think about investor-state arbitration In my experience, probably the best indicator is whether or not the person works, or aspires to work, as an investor-state lawyer or arbitrator.

CHAPTER 36.

THE GOVERNMENT'S SPIN, PART ONE

How did the Harper Government spin the FIPA? It would take another book to count all the ways. I discuss four examples in the next few chapters.

The first example is the prime minister's spin when the FIPA was signed. The second is a Conservative member of parliament's answers to a letter from constituents. The third is the federal trade ministry's answers to questions from a political party. The fourth is a federal trade official's testimony to a judge.

After the FIPA was signed in September 2012, in Vladivostok, Russia, the Prime Minister's Office released a statement that said what most governments say when they do things. The government was "creating the right conditions for Canadian businesses to compete globally" and the FIPA would "create jobs and economic growth in Canada" and "provide stronger protection for Canadians investing in China."

The last of these claims was true because it used the word stronger instead of strong, but important caveats were left unsaid. The other claims were dubious, if one thinks that a claim should follow from evidence. I am not saying the claims were outright wrong, only that they were mostly hot air. I expect the government would have said them no matter what happened in Vladivostok.

Not surprisingly, the Prime Minister's Office did not identify what the government had given up to get the deal or explain why the concessions were necessary. It also played up the potential opportunities for Canadian investors in China, while downplaying the FIPA's protections for Chinese investors and what those protections mean for Canadians. On the latter issue, the Prime Minister's Office said simply, "Chinese firms have also expressed a desire to invest in Canada. Sectors of interest include mining, and oil and gas extraction."

In an earlier news story about the FIPA, the *Globe and Mail* correspondent Mark MacKinnon included a quote from Charles Burton, a Canadian expert on China. Burton said he was worried that Canada's delegation may have signed a weak deal to show dividends from Harper's trip to Beijing in February 2012. It turned out that he was right to be worried, as became clear when the FIPA's text was finally released.

Within a few weeks of the FIPA's text being made public, many Canadians educated themselves about it and objected. This opposition made it possible to have more of a public debate about the FIPA, even though a proper review of what the deal meant never took place.

In this chapter, I highlight one part of the debate at the time and the reasons why a further review was important, by reproducing a series of claims made by the Conservatives—here, in a letter from Conservative Member of Parliament Blake Richards to constituents—and my replies to those claims at the time. The exchange was published by *The Tyee* in November 2012; to capture that record, I have reproduced all of the Conservative claims and a trimmed version of my replies, even though much of the exchange repeats things said elsewhere in this book.

Claim #1: *Our Conservative Government is committed to creating* *the right conditions for Canadian businesses to compete globally. Canada's Foreign Investment Promotion and Protection Agreement (FIPA) with China—the world's second largest economy—will provide stronger protection for Canadians investing in China, and facilitate the creation of jobs and economic growth here at home.*

Reply: Chinese investment may facilitate the creation of jobs and growth in Canada. On the other hand, if it removes value-added benefits from Canada's resource sector or other areas of the economy, Chinese investment may undermine jobs and growth.

A problem with the FIPA is that it will hamper the ability of Canadian governments to ensure that benefits of resource extraction in Canada accrue reasonably to Canadians. On the other hand, China will retain a wider range of policy tools to discriminate in favour of its own companies in China.

Also, the potential role of the FIPA in protecting Canadian companies in China is overstated by the government and other promoters of the deal, some of whom are lawyers at firms that offer investor-state arbitration. If anything, Canada appears more vulnerable to being sued and having to pay compensation to Chinese investors under the treaty.

The arbitration mechanisms under these treaties enrich lawyers and arbitrators, but there is little evidence they can protect Canadian business in a meaningful way against a major player like the Chinese government, especially when China has retained the right to continue to discriminate in favour of its own companies.

Claim #2: *Our government's ambitious pro-trade plan is opening new doors for Canadian businesses in dynamic, high-growth markets like China, and our FIPA with China provides important benefits for Canadian investors.*

Reply: Unlike NAFTA, the FIPA does not reduce tariffs for Canadian exports to China. Its main role is to protect Chinese investors in Canada and vice versa. Because there is more Chinese investment in Canada than the other way round, the FIPA puts more risks and constraints on Canada.

It is the government's responsibility to indicate how much Chinese investment is anticipated under the treaty and in what areas so the risks and constraints can be assessed and debated in an informed way.

Claim #3: For businesses looking to set up in China, China cannot treat a Canadian company less favourably than they would any other foreign company looking to do the same.

Reply: The FIPA does very little to protect Canadian investors from discriminatory treatment in China. In fact, it locks in an uneven playing field. Under the FIPA, Canada and China can keep their existing laws and practices that discriminate in favour of their domestic companies, and these existing laws and practices are then locked in. Because China has more discriminatory laws and practices than Canada, the treaty freezes an uneven playing field in China and a relatively even one in Canada.

Claim #4: Fundamentally, this investment treaty will help protect the interests of Canadians.

Reply: Perhaps the treaty will protect Canadian interests. However, on each of the key issues of market access, investor protection, and levelling of the playing field, the treaty favours China. The federal government needs to acknowledge this and explain why it is in Canada's interest. Before locking in the treaty, the federal government and other governments in Canada should make public their risk assessments and cost-benefit analyses of the treaty to allow for scrutiny and informed debate. If they have not done those assessments, then frankly it would be negligent to ratify the treaty.

The treaty will allow Chinese companies to challenge democratically authorized decisions in Canada via arbitration processes that are not open, fair, or independent in the manner of a court. Canadians deserve to learn more about these arbitrations and the lawyers who control them before their sovereignty is conceded to the arbitrators for thirty-one years, for the purpose of protecting Chinese state companies in Canada.

Claim #5: Creating a secure, predictable environment for Canadian investors is why, since 2006, our government has concluded or brought into force FIPAs with fourteen countries, and are actively negotiating with twelve others. The Canada-China FIPA is very similar to the other FIPAs that Canada is a party to. It contains all of the core substantive obligations that are standard in our other FIPAs.

Reply: The Canada-China treaty is vastly different from Canada's other FIPAs with countries like Armenia, Costa Rica, and Romania, all of which invest relatively little in Canada. Chinese ownership of assets in Canada dwarfs that of these other countries. Thus, the FIPA's liabilities and constraints are much greater for Canada. Unlike Canada's other FIPAs, Canada is the capital-importer, to a very significant extent, in its relationship with China.

Before ratifying the treaty, the government should make clear whether it expects tens or even hundreds of billions in Chinese investment in Canada over the foreseeable future. It should allow for independent assessments of the risks for Canada in relation to Chinese assets in different scenarios. These risks, and the costs of an uneven playing field on market access and discriminatory practices, could then be weighed against the benefits of investor protection to Canadian assets in China.

Claim #6: Our Conservative government has introduced an unprecedented process for putting Canadian international treaties to the scrutiny of the House of Commons. In 2008, our Government announced that treaties between Canada and other states or entities, and which are considered to be governed by public international law, will be tabled in the House of Commons. Accordingly, the Canada-China FIPA was tabled in the House of Commons on September 26, 2012. This reflects our government's commitment to transparency and accountability.

Reply: The treaty's constraints on Canada will last for thirty-one years, with major implications for Canada's relationship with one of the largest economies in the world. It is as yet unclear how China will act as a major capital-exporter and how it will use these sorts of treaties to protect its interests.

Rather than release assessments and analyses of the treaty, however, the government has limited Canadians to about five weeks' notice of the treaty text with little opportunity for scrutiny and debate. If the government was serious about making a well-informed decision, it could, for example, set up an independent review of the FIPA.

Claim #7: With regards to investor-state dispute settlement, it is Canada's long-standing policy to permit public access to such proceedings. Canada's FIPA with China is no different. As we do with all other investor-to-state disputes, this FIPA allows Canada to make all documents submitted to an arbitral tribunal available to the public. All decisions of the tribunal will be made public.

Reply: The federal government still has not released a NAFTA award in an important case that Canada lost in May 2012, *Mobil/ Murphy Oil v. Canada*. [The award was later released after about a six-month delay.] This undermines the federal government's credibility when it says that it will make public decisions and documents under the FIPA. It also raises the question of why the government in the treaty with China, unlike other FIPAs, retained the right to withhold documents relating to Chinese lawsuits against Canada.

By retaining this right, the government will be able to shield itself from embarrassment by not telling Canadians about cases in which a Chinese company has sued Canada. The government's response, in the face of the clear language in the treaty, is to ask Canadians to trust that the government will release all documents in all cases over the next thirty-one years.

Claim #8: Ultimately, access to international arbitration will provide Canadian investors with the confidence that comes from recourse to an independent, international body to adjudicate any disputes.

Reply: Again, no foreign investor has ever resorted to these arbitration processes in a known case against China, despite hundreds of lawsuits against other countries over the last fifteen years. Also, the arbitration process lacks institutional safeguards of independence that apply in courts. Based on the arbitrators' decisions to date, there is reason to suspect that the arbitration mechanism may favour major capital-exporting countries and their investors to the detriment of Canada under this treaty. Canada should have insisted on a dispute settlement process that accords with the rule of law and ensures a fair, rules-based system.

Claim #9: *It is also important to note that under this treaty, both Canada and China have the right to regulate in the public interest. Chinese investors in Canada must obey the laws and regulations of Canada just as any Canadian investor must.*

Reply: This is misleading. Both countries maintain the right to regulate in the public interest only to the extent that the arbitrators agree with how that right was exercised. The arbitrators are largely a power unto themselves and have regularly rejected interpretations of these treaties that were proposed by governments, including by Canada. In many ways, they have expanded their own power to award public compensation for foreign investors. It should also be kept in mind that these are adjudicators who are paid by the case, not tenured judges who receive a set salary from the state.

A government may face intense pressure not to exercise its right to regulate, due to the power of foreign investors to threaten lawsuits for hundreds of millions or billions of dollars. Even if the government thought it had a strong defence in a case, it would run the risk of being ordered to pay massive compensation to an investor. Unlike at the World Trade Organization, the compensation order tracks back to the government's original decision, creating uncertain but potentially catastrophic fiscal risk for governments. Although governments maintain the right to regulate, subject to the arbitrators' authority, their bargaining power can be undermined significantly in closed-door discussions, especially in relation to expensive projects.

Claim #10: At the same time, Chinese investment in Canada will continue to be subject to the Investment Canada Act for both the net benefit test for acquisitions above the applicable threshold and for national security concerns with respect to any investment. Decisions by Canada under the Investment Canada Act are excluded from challenge under the provisions of the FIPA.

Reply: This is true. Indeed, if the treaty comes into effect, the primary protection for Canadians from the treaty's risks and constraints will be the federal government's power to limit Chinese investment under the Investment Canada Act. That said, there are weak points that could potentially be exploited by Chinese firms to buy assets in Canada outside the framework of the act. Also, Canada excluded only the Investment Canada Act from the treaty, whereas China excluded unspecified "Laws, Regulations and Rules relating to the regulation of foreign investment" that allow China to block Canadian investments. As a result, in Canada—but not in China—a subnational (e.g. provincial) government could not rely on this carve-out to block takeovers by foreign investors, if the federal government approved the takeover. This is another example of how the treaty is lopsided in China's favour.

Claim #11: We've been clear that Canada wants to continue to expand its relationship with China, but we want to see it expand in a way that produces clear benefits for both sides. By ensuring greater protection against discriminatory and arbitrary practices, and enhancing predictability of a market's policy framework, this FIPA will allow Canadians to invest in China with greater confidence.

Reply: What are the benefits for Canada? The treaty does not lower tariffs for Canadian exports to China's market. It does not open China's economy to investment by Canadian companies, beyond what governments in China already allow. It does not level the playing field for Canadian companies. On the contrary, the treaty allows China to continue to discriminate in favour of its own companies in China, while locking in the relatively level playing field in Canada.

On investor protection, the treaty favours China because Chinese investment in Canada is more extensive than Canadian investment in China and because Canada appears more vulnerable to being sued in arbitration proceedings. Thus, Chinese companies—and presumably the Chinese government—will have more bargaining power over governments in Canada and, in turn, an apparent competitive advantage over Canadian companies in their own country.

As the debate about the FIPA proceeded in the fall of 2012, I called for a delay in ratification to allow for a thorough, independent, and public review. Each of these adjectives was important. A review that was not thorough, for example, was not enough. The review needed to consider the FIPA's implications for Canadians in general. It needed to be independent of political parties and the federal trade ministry that negotiated the deal. It needed to be public, of course.

Had the government allowed for a proper review, Canadians would have been able to access accurate and reliable information before the FIPA was locked in. The review never happened, which in itself is telling.

CHAPTER 37.

THE GOVERNMENT'S SPIN, PART TWO

The Harper Government did not allow time for study and debate of the FIPA in Parliament. This was one way in which the FIPA was hastily pushed through.

However, in 2012, the Conservatives did allow for a short briefing on the FIPA by federal trade officials at the House of Commons' trade committee. It appears that Conservative members of the committee used their majority to block other witnesses from appearing at the hearing. That meant that trade officials were able to put misleading information on the record, without it being corrected by any independent experts, as I discuss on my blog, gusvanharten.wordpress.com.

Despite the Conservatives' efforts to limit debate, other politicians were able to use the process at the House of Commons trade committee, and elsewhere in Parliament, to put important questions about the FIPA to the government. From what I saw, the federal members of parliament who did so most actively were the Green Party's Elizabeth May, the NDP's Don Davies, and the Liberals' Wayne Easter. As another example of the government's spin, I reproduce below some questions from Wayne Easter, and explain why many of the government's answers were duck-and-weave exercises.

Among his questions, Easter asked the federal government (1) if it would commit to pay any awards under the FIPA if they related to provincial, territorial, or local government decisions, and (2) how the federal government would manage its potential liability for decisions of other levels of government. He also asked for any federal communications or agreements with provincial governments on the matter.

The government replied that "Canada" (not the federal government) was responsible for its treaty obligations, adding that the provinces and territories "were updated" on the FIPA negotiations "on a regular basis" in an inter-governmental trade committee and that none had raised concerns about the FIPA. Assuming that this was true, it did not explain who would pick up the tab, if a province or territory does something that is later found by arbitrators to have violated the FIPA. Which level of government in "Canada" has to pay? It would have been sensible to work out that question before Canada took on the risk of a major FIPA award.

Easter also asked if Chinese state-owned companies would be able to sue under the FIPA, where a law in Canada impacted their expectation of profit. The government's reply was a long-winded yes:

> As in all of Canada's FIPAs, this Agreement provides mechanisms for resolution of disputes. This provision provides rights to foreign investors to seek redress for damages arising out of alleged breaches by host governments of investment-related obligations.
>
> When a government takes measures or a series of measures . . . investors have the right to seek dispute settlement if there has been a "substantial deprivation" of an investment—that is, a mere reduction in profits *would not likely give rise to a successful claim, as the value of the investment must be significantly affected* by the government measure (emphasis mine).

In other words, Chinese state-owned companies can use the FIPA to challenge Canadian laws, but federal trade officials thought the companies would "not likely" win, if a law merely reduced their profits. However, it was a different matter for Canadian laws that "significantly affected" a Chinese investor, an admission that is not reassuring for voters and taxpayers.

In case any Canadian is thinking about trying to get compensation for a new law that "significantly affects" him or her, at this point I'll tell you, you can put that thought in the bin. Canadians don't have any such option. Except for foreign investors under investment treaties, the passage of a law in Canada is final, subject to constitutional review in the courts. That's as it should be, since a law is the outcome of the formal democratic process. If there was an accounting for every law's financial cost to everyone "significantly affected," then elected officials would find it hard to pass all kinds of important legislation.

If not for the FIPA, Chinese investors would be taken to have accepted this democratic principle and way of government in Canada, and the benefits (and costs) that it brings for everyone in the country. Like other foreign nationals who come to Canada, they would be assumed to have accepted these things when they chose to come. With that in mind, the government's reply to Easter, as I read it, essentially asked people not to think about how the FIPA changes democracy in Canada.

In another question to the government, Easter asked how the FIPA would impact Canada's laws protecting consumer safety, the environment, labour rights, privacy, agriculture, and so on. The government dodged this question too:

> With respect to the above noted public policy areas, the Canada-China FIPA, like our other FIPAs, ensures that all foreign investors in Canada, including those from China, are subject to the same laws and regulations as domestic investors. Nothing in the FIPA prevents federal, provincial and territorial governments

from regulating in the public interest, as long as it is done on a non-discriminatory and not wholly arbitrary manner.

Did you catch the dodge? It lay in the statement that Chinese investors are "subject to" Canadian laws. That choice of words avoided the issue of Chinese investors' new right to sue under the FIPA if they didn't like the laws, and to get compensation for laws when Canadians could not.

In other words, Canada's laws protecting consumer safety, the environment, labour rights, privacy, agriculture, and so on do still *apply* to Chinese investors. It's just that they may cost a whole lot more for Canadian taxpayers—or they may get watered down—if a big Chinese company objects to them.

The government's reply was misleading in another way. It reassured Canadians that FIPA arbitrators would only order compensation for "discriminatory" or "wholly arbitrary" laws. This choice of language sidestepped Chinese investors' many other FIPA rights—fair and equitable treatment, compensation for indirect expropriation, free capital transfers, immunity from the cost of performance requirements—that go beyond discrimination or arbitrariness.

Easter also asked if the FIPA would give China the ability to bring in Chinese workers. Perhaps as a surprise to many, the answer was a qualified yes:

> The FIPA has a provision whereby citizens of the other country that are employees of an investor or a covered investment are to be permitted to enter and remain temporarily in the country in which the investment is located and work in a capacity "that is managerial, executive or that requires specialized knowledge." All foreign investors in Canada, including those from China, are subject to the same laws and regulations as domestic investors and this includes labour and immigration laws.

To which one might ask further, which country has higher labour costs for foreign investors, Canada or China? The challenge for Canada is that, over time, Chinese investors will have more incentive to use Chinese workers in Canada, than Canadian investors will have to use Canadian workers in China. The incentive comes from the low cost of labour—and often brutal working conditions—in China, compared to Canada.

Canadian and Chinese companies are already bringing in tens of thousands of foreign workers into Canada, through the government's temporary foreign workers program. Chinese investors now have a special right under the FIPA to defend their interests in that program, in case future governments wanted to end it.

Indeed, it is not far-fetched to think that Chinese investors have already used their FIPA rights to challenge labour and immigration laws in Canada, at least behind the scenes. Consider the *Globe and Mail* story called "Canada's immigration policies hurt bottom line, China says," which ran in November 2014, two months after the FIPA was ratified. According to that story:

> China's state-controlled energy firms are struggling to turn a profit in Canada in part because of the federal government's immigration laws, a senior Chinese diplomat says.
>
> Wang Xinping, China's consul general, based in Calgary, said his country's energy companies want to bring in their own employees to reduce costs. But Ottawa has been stingy in issuing work permits, he said, making it harder for Chinese companies to develop their projects.

The FIPA does not necessarily mean that these Chinese complaints about laws in Canada will change how the government applies the laws. But it makes that outcome more likely, because Chinese complaints are now a lot more risky for the government to reject. It is also going to be very hard for Canadians to know how the complaints are resolved. The same *Globe* story reported that it was not possible to verify how many work visas have been granted to a company, since the federal immigration department does not release that information. Meanwhile, the FIPA lets the government keep a Chinese lawsuit against Canada's labour or immigration policies secret, so long as the lawsuit is settled before the FIPA arbitrators issue an award.

Considering the possibility of FIPA lawsuits against Canada, Easter also asked if the federal government had assessed the fiscal liabilities associated with the FIPA's protections for Chinese investors. He requested that the government explain its analysis and share a copy of the assessment.

The government's answer is one of my favourites: "Canada has not estimated a potential fiscal liability under the Agreement because it has no intention of violating the terms of this or any other International agreement to which it is a Party."

Yet, Canada has already been found to have violated similar rules in NAFTA and been ordered to compensate U.S. investors. Innocent intentions were not an excuse. It's the FIPA arbitrators who decide if Canada must pay huge amounts of compensation, not the federal government.

I suppose it goes without saying that it is not wise to lock Canada into potentially billion-dollar liabilities, without trying to estimate them first. We don't intend to slip on the sidewalk in winter, but we still check for ice.

CHAPTER 38.

THE GOVERNMENT'S SPIN, PART THREE

My last example of the government's misleading responses to concerns about the FIPA comes from the legal challenge brought by the Hupacasath First Nation. In that court case, a federal trade official testified that the FIPA followed Canada's past practice:

> [O]ur China [FIPA] stuck to the model, the model [FIPA] . . . This is a perfect example of . . . a family of investment agreements that Canada has had in place since 1994 in terms of [FIPAs] or . . . investment chapters of free trade agreements. So there is no departure from our past practice in that regard.

In key respects, this statement wasn't true. In fact, the China FIPA departed dramatically from Canada's past practice in other FIPAs and trade agreements. One remarkable departure was the China FIPA's unequal approach to market access. Another was its express right for the federal government to keep FIPA lawsuits secret until an award is issued. I discussed these aspects in chapters 6 and 14. In this chapter, I focus on another departure in the China FIPA that was relevant to the legal challenge itself.

For aboriginal peoples in Canada, there is a key difference between the China FIPA and all of Canada's other treaties that allow for investor-state arbitration (and that, like the China

FIPA, include a rule against performance requirements). The difference is that the China FIPA does not have as broad a carve-out for measures that treat aboriginal peoples more favourably than Chinese investors and that would otherwise violate the deal's rule against performance requirements.

This sounds impossibly legalistic, I know. However, it is important for anyone, aboriginal or not, whose job or business depends on a government policy of favouring local over multinational companies. In trade lingo, such policies are called performance requirements. They are often restricted by trade deals, largely because U.S.—and apparently Chinese—multinationals like it that way.

For Canada, performance requirements are a potentially useful option in a lot of areas of the economy, perhaps especially in the resource sector. For example, Canada's priority obviously should be to increase the benefits, for Canadians, of resource extraction in Canada. To do that, governments in Canada have historically required foreign investors to make commitments to use local materials and suppliers, for example. The federal government still does this sometimes, through the undertakings it expects from foreign companies under the Investment Canada Act. That is, to get approval for takeovers of large Canadian companies, foreign investors usually commit to keep jobs, a head office, or research and development in Canada.

Guess what? Multinational companies don't like these requirements. They no doubt would prefer the freedom to pursue their own global business strategy, often centred in another country, no matter if it guts Canadian jobs and businesses. And, if you recall, the judge from the legal challenge against the FIPA—when he was a Bay Street lawyer—also dismissed these Investment Canada Act undertakings. He called them "embarrassing" for Canadian lawyers who advise foreign companies, and encouraged the Harper Government to make it harder for Industry Canada to negotiate them.

I am guessing that Canadians who have their jobs or business thanks to these undertakings might have a different view.

Since the 1980s at least, the U.S. government has pressured other countries to give up their sovereign right to put performance requirements on foreign companies. Canada conceded to this pressure, especially in NAFTA. Since then, U.S. corporate priorities have often led to closures of plants and offices in Canada. This is presumably connected to a lot of things, but one basic reason is that it is easier for U.S. companies to treat Canada merely as an extension of the U.S. market. The U.S. government's Buy America rules encourage this strategy even more.

Ultimately, any country will be in bad shape if it can't promote linkages between its economy and the foreign investors that operate within it. Like many things, a government can play a useful role in supporting these linkages, or it can hurt the situation.

Consider this scenario. A Chinese company brings in Chinese workers to develop a mine in northern Canada. The company ships out the resources on a railway that it built and owns. The railway leads to a port, also built and owned by the company. At the port, the resources are loaded onto Chinese-owned ships bound for Asian markets, where the minerals will be processed and used as inputs for manufactured goods, which are then exported to Canada. This is an extreme example, but it is not unrealistic.

If the FIPA allowed performance requirements to be imposed on Chinese investors, then governments in Canada could require Chinese investors to use a certain proportion of Canadian materials and suppliers, to process a certain proportion of the resources in Canada, and so on, so that more wealth was generated in Canada. These requirements might also have costs, such as lost foreign investment; not all Chinese investors would necessarily accept such performance requirements. That is part of the challenge faced by a government when it decides how to tailor its policies in different cases. That is, it is a challenge that used to face governments in Canada, until deals like NAFTA and the FIPA limited Canada's right to use these policies.

I turn now to some of the details of the China FIPA's handling of performance requirements.

There are two key details for our purposes. The first is that the FIPA has a rule prohibiting performance requirements, albeit on a more limited basis than the comparable rule in NAFTA. The second is that the FIPA's prohibition on performance requirements does *not* come with an exception—contained in Canada's other investment treaties that prohibit these requirements—for decisions that favour aboriginal peoples over foreign investors. As a result, the FIPA changes how investor-state arbitration affects aboriginal rights, for reasons I'll explain a bit later in this chapter. In the rest of this section, I will explain some technical aspects of the FIPA's handling of performance requirements.

In the FIPA, the prohibition on performance requirements for foreign investors is limited to Canada's obligations under the World Trade Organization's TRIMs Agreement, a trade deal that dates from 1994. The TRIMs Agreement prohibits countries from putting performance requirements on foreign investors, but only for their activities related to trade, which is a narrower concept than investment.

By putting the WTO TRIMs obligations into the FIPA, the obligations become much riskier for governments. For one, the WTO TRIMs obligations are made enforceable through investor-state arbitration instead of country-to-country dispute settlement that would otherwise apply at the WTO. In turn, the FIPA exposes Canada and China to foreign investor claims and backward-looking orders of compensation. In contrast, at the WTO, lawsuits can only be brought by countries and WTO panels can only order forward-looking penalties. Thus, under the FIPA, Canada gave up the opportunity it would otherwise have had to avoid an economic penalty by changing its policies to comply with a WTO panel's decision, at the end of a dispute with another country. In investor-state arbitration under the FIPA, Canada may rack up massive liability while it waits for the arbitrators to decide, with no right to change its policies and avoid the liability after the arbitrators make up their minds.

I have laid this out in detail, partly to counter the federal government's spin about the FIPA. When the narrowness of the FIPA's carve outs on this issue were highlighted, the government claimed that it was not a problem because the FIPA merely incorporated Canada's existing WTO obligations. For the reasons I've noted, the WTO obligations change in important ways when they are put into a FIPA.

This brings us back to the question of how the China FIPA differs from Canada's other treaties that put limits on performance requirements and that allow for investor-state arbitration. Among other things, the difference shows how the Harper Government sacrificed aboriginal rights in its negotiation of the China FIPA.

Canada's other relevant investment treaties have a carve-out like this (I am quoting the version in NAFTA): "Canada reserves the right to adopt or maintain any measure denying investors of another Party and their investments, or service providers of another Party, any rights or preferences provided to aboriginal peoples." The China FIPA has a carve-out with a more limited scope, which does not apply to the FIPA's rule against performance requirements. As a result, the FIPA uniquely bars any Canadian requirement for Chinese companies to use local aboriginal content as a condition of operating in Canada. Importantly, the change will almost certainly extend to U.S. companies in Canada because of their right to most-favoured-nation treatment under NAFTA.

This narrowing of the aboriginal carve-out in the China FIPA seems especially important for so-called "impact and benefit agreements," which are common in Canada's resource sector. Impact and benefit agreements are usually done between a resource company and an aboriginal entity. They are a way to balance resource development and aboriginal rights, and avoid disputes. In some cases, they are required by law; in others, they are voluntary. Most importantly, impact and benefit agreements typically include commitments by the company to use aboriginal workers, materials, or suppliers so that the economic benefits of a resource project are shared with local and aboriginal communities.

Why would the federal government want to give away its ability to require Chinese investors to make commitments like that, as it has done in the FIPA? I assume it is because China wanted it that way. That is, China wanted its companies to be able to avoid using aboriginal (or other Canadian) workers in Canada. To me, it is not a good sign.

From the point of view of aboriginal peoples, this change to the FIPA was made even worse by the federal government's failure to consult with aboriginal organizations (and with other constituencies) about the FIPA.

According to the federal trade official, whose testimony was quoted at the outset of this chapter, the decision not to consult was excusable because the China FIPA "stuck to the model" and was "a perfect example" of Canada's trade agreements and FIPAs since 1994, with "no departure from our past practice in that regard." But the FIPA clearly did depart from Canada's other FIPAs and trade agreements, among other things in its handling of aboriginal rights. By itself, that was a good reason for the government to consult with others before charging ahead with the deal.

Presumably, the federal trade official who gave this testimony believed in the truth of what he was telling the court.

One should not conclude that anyone failed to testify truthfully, without giving him or her an opportunity to reply, and I do not want to imply that he did.

Even so, it is very troubling that this inaccuracy was given as evidence in a legal challenge that sought to delay the FIPA's ratification so that consultation could take place. As I discussed in chapter 23 of this book, the Hupacasath First Nation's legal challenge was dismissed because the court did not think there was enough evidence of a link between the FIPA and adverse impacts for the First Nation. Would things have been different if the unique aspects of the FIPA had been spelled out to the judge by the federal government? It is hard to say.

For our purposes, the federal trade official's inaccurate testimony is just another example of how the FIPA was pushed through, without a proper review of its implications.

The FIPA's approach to performance requirements is relevant to many others in Canada, besides aboriginal peoples.

The possibility for conflict between foreign investors and provincial governments, for example, was shown in 2012, when Canada lost a NAFTA lawsuit brought by ExxonMobil and another oil company called Murphy Oil. The companies launched the lawsuit after a Canadian regulatory agency tightened its rules on research-and-development (R & D) spending by companies in Newfoundland and Labrador's offshore oil sector. The tighter rules required the oil companies to spend a share of their earnings on R & D instead of filing R & D plans for approval which, as far as the regulators were concerned, were not as reliable.

The regulators' decision was upheld in Canadian courts, but NAFTA allowed ExxonMobil and Murphy Oil, as U.S. investors, to keep on suing. The NAFTA tribunal decided that the regulators' decision to tighten the rules violated NAFTA's prohibition on performance requirements. A majority of the tribunal members also decided that the tighter rules were not protected by Canada's special NAFTA carve-out for the Canadian law that allowed the R & D rules in the first place. The tribunal's majority got to this conclusion by interpreting Canada's NAFTA carve-out very narrowly. This last aspect of the majority's decision was particularly controversial.

The NAFTA tribunal's decision meant that Canada had to pay compensation for changing its R & D rules, but only as they applied to U.S. companies, not Canadian ones. Recently, the tribunal reportedly awarded about CDN$17 million in compensation to the U.S. oil companies and indicated that Canada will have to pay more compensation in the years to come if the tighter R & D rules are kept in place.

The federal government's loss in this case demonstrates how the FIPA's rule against performance requirements may clash with policies in Canada. Despite this risk, provincial, territorial, and municipal decision-makers—like aboriginal organizations—were not consulted about the FIPA's approach to performance requirements. Once again, according to the federal trade official who testified during the legal challenge, there was no consultation because the China FIPA "did not depart from our FIPA model" and because federal officials "are very comfortable with the impacts of that FIPA model on the various policy communities that are covered by this treaty." I expect federal officials may have been a lot less "comfortable" with the China FIPA, if Canadians had had more of an opportunity to learn about it.

CHAPTER 39.

LAURA DAWSON'S LAWN DARTS

The Harper Government announced that it had ratified the FIPA on a Friday afternoon, September 12, 2014. Unlike the FIPA's announcement two years earlier, the prime minister did not appear publicly; the federal trade ministry merely issued a short press release.

However, other promoters stepped up to defend the government's decision. One forum for the new round of promotions was a CBC Radio show called *The 180*. The show is styled as a place for airing contrarian views and provoking debate. It certainly provoked me when I heard the show's spot on the FIPA.

At the outset, one might have thought that a contrarian view of the FIPA would not just track the government's position. By that time, the government's deal had been backed by big-time columnists, Bay Street lawyers, and the Conservative spin machine. Yet, the only guest on *The 180* was a FIPA proponent from the early days of its public controversy: Ottawa-based trade consultant Laura Dawson. Dawson reportedly has clients that may use investor-state arbitration, and is a former economic advisor to the U.S. state department.

In her guest spot, Dawson explained why, in her view, people who questioned the government's decision to conclude the

FIPA were wrong. She began with the usual tactic of putting up a straw man and knocking it down, saying that criticisms of the FIPA were "almost completely unreasonable" and that there was no basis for the "sky-is-falling attitude" of critics. She labelled the critics "opponents to trade and investment." I wondered, why not call them enemies of land, labour, and capital too? Neither Dawson nor the show's host, Jim Brown, mentioned any specific examples of the FIPA's lopsidedness, which had been pointed out by critics since 2012.

In her opening, Dawson used another familiar line: "We have this kind of agreement with more than twenty-seven, I think, different governments around the world and they're a fairly straightforward agreement. There's nothing that's particularly new or dangerous here." As we have seen, the FIPA differs from Canada's other relevant treaties in important ways. An obvious point is that it was the first time that Canada was made subject to investor-state arbitration—while Canada was the host to substantial investment from the other country—since the explosion of foreign investor lawsuits began in the 1990s.

The host did not put this criticism of the FIPA to Dawson. Rather, he asked her to give an overview of FIPAs. She replied that the FIPA did not "give anybody permission to invest in Canada," and added:

> It does not give China access to the Canadian market. It doesn't say that a particular company can buy an oil field or a factory. All it does is determine the conditions under which that investor will be treated once he or she is actually in the country.

Well, that was wrong, as we saw in chapter 6 of this book: the FIPA does "give China access to the Canadian market." It was an easy mistake to make because China's one-way right of market access is not obvious in the FIPA's text. But Dawson missed this critical point two years after the FIPA was released.

Since Dawson claimed to have specialized knowledge in investment treaties, it was a serious error.

Next, Dawson talked about FIPA arbitration. She said the process allowed foreign investors to take a dispute "to a recognized legal court and have that court hear that dispute." However, FIPA arbitration is very different from a court because it lacks the usual safeguards of judicial independence and fair process. The lack of judicial hallmarks in investor-state arbitration has been discussed in the field for at least seven years. It is clearly wrong to call FIPA arbitration "a recognized legal court."

The host did not challenge Dawson on this claim. Instead, he asked her a series of softball questions; that is, he asked her questions that appeared to stress exaggerations or mis-statements by non-expert critics of the FIPA, while avoiding accurate versions of the same basic criticism.

Once again, the host did not challenge Dawson on her misleading claim (flagged by the host from an unnamed online source) that "China can now sue Canada in secret tribunals to repeal national and provincial laws if China feels that those laws interfere with their investments." To put that criticism more precisely, one would need to say lawsuits instead of "tribunals," Chinese investors instead of "China," and attack or condemn instead of "repeal."

Because the criticism was not put precisely, Dawson could reply in this disparaging way: "Gosh, there's so many mis-statements and mis-directions there. It's hard to say where to start." She continued, "Okay, let's say, let's start with the secret part. Is it a secret tribunal? No, it's a tribunal that's set up according to some very well-publicized, well-established legal standards." Thus, Dawson shifted from the question of "secret tribunals" to an issue not raised by FIPA critics, to my knowledge: are the "standards" applied by FIPA tribunals public?

Well, of course, the *standards* are public. They are written in the treaties! The real issue has always been whether the *documents and evidence* put before FIPA arbitrators—and the mere fact that a lawsuit exists—will be public. This criticism of secret tribunals had been laid out since the early stages of the FIPA debate in October 2012, such as in my open letter to the prime minister:

> This heightens my concern that *you have, in the Canada-China treaty, retained the right of the federal government not to release documents filed in Chinese investor lawsuits against Canada under the treaty if the government deems it not "in the public interest" to do so.* This is not consistent with longstanding Canadian government policy to make such documents, and the arbitration hearings, public as a matter of course. If you intend to release the documents in any event, then why have you retained the right not to do so in the treaty? Other Canadian FIPAs state very clearly that all of the documents will be made public.

Yet, Dawson did not even mention the FIPA's shift to secrecy, and the host did not press her.

Dawson continued her answer on FIPA secrecy by saying that "some of these [FIPA] tribunals are supervised by the United Nations." What she meant by this is hard to say. FIPA tribunals certainly are not supervised by the United Nations.

The best I can make of Dawson's claim—and getting into some technicalities—is that, if a foreign investor chooses to bring a FIPA lawsuit under the ICSID Convention (see Article 22(1) of the FIPA), then the tribunal would be supervised in a limited way by an ad hoc annulment panel of the World Bank. The World Bank is a Bretton Woods institution, as are the United Nations and the International Monetary Fund.

That loose connection between FIPA tribunals and the UN puts Dawson in the wrong ballpark.

Or, Dawson might have meant that if a foreign investor chooses to bring a FIPA lawsuit under the arbitration rules of either the Additional Facility or UNCITRAL (for UN Commission on International Trade Law) (see again Article 22(1) of the FIPA), then the FIPA tribunal would be supervised in a limited way by courts in a jurisdiction, somewhere, that would be picked—by the FIPA arbitrators themselves—as the formal "place" of the arbitration. If that were the case, there is still no supervision by the United Nations, as Dawson claimed. However, the UNCITRAL arbitration rules were developed, originally in the 1970s, by a UN body in order to help resolve international commercial disputes, and were subsequently imported into treaties like the FIPA.

That connection to the UN puts Dawson near the ballpark, although it seems again to be the wrong ballpark.

Either way, Dawson's statement showed at best a lack of basic knowledge about investor-state arbitration, though it takes time to explain why. Once again, her claim went unchallenged by the host.

Dawson concluded her answer on FIPA secrecy: "Because some of these processes include discussing commercial information, which we like to hold confidential, there are some business secrecy elements, but these are not secret tribunals that are held by guys in black cloaks."

This completely missed the key criticism. Like other investment treaties, the FIPA lets arbitrators decide to keep commercial information confidential. That is fine (except that those decisions should be made by a judge, not arbitrators). More important, in fifteen years of following the field I cannot recall ever hearing a critic raise this issue when discussing the problem of secrecy in investor-state arbitration.

For the FIPA, the key concern was that the federal government—when Canada is sued—kept for itself a right to keep the documents in the lawsuit secret, until a FIPA award is issued. All the government has to do is to decide that it is not "in the public interest" to reveal the lawsuit or the documents to Canadians, and they can be kept secret. In the courts, a government power to impose near-blanket secrecy over the process would be scandalous. It is also unacceptable in FIPA lawsuits against Canadian laws and regulations. In the debate about the FIPA, this particular issue was a widespread concern. Dawson and the host did not mention it, even in a discussion of secrecy and the FIPA.

With his next question, the host asked Dawson if FIPA tribunals could "repeal" Canadian laws. Whether intended or not, this choice of wording was another set-up. Arbitrators under investment treaties usually order damages for the laws they condemn. They don't order laws to be repealed.

By asking the question in this way, the host enabled Dawson to say "absolutely not," and then to continue, "a worst case scenario is that if a country changes its law for some reason and . . . that change affects the value of the investment, that investor is entitled to be compensated." To illustrate her point, Dawson gave an example that revealed—apparently inadvertently—the core problem. She highlighted the scenario in which a law in Canada prohibits something unsafe for the first time (her charming example was lawn darts). She said that the FIPA could require compensation for such a law, if a foreign company made the unsafe product:

> So, let's think about lawn darts . . . when I was a kid, lawn darts were legal and now they're illegal, and unsafe. They probably should be.
>
> But if a foreign company was the lawn dart manufacturer in Canada and was selling its lawn darts happily in Canadian Tire and the government of Canada said, "Hey wait a minute, we don't think those are safe anymore. We're not going to let you sell lawn darts in Canada," well that would negate the value of that investment, right?
>
> So that investor should have some recourse to either compensation or, at least should be heard in court and say, "Hey wait a minute, my company's not worth anything anymore, you guys changed the rules."

That makes sense, doesn't it? The foreign company lost out because of a law. All the company did was manufacture a product that the legislature later decided was unsafe. Why shouldn't the company be compensated for its lost profits?

Now, replace "lawn darts" with "drugs," newly found to be dangerous. By Dawson's account, a foreign drug manufacturer (but not a Canadian one) should be able to bring an international lawsuit against Canada, and perhaps get compensation, if Parliament prohibits the dangerous drug.

Presumably, no sane arbitrator would order compensation in this situation, though I wouldn't rule it out completely having read a lot of hawkish awards. Even so, that's not the point. The point is that these are important policy choices for the country. They should be made by the elected government, subject to review in the courts. They should not be decided by FIPA arbitrators who, among other problems, stand to make money if foreign investors bring more lawsuits. Worse, the FIPA allows the government to settle the Chinese investor's lawsuit secretly, to avoid political embarrassment. Canadians would never learn how much it cost them to change the law to protect Canadians.

So, Dawson's example is actually very worrying. It shows the importance of the FIPA's change to the role of Canada's legislatures and courts. Their institutional power is diminished to protect and insure Chinese investors against the dangers of Canadian democracy and judges. Over time, Canadian taxpayers could be on the hook for all kinds of things that Canadians might vote for: new labour laws, bans on dangerous chemicals, tougher mine safety regulations, tighter rules for railways—the list of possible liabilities goes on and on. Should Chinese investors and FIPA arbitrators have the final word on whether new laws are allowed, and the price for having gone ahead with them?

The host went on to ask Dawson if there should have been

more public debate about the FIPA. She responded with the same line as the trade official whose testimony I discussed in the previous chapter: "We've had FIPAs for decades," she said. "There's nothing that's different in this agreement." Except, as we have seen, the FIPA is different. The real question was, are the differences good for Canada?

Instead of pursuing that issue, the host pointed to an obviously rhetorical description of the FIPA, by Diane Francis in a *Financial Post* column, as reflecting "the worst negotiating skills since Neville Chamberlain." This question made it easy for Dawson to trump Francis' lack of expertise, and to leave the impression that the FIPA is unremarkable: "Well, I don't know how Diane was reading the agreement, and I've only been doing international trade agreements for twenty years, so I've got some stuff to learn." Dawson added that she had gone through the FIPA and "just didn't see anything that was unprecedented or outside the realm of possibility." She downplayed the deal as "a very standard, boilerplate agreement."

Next, the host asked Dawson why people were "so fearful" of the FIPA. In her explanation, she was able to assume—because the host helpfully added—that "the actual text of this agreement doesn't support some of the more strident things that we're hearing."

Canadians were fearful, Dawson said, because "China is such a big economy" and "you can attach a lot of fear and concern about a lot of different issues to a trade agreement." Then she went into a lengthy discussion about the global economy over the last twenty years, lost manufacturing jobs, cross-border immigration, and Canada's less stable economy. Apparently, these things had helped FIPA critics play on "people's fears about what's gonna happen next" which "are reflected in these concerns about free trade agreements," as Dawson put it. The FIPA was "a lightening rod or a scapegoat for much that people think is wrong with the global economy."

That was all very interesting, but it had little to do with

the specific concerns identified by critics of the FIPA. Those concerns centred on the deal's lopsidedness and the role of investor-state arbitration. They provided a credible basis for anxiety, even fear. Dawson was speculating about how easily Canadians could be spooked by critics, but avoiding their actual criticisms.

Dawson (and the host) also sidestepped the call for a review of the FIPA, before it was ratified. Instead, she reassured listeners that the FIPA would not cause more lost jobs or precarious work, offering the usual view that Canada's experience in NAFTA investor-state arbitration had been fine. As you can guess, I think Dawson's view of this experience was too rosy. More importantly, what was the Canadian public to make of competing claims about Canada's experience, without reliable information from an authoritative source? To this day, the federal government has not done a thorough, public review of how decision-makers have been affected by investor-state arbitration, whether in relation to the FIPA or any other investment deal.

Toward the end of the radio show, Dawson was asked whether, "if it's the fact that it's China that has people so concerned," there is "anything to that as far as you're concerned?"

Dawson replied with some speculation about China's mind and maturity. She said China is "not really aware of its own strength" and "is kind of like, you know, a big adolescent stomping through the global economy." This prompts me to respond that I found Dawson's statements to be quite naive about the negotiating skill and effectiveness of Chinese officials. I think the terms of the FIPA show that China "stomped" maturely, compared to Canada.

Also toward the end of the show, Dawson stated—at the host's suggestion—that she would "watch very closely to see how they [the Chinese] act" in Canada as "a matter of scale and a matter of novelty." She added that "until Chinese companies operating in the world become more familiar with what the rule of law is, what are acceptable behaviour and practices, we all have to be watching."

Did you get that? *After* the FIPA was locked in, Canadians should all be watching Chinese investors closely because they are big, new, and not as familiar with acceptable practices. On the other hand, there was supposedly no need to review the FIPA before it was ratified because, according to Dawson, the deal was just like Canada's other FIPAs. At least this upside-down assessment seemed to fit with a show called "The 180."

From this interview, I had the impression that, for Dawson, almost any FIPA would be a good FIPA. All FIPAs have rules and, according to her, we want a "rules-based agreement." Why bother with the details and whether the rules favour China? Dawson said, "We need more agreements with China, not fewer."

Ironically, Dawson's appearance on *The 180* seemed to be more about throwing water on a hot debate about the FIPA than provoking a debate. Timed as it was, the interview sounded to me like an exercise in damage control for the government's decision to finalize the deal. That was too bad. Two years earlier, other CBC shows had played an important role in flagging the debate about the FIPA and helping to inform Canadians.

Am I being too hard on Dawson? Perhaps she wasn't aware of the background of investor-state arbitration and how it can be used to pressure governments?

I don't think I am, especially for this reason. Not long after she defended the ratification of the FIPA, Dawson reportedly co-authored a report that was delivered to federal officials. According to the *Globe and Mail*, it was advised in the report that if the government went ahead with plans to tighten federal anti-corruption rules, then Canada could be sued by foreign companies under NAFTA. Also, according to the *Globe*, the report warned that federal plans to apply anti-corruption rules to Canadian affiliates of foreign nationals, and administrative bans on selling to the Canadian government, would be particularly vulnerable to investor-state challenges.

The report was commissioned by the Canadian Council of Chief Executives, headed by another FIPA promoter, John Manley. One of the corporations reportedly affected by the new rules—which has a member on Manley's Council—was the German multinational Siemens. Coincidentally, Siemens previously used an investment treaty to sue Argentina for annulling a contract with Siemens, and then settled the lawsuit after an international scandal broke out about Siemens' corrupt activities. In light of this history, it is fair to ask why the federal government's plans to tighten anti-corruption rules in Canada, and the option of bringing a foreign investor lawsuit in response, would be of such interest to Manley's Council.

For her part, Dawson appears to have written several reports for the Canadian Council of Chief Executives, over the course of just a few years preceding the FIPA's ratification. It seems reasonable to expect that she might one day write a report about how Chinese investors can use the FIPA to sue Canada, for one reason or another. Also, Dawson evidently knows how foreign investors can use investor-state arbitration to oppose or frustrate proposed decisions in Canada. Yet, in an opinion article on the FIPA in 2012, she associated the FIPA's critics with "hysteria" and "anti-NAFTA zealots" after they warned about the threat of Chinese lawsuits against Canada.

I can't help wondering: how quickly will this "hysteria" find its way into one of Dawson's consultant's reports?

CHAPTER 40.

THE STRANGE CASE OF STEPHEN GORDON

Another example of poorly informed spin, after the FIPA's ratification, was an article by Stephen Gordon in *Maclean's* magazine. Gordon is an economics professor at l'Université Laval.

Gordon's pitch began, once again, with labels for unnamed critics. They were "excitable nationalists" with "wild imaginings" who spouted "fantastical nonsense." Gordon then said—apparently without tongue in cheek—it was "time to tone down the rhetoric."

Gordon then promised to educate readers about why "FIPAs are not so scary when you take the time to look at them." I agree with him, looking at a FIPA isn't scary. But riding the roller coaster of investor-state arbitration—and seeing countries ordered to pay vast sums in an extra-judicial process—can be, shall I say, unsettling.

Gordon also used the familiar line that—to sue under the FIPA—"foreign firms have to show that they've received different treatment than their Canadian-owned competitors." As we have seen, this was wrong. Indeed, it was Gordon's article that triggered the exasperated correction from a U.S. investment law specialist, Simon Lester, that was highlighted in chapter 29 of this book.

Gordon next noted the obvious point that "all international agreements involve ceding sovereignty." He appeared not to appreciate how the degree of a cession of sovereignty can be important, as I discuss later in this chapter. Instead, he quickly linked sovereignty to expropriation, saying: "Wanting to retain the power to expropriate foreign-owned assets is probably the most petty and diminished notion of what sovereignty means."

When he condemned the sovereign "power to expropriate," I assume Gordon meant the power to expropriate *without paying compensation*, and not simply the power to expropriate. By itself, the power to expropriate is used commonly in all countries, especially to build infrastructure. As for the power to expropriate without paying compensation, like Gordon I sympathize with a foreign investor—or anyone else—who is hurt by a government because of this power of the state. Yet, even a direct expropriation of property, without paying compensation, can be an important part of a country's sovereignty.

Think of a colony of slaves who succeed in freeing themselves from their foreign owners. They declare themselves and the colony to be an independent country. Should they have to compensate the former owners for the "expropriation" of their newly freed "property," the slaves' own persons? Would it be "petty and diminished" if they refused to compensate the former slavers?

This is not an absurd example. It reflects the history of Haiti, the only country whose sovereignty came from a successful slave revolt, in the early 1800s. Eventually, Haiti succumbed to European and U.S. demands—backed by military threats and an economic blockade—to compensate the "expropriated" slave owners, most of whom were French. Haiti's long struggle to pay back the slave owners helps to explain the country's poverty, even today.

Before someone accuses me of it, let me make clear, I'm not saying that Chinese investors will use the FIPA to enslave

Canadians! The Haitian example simply shows how important moral questions can arise in a debate about sovereignty and expropriation, and that Gordon's attitude was simplistic.

Gordon continued, more or less as usual, by flagging the uncertain questions of how often Chinese investors will sue or win under the FIPA, and by tripping over the facts. He focused on Canada's NAFTA experience, as if it was the only source of relevant information to gauge how the FIPA will be used, and then botched basic information about the NAFTA experience.

Gordon claimed that Canada had lost only one NAFTA case and then seemed confused about the very case he chose to highlight. According to Gordon:

> Initiating a lawsuit is not the same thing as winning one. . . . In [the federal government's online] archive of NAFTA Chapter 11 lawsuits, I count 15 lawsuits that were withdrawn or abandoned, 10 cases where Canada's position was upheld (often with costs), and one defeat. The defeat was the S.D. Meyers case, in which the federal minister for the environment (Sheila Copps, if you must know) overturned a contract won by S.D. Meyers to dispose of PCBs in favour of a Canadian competitor. No one—including her own advisers and the arbitration panel—could see what public purpose was served by shipping PCBs 3,500 km from Toronto to Edmonton instead of 500 km to Cleveland.

If Gordon looked carefully at the federal government's online archive, then he should have known that Canada has lost other NAFTA cases besides the *SD Myers* case. Also, Gordon appeared not to realize that a withdrawn NAFTA case in the government's online archive may have been settled on confidential terms, reflecting a loss for Canada, and that the FIPA gives much more scope for this kind of secrecy.

Moreover, if Gordon read the *SD Myers* decision (he misspelled its name), then he should have known that the case arose after the federal government banned exports of toxic

PCBs from Canada to the United States. The government's ban was prompted by an unexpected and short-lived decision of the U.S. Environmental Protection Agency to lift a U.S. ban on PCB imports, for certain companies including SD Myers that had lobbied against the U.S. ban. A motive for Canada's export ban was to ensure there was a sufficient supply of PCBs in Canada to support the only company in Canada—in Edmonton—that could dispose of PCBs.

The NAFTA tribunal awarded compensation to SD Myers by framing Canada's export ban as an attempt to disfavour the U.S. company. In doing so, the tribunal gave short shrift to one of the export ban's purposes, which explained its "discriminatory" effect. As the federal government had pointed out to the tribunal, Canada's newly agreed commitments under the Basel Convention on the international shipment and disposal of hazardous waste called on countries to ensure adequate disposal facilities for hazardous waste in each country's territory. Canada was caught between its commitments to protect the environment and its (far more powerful) obligations to compensate U.S. investors.

For our purposes, Gordon's inaccurate summary of the SD Myers case was a good example of how promoters of investor-state arbitration often spin individual cases to downplay concerns about NAFTA and arbitrator power. If Canada lost a case, it was our fault; if Canada won, NAFTA worked.

After his quick peek at NAFTA, Gordon turned to his economic case for the China FIPA. It was a simplistic argument, and had little relevance to any research or debate on investment treaties and investor-state arbitration that I have encountered. But, to be fair to Gordon, I'll reproduce his explanation in full:

> So the first point I want to make here is that *capital flows are the obverse side of trade flows*. It makes no sense to claim to be in

favour of international trade but against international flows of capital. You can't have trade flows without corresponding flows of capital.

As it happens, Canada runs a fairly large trade deficit with China: roughly CDN$30 billion per year. This means that as far as China is concerned, trade with Canada is essentially a matter of them accumulating large amounts of Canadian assets.

Once you realise that capital flows are essentially the same thing as trade flows, the logic behind FIPAs become[s] clear. Countries that are exporting goods in return for assets can reasonably expect to ask that these assets won't be effectively expropriated by governments pandering to anti-foreign bias.

It's not enough to simply promise to treat foreign-owned firms the same as domestically owned firms. Even if discriminatory regulations and/or fees are subsequently overturned, the lost revenues—not to mention the legal costs—still amount to an effective expropriation. What FIPAs do is ensure that governments can't expropriate foreign-owned assets without compensation. . . .

The above explains why FIPAs exist, and what they are designed to do. Once you understand these points, you start to see that much of the criticisms of FIPAs consist of fantastical nonsense, especially when you take the trouble to read the text of the treaties (emphasis his).

Basically, as it appears to me, Gordon was arguing that because Canada imports more from China than vice versa, China must own assets in Canada that are equivalent to the value of China's trade surplus. As he chose to put it, China's trade with Canada "is essentially a matter of... accumulating large amounts of Canadian assets," and capital flows "are essentially the same thing as trade flows." As a result, for Gordon, it was logical and sensible to have a FIPA to protect Chinese assets in Canada.

That strikes me as a very strange argument. Obviously, Canadians must pay for imported goods from China. But Gordon seemed not to appreciate that China can obviously take payment for such goods in, say, U.S. dollars and then stash the money in China's currency reserves or use it to buy assets outside of Canada. It does not have to be a simple exchange of imports from China for assets in Canada.

At a low point in this argument, Gordon declared that it made "no sense to claim to be in favour of international trade but against international flows of capital." FIPA critics have been called a lot of things, but that was the first time I saw them accused of being "against international capital flows."

Gordon's approach was not new or interesting. He lampooned the critics. He claimed to have accurate information. He got his facts wrong.

The problem is, all these Gordons can add up to some serious misunderstanding.

The same goes for misinformation spread by the FIPA's critics. However, by my reckoning, theirs was not nearly as wide-ranging as the promoters' and, in the critics' defence, it was under the pressure of a short and uncertain deadline for expected ratification. I think FIPA promoters have more to answer for. They spread misinformation to support ratification, without calling for a proper review of the deal.

Not everyone who talks about the FIPA has to be an investment law expert. But Canadians deserved reliable information on what the deal means. Unfortunately, it was too easy for poorly informed commentators to fill the gap. Take this example of an argument for the FIPA: all treaties limit a country's sovereignty, so what's the big deal? Gordon and other promoters often made this point. It's an important issue but a bad argument, mainly because of the uniqueness of investor-state arbitration.

Briefly, investor-state arbitration is the only form of international adjudication that gives arbitrators—instead of judges—the ultimate power to review a country's sovereign decisions in such a wide-ranging way based on claims by private actors. It is also the most powerful form of international court or tribunal, by a long shot, as measured by its scope, its unavoidability (for countries, not foreign investors), and the enforceability and sheer size of its penalties. Did FIPA promoters ever acknowledge how investor-state arbitration is so different from other forms of international adjudication? Not that I saw. As a result, they missed a point of vital importance for people in Canada, China, and many other countries.

As I said earlier in this book, treaties like the FIPA create a world supreme pseudo-court whose sole purpose is to protect the property rights of foreign investors, especially large multinationals and very wealthy individuals. Protect them from what? The main threat against which the treaties protect them is interference from the democratic, judicial, or sovereign institutions that represent and protect everyone else. And, by the way, the new pseudo-court is staffed by arbitrators instead of judges, it is not open in the manner of a court, and no one but the foreign investor and the national government has a right of standing in the process.

When such an important change is rushed through, we should all be concerned.

PART 5.

_____

REASONS WHY, AND WHAT TO DO

_____

CHAPTER 41.

"THE LARGEST ENERGY PROJECT IN THE ENTIRE WORLD"

If the FIPA is lopsided, which it obviously is, why did the Harper Government agree to it?

This question is impossible to answer conclusively. There is no *Being Stephen Harper* portal into the Prime Minister's head; we cannot access the closed discussions of the federal Cabinet. Unlike in the other parts of this book, the answers cannot be based on verifiable examples from the FIPA's text, other treaties, or arbitration awards. Even so, it is a burning question, so I will offer some possible explanations, starting in this chapter with the one that seems the most likely.

My best informed guess for why the Harper Government accepted a lopsided FIPA was its anxiousness for China to buy Canadian oil and gas and to invest in Canada's resource sector, especially the oil sands (also known as tar sands) in Alberta. This overriding priority of the government gave China a very good hand to play, and China played it well.

It almost goes without saying that the oil sands have been at the top of the Harper Government's priorities. The government has pushed hard for new pipelines and overseen a massive expansion of shipments of oil by rail. Its first budget—after Harper won his first majority—brought in omnibus reforms of federal environmental and fisheries laws that could have gotten in the way of big projects. By cutting programs and laying off staff, the government reduced the federal government's capacity for well-informed regulation of the environmental impacts of resource exploitation. The government pooh-poohed concerns that its focus on the resource sector was inflating the Canadian dollar and possibly hurting other parts of the economy. For years, it has run a major public relations and diplomatic campaign to discourage U.S. and European decision-makers from taking decisions that would disadvantage the oil sands.

Of course, one can debate the merits of these policies and the accuracy of my summary. My point is simply that the oil industry has had a supportive government in Ottawa, especially since the Conservatives' election win in 2011.

So, how might the oil industry benefit from a new relationship—including a lopsided FIPA—with China? Two things stand out. First, the industry stood to benefit from new markets in Asia in order to break from its near-complete dependence on the U.S. market; second, the industry needed money to finance oil sands facilities and infrastructure. When the Harper Government was turning its attention to a FIPA in the summer of 2011, China offered a potential fix for both problems. The oil industry needed a new market, China appeared to be the prime new buyer in the world. The oil sands needed over CDN$500 billion in investment over the next few decades, China was expected to invest as much as USD$1 trillion globally by 2020.

To illustrate the mood at the time, in April 2011 John Carruthers—the president of Enbridge Northern Gateway (a major pipeline project)—stressed China's importance in a speech to a Calgary oil conference. Of Canada's dependence on the United States to buy Canadian oil, he said: "They have a world of options and we only have one." He continued, China is "looking for supply diversity the same way we're looking for market diversity."

Yet, there was an important difference between Canada and China in this equation. China imports its oil from many countries, whereas Canada exports nearly all its oil to only one market, the United States. Thus, Canadian oil was not nearly as important to China as China was important to the Canadian oil industry. That put China in a strong position to demand a good deal and, most importantly, an ownership stake on China's terms.

Was China thinking this way? A few reports indicate Chinese officials were well aware of the oil industry's need to diversify its markets. As Carruthers was giving his speech in Calgary, for example, he was "flanked by representatives" from the China National Offshore Oil Corporation, according to the *Calgary Herald*. Just before Prime Minister Harper's visit to Beijing in February 2012, *Globe and Mail* correspondent Campbell Clark reported that China wanted Harper to deliver "consistent access to buying companies in Canada, in the oil sands and elsewhere." And, when the FIPA was announced during that same visit to Beijing, Chinese officials were gung ho about buying oil from Canada.

Perhaps even more telling, just a few months after the FIPA was announced, Chinese officials were delivering another message, reminding Canadians that they have lots of other options. In May 2012, according to the *National Post*, China's ambassador, Junsai Zhang, said:

It's too early to say China imports your oil and gas. We are in a very good collaboration with Australia, with other Western countries. No problems. If we don't import from here, we import from other countries. It's OK.

Having heard the same message, *Calgary Herald* columnist Deborah Yedlin wrote:

Canada should not see itself as the only option for China to meet its growing energy needs.

That reality check was one of the messages that emerged during a wide-ranging interview with China's ambassador to Canada ...

"It's not definite that China needs Canadian oil. It's a wrong perception. . . .Yes, China needs energy. But they (Chinese companies) can find it everywhere—Russia, Pakistan, Middle East. They are doing this," Junsai Zhang said while in Calgary last week.

When I reviewed Canadian media reports on China as part of the research for this book, I saw this message—delivered on other occasions too—as a tactic to pressure the Harper Government to approve more Chinese takeovers in the resource sector, to facilitate Chinese-owned projects in Canada, and to not push for Alberta bitumen to be refined in Canada.

Whether or not China intended to apply pressure this way, the media reports indicate that when the FIPA was negotiated in 2011, China was in a strong position to make demands of the Harper Government in return for promises to help the oil industry deal with its dependence on the U.S. And, there can be little doubt that China Inc. was pursuing a major ownership stake in Canadian oil. Since 2010, the China National Offshore Oil Corporation (CNOOC), Sinopec, PetroChina, China Investment Corporation, and China Oil and Gas Group Limited have taken over Canadian oil firms. Chinese companies like CNOOC and Sinopec have also bought into the proposed Northern Gateway pipeline, whose main purpose appears to be to ship bitumen from Alberta to refineries in China.

Indeed, these deals may be just the tip of the iceberg for Chinese ownership of Canada's resources. If Chinese outflows of investment reach USD$1 trillion globally, a prediction cited by federal trade officials in 2012, Chinese investors may realistically come to own hundreds of billions of dollars in Canada. That would mean widespread Chinese ownership, and corresponding outflows of wealth from Canada long-term, while much of China's economy remains closed to Canadian ownership. And, of course, with ownership comes influence over Canada's economic and environmental future.

How much one-way Chinese control would Canadians accept, and with what long-term guarantees for China? Enter the thirty-one-year FIPA.

FIPA promoters stressed that the FIPA with China had been discussed for eighteen years before it was finally agreed in February 2012. But the key period for hashing out the final deal seems to have been the summer and fall of 2011, around the time when the oil industry was signalling its interest in closer links with China.

In July 2011, soon after the Harper Government won its majority in May of that year, Foreign Affairs Minister John Baird made an official trip to China. During the visit, he reportedly called China "a strategic partner, whether it's on energy, natural resources or international affairs." That month, International Trade Minister Ed Fast flagged the possibility of finalizing a FIPA with China. Reportedly, he said that a FIPA would give Chinese investors "the security that knowing when they invest in Canada, there's a clear set of rules." Thus, he acknowledged—before the FIPA became controversial—that its purpose was to protect Chinese assets in Canada, as well as Canadian assets in China.

In August 2011, the *National Post* reported that the Harper Government was formally pursuing a FIPA with China. Similarly, the *Globe and Mail* reported:

> Since winning a majority this spring, the government has ramped up its focus on China.
> In the fall, Mr. Harper is expected to travel to China, where he will be under pressure to win an investment-protection agreement that would shield Canadian businesses operating in China from unfair treatment.

> In return, China hopes Canada will permit Chinese companies to increase the amount of investment in Canadian resource companies producing minerals, lumber, oil and gas and other commodities needed to fuel China's fast-growing economy.

Soon after, in October 2011, the *Ottawa Citizen* reported that Fast was expecting that "negotiations with the communist government on a foreign investment and protection agreement will be completed soon." Thus, a deal that was flagged as a possibility in July was nearly complete, only three months later.

Prime Minister Harper visited Beijing and announced the FIPA in February 2012. Media reports give an impression of his focus on the oil industry's priorities during this trip. The *National Post* reported:

> Harper's second official trip to the Middle Kingdom comes at an important juncture in Canada-China relations....
>
> The prime minister is courting China as a customer for Canadian natural resources—insisting it's in Canada's national interest to send oil and gas to Asia—and looking to sew stronger economic ties with the world's fastest-growing economy.

This story included a comment from Joseph Caron, Canada's ambassador to China from 2001 to 2005, on the Canada-China energy relationship: "We Canadians are more impatient than the Chinese. . . . The Chinese are masters of the long game." On the prospects for a FIPA, the story said:

> [O]bservers and government officials acknowledge it could be difficult for Harper to finally secure a foreign investment promotion and protection agreement (FIPA) that has been negotiated since the mid-1990s.

On the same issue, China specialist Charles Burton, of Brock University, added: "My understanding is the Chinese are not prepared to give us terms that Canada is prepared to sign at this time."

Yet, Harper clearly was prepared to accept a FIPA and, as we have seen, its terms favour China in extraordinary ways. What was on the prime minister's mind at the time?

During the February 2012 visit, Harper gave a speech in Guangzhou, China, to a Chinese and Canadian business audience. He stressed that Canada was offering its resources to China:

> Those natural resources are critical things that China needs, and will continue to need, to power the kind of industrial growth that you are witnessing . . . minerals, food, lumber, advanced expertise in a wide spectrum of activities . . . And of course, Canada has energy.

He put a lot of emphasis on this last point:

> Let's just talk about that for a moment. Canada is not just a great trading nation. We are an emerging energy superpower. . . . We have abundant supplies of virtually every form of energy. And you know, we want to sell our energy to people who want to buy our energy. It's that simple.

After discussing energy some more, he turned to the FIPA:

> But taking things to the next level means more than just increasing energy sales. . . . This week, I was truly delighted to announce with Premier Wen the conclusion of negotiations on a foreign investment promotion and protection agreement between our two countries.

So, when the FIPA was first announced, Harper was very focused on encouraging China to buy Canada's resources, especially energy. Perhaps this is as close as we can get to understanding his thought process when he accepted a lopsided deal. The FIPA was connected to his effort to solve one of the oil industry's problems, and to boost the resource sector.

What about the oil industry's other problem, its need for more capital?

Joe Oliver, then the natural resources minister, went with Harper on the February 2012 trip. His role as minister was to promote the resource sector. On the oil question, a few days after the FIPA was announced, he was reported in the *National Post* as having said that Canada needed more capital to develop its oil reserves:

> As their [Chinese] investments get larger, they are watching to see whether we continue to be welcoming. We've told them we are welcoming . . .
> Our oil sands are the largest energy project in the entire world. We simply don't have enough capital in Canada.

As well, the story signalled what China wanted from Canada: "Oliver said Chinese officials raised foreign ownership issues in Canada during the trip."

These reports give clues as to what priorities were top of mind for the Harper Government when the FIPA was announced in Beijing. Of course, they do not prove why the government accepted a lopsided deal. But they offer the best explanation I've been able to find, having reviewed the record and racked my brain about Canada's capitulation on key facets of the FIPA. The government's fixation on the resource sector—especially the oil sands—made it vulnerable to pressure from China; as "masters of the long game," to borrow Joseph Caron's description, the Chinese played their hand well.

CHAPTER 42.

OTHER EXPLANATIONS FOR A LOPSIDED DEAL

What other things could explain the Harper Government's decision to do the deal? I outline some ideas in this chapter, partly to explain why I eventually concluded that the leading factor was the government's overriding commitment to the oil patch.

For example, a lot of information communicated to Canadians about the FIPA was inaccurate. Did the federal government buy its own spin? Was it confused about what the FIPA actually does? I doubt it. The government has a large staff of lawyers and analysts. It would not have missed key implications of the deal, even if the implications were buried in legal details.

Perhaps the government's trade officials were aware of the implications, but did not inform political decision-makers in the Harper Cabinet? That seems slightly plausible. In statements on the FIPA, the prime minister appeared to misunderstand key aspects of the deal, especially its anti-discrimination rules. International Trade Minister Ed Fast also did not seem well-informed when I heard him speak about the FIPA after it became controversial.

Even so, it is hard to believe that trade officials pulled a fast one on the politicians. The FIPA's ratification was apparently delayed for about two years, allowing time for Cabinet members to examine it closely. If they were doing their jobs, the politicians should have had their staff collect criticisms of the FIPA and study the treaty's lopsidedness, the expansion of secrecy, the risk of Chinese lawsuits, and so on. Politicians, like other Canadians, are vulnerable to being misled. But it would require a serious failure of competence for a lopsided deal to be concluded primarily on that basis.

Another possible explanation is that the ideology of individual officials made them predisposed to make concessions, out of a faith in the general goodness of all trade and investment agreements. I think this may be part of the story, but only in the background. That is, trade officials—being predisposed to investment treaties—may have had a bit of a blind spot on the FIPA's lopsided elements, and this may have helped lay the groundwork for China to win more concessions and—especially—for the government to avoid a public review of the FIPA before it was ratified. However, I tend to think this is too diffuse a factor to explain why this particular deal was done.

Another possibility is that the government wanted to be able to celebrate getting a deal with China, without caring too much about the terms. In fact, the government said over and over again, without giving any evidence, that the FIPA would create jobs, help the economy, and so on. That might have been seen as an easy political win, since very few people outside of the government and the investor-state legal industry have the specialized knowledge to uncover how the deal is lopsided. However, I find it hard to believe that the government would be so shallow as to accept major concessions in a long-term agreement, merely for the bragging rights. To be sure, the FIPA was spun for political effect, but I expect this was an after-the-fact justification for a decision taken for other reasons.

Some have offered another explanation for the FIPA, saying that Canada wanted to build better relations with China. For example, when the FIPA was ratified, the director of a Canada-China energy group, Wenran Jiang, was quoted by Canadian Press: "This is a major step by the Canadian government—and to be more specific, by Harper himself and the Cabinet—to mend the fence prior to his November China trip." Jiang added that the FIPA's ratification would help the prime minister to plan a successful bilateral visit with his Chinese hosts in November 2014.

It could be that the Harper Government came under pressure from China to ratify the FIPA in advance of this bilateral visit. However, I find it hard to accept that "making nice," so to speak, could be the main rationale for negotiating and ratifying a lopsided deal. I am guessing the prime minister—like any Canadian—would want Canada's interests to be favoured in the FIPA, and would want China to be the one hoping for mended fences. However, this possible explanation brings me to a part of the record of Canada-China relations that is both troubling and hard to explain.

In August 2014 (a few months before Canada ratified the FIPA), two Canadian missionaries who owned a coffee shop near the Chinese border with North Korea—Kevin and Julia Garratt—were detained in China as accused spies. By coincidence, their detention came soon after Canada's Treasury Board reportedly blamed what it called a "highly sophisticated Chinese state-sponsored actor" for trying to hack into the computers of the National Research Council.

The question I have is, even if the government were to avoid questioning China's allegations against the Garratts, why did it not secure their release in exchange for Canada's ratification of the FIPA in September 2014? This would have been a small gesture by China to close the deal on Canada's long-term concessions. On the other hand, securing the Garratts' release would be important for a family and community in Canada, and a reflection of the supposedly good relations between Canada and China.

Instead, on the very day that the government announced the FIPA's ratification, the *Globe and Mail* reported:

> The Canadian government has threatened to have the prime minister back out of a high-profile meeting with the Chinese leadership if Beijing does not release a couple it accuses of stealing state secrets. . . .
>
> In a series of conversations with Chinese officials, Ottawa has made clear that if the couple is not released, it will decline an invitation to a meeting between Mr. Harper and Chinese leadership in Beijing around the time of the Asia-Pacific Economic Cooperation (APEC) conference in early November.

I find this timing confounding. The Harper Government had a bargaining chip; it could have delayed the FIPA until the Garratts were back in Canada. Instead, the government ratified the FIPA, and then threatened to snub the Chinese at a planned meeting in Beijing if the Garratts were not released. Even that relatively meek threat didn't pan out. Harper went to China for the conference and returned, without the Garratts being released. Ironically, this was the same visit the prospects for which, according to Wenran Jiang's quote, had brightened considerably after the FIPA was ratified.

I think more viable explanations for the lopsided FIPA track from the question of who benefits. On that question, the role of investor-state lawyers looms large.

Lawyers and arbitrators can make millions of dollars from treaties like the FIPA. Over the last fifteen years, foreign investor lawsuits worldwide have led to billions in legal and arbitration fees. This boon has come from the treaties' arbitration mechanism and the high stakes that foreign investor lawsuits create for countries and their people. Few companies would ever litigate under an investment treaty, without the prospect of a substantial payout from taxpayers.

Also, many lawyers and arbitrators have actively promoted the treaties. That was true for the FIPA, and it has been true for other investment treaties too. In Canada, I have observed it done, for example, by lawyers associated with the Canadian Bar Association in relation to Canada's ratification of the ICSID Convention in 2013. Sometimes, the lawyers move in and out of the government agencies that negotiate the treaties. This usually would not create any direct conflict of interest, but it can boost a mentality in government that supports investor-state arbitration as well as bolster private lawyers' claims of credibility when they promote investor-state arbitration to the public.

For sure, the interests of lawyers and law firms must not be taken lightly as an explanation for the FIPA, especially in helping to reassure decision-makers and discredit critics who aren't lawyers themselves. Even so, it is still a stretch to think that the legal industry could have captured so much of the federal government's decision-making as to be the prime driver of a lopsided deal.

What about other interests? FIPA promoters often identified Canada's interest as being to protect Canadian investors in China. That is clearly an important part of the FIPA, even if the deal's role in this respect was often overstated. However, I doubt that this priority drove the Harper Government's acceptance of the deal, for two reasons.

First, the benefits to Canadian investors are limited based on the terms of the FIPA itself. Even for very large Canadian companies, the FIPA may not change the landscape much. They still have to reckon with potential discrimination in favour of Chinese competitors. They still have to focus on friendly relations with Chinese partners and officials. If a Canadian company is not deep-pocketed, the option of FIPA arbitration offers little hope to fix problems in China. As some

Canadian lawyers have worried, it could make things worse if the FIPA gives an excuse for Canadian officials to put less energy into diplomatic protection of Canadian investors.

Second, the government made a huge concession to China on market access, at the expense of Canadian investors. That is, the government let China keep its barriers to Canadian investors, even after giving up a general right of market access for Chinese investors. That cave-in is very good evidence that Canadian investors' interests in China were not a deal breaker for the Harper Government.

Before the FIPA became controversial, market access had been highlighted as a key objective for Canada. Even as the FIPA was announced in February 2012, Harper was reportedly pushing for Chinese approval of proposed Canadian investments in China. This report was deceptive because, as we know now, the government had just conceded on Canada's goal of reciprocal market access in the FIPA itself.

To illustrate the significance of this concession, one of the proposed Canadian investments noted by Harper—when the FIPA was announced—was a Scotiabank bid to buy a 20 per cent stake in the Bank of Guangzhou for CDN$719 million. The bid was reportedly expected to have closed months earlier, but hadn't been approved yet. According to the *Globe and Mail*:

> Investing in Chinese banks isn't easy for foreign companies, with the government choosing carefully which suitors are allowed into the market. Rather than announce the deal as an acquisition, Scotiabank said in a press release that it had "been selected" to buy a stake in Bank of Guangzhou.

Fast forward a year. The Scotiabank bid still hadn't been approved. At that point, it was suggested that China's approval might be linked to the Harper Government's review and eventual approval of the China National Offshore Oil Corporation's takeover of Nexen. The *National Post* noted this was "not the only move by a Canadian bank or insurance company that's faced hurdles in China," and reported that Canadian financial companies were "frustrated by their limited ability to grow" in China.

Fast forward another six months. The bid still hadn't been approved, and Scotiabank abandoned it. *Bloomberg* reported that political changes at the federal and municipal level in China had affected the deal. This collapse of the bid came more than a year after Harper pressed the Chinese to approve it during his FIPA visit in February 2012, and two months before Canada ratified the FIPA in September 2014.

Did promoters of the FIPA at any point think the federal government should have driven a harder bargain on market access, when negotiating the FIPA? Did they tell the government to re-think the FIPA's ratification, after the Scotiabank bid fell apart? If so, they didn't do these things publicly.

One failed bank bid doesn't explain the lopsided FIPA. But it hammers home that the government did not insist on binding market access commitments from China, even though it gave them up to China. The fate of Canadian investors in China just wasn't the top priority.

CHAPTER 43.

THIRTY-ONE YEARS AND A HYSTERICAL SCENARIO

The FIPA is not just lopsided, it is also locked in. If things go badly for Canadians, no one will be able to get us out of the deal for at least thirty-one years. That is, once the FIPA was put into force, no legislature, government, or court in Canada could change any of its terms, without China's consent, for the treaty's mandatory lifespan.

How can the Harper Government bind future governments in Canada in this way? I know it sounds hard to believe. The simple answer is: by agreeing with another country to do so, and by making that agreement enforceable for a long time in an extraordinarily powerful way.

In international law, it's quite easy for a country to give up core aspects of its sovereignty. A country's leader or foreign minister simply has to sign on the dotted line with another country. This creates a binding agreement with the other country, which international law says cannot be broken regardless of each country's own laws and decisions. For this reason, in Canada, we depend almost entirely on the federal government to protect the country's sovereignty. Usually, it does so with care, by avoiding long-term commitments.

Indeed, almost all international treaties have no minimum

term at all, beyond six months' or a year's notice for termination by either side. The absence of a minimum term in other treaties makes it legally easy for countries to abandon them. For example, in 2011, the Harper Government was able to withdraw from the Kyoto Protocol, a treaty aimed at reducing climate change. In 2013, it pulled out of the UN Convention to Combat Desertification. The Harper Government could terminate these relatively weak and low-cost treaties because the treaties in question allowed for it, based on their terms.

Thus, on topics like the environment, human rights, and anti-corruption, countries have been careful to protect their sovereignty in international treaties. Even though the treaties have much weaker enforcement processes, compared to investment treaties, they do not have a long minimum lifespan. Investment treaties, in contrast, have strong enforcement processes *and* often a long minimum term. In theory, that helps foreign investors make investments abroad, knowing they will be safeguarded against changes to a country's laws and regulations. In other words, and as I have said before, it gives large companies a long-term, public guarantee against risks of democracy and politics.

Turning to Canada's investment treaties, the China FIPA has the longest lock-in period of them all (alongside the Canada-Egypt FIPA). Canada can withdraw from NAFTA on six months' notice. Most of Canada's FIPAs allow for termination on one year's notice, and have a survival clause that extends the treaty for another fifteen years after termination, for existing foreign investments. This structure creates a minimum lifespan of sixteen years. By comparison, the China FIPA has a minimum term of fifteen years, plus one year's notice to terminate. After that, there is a fifteen-year survival clause, making for a minimum lifespan of thirty-one years—about double that of most FIPAs.

The China FIPA is especially constraining in its first sixteen years. During that period, no future government in Canada can change or abandon the deal, without China's agreement to do so. Under almost all other FIPAs, the equivalent period is only one year. Thus, there is a very long window under the China FIPA for Chinese ownership in Canada to grow and grow, subject to automatic long-term FIPA coverage. So, it is not an exaggeration to say that Canada has been put in a FIPA straightjacket until 2045.

What if Canada just cancelled the deal, without China's consent?

The simple answer is, the lawyers clearly thought of that possibility when they designed investment treaties to provide lopsided protections for foreign investors. If Canada tried to cancel the FIPA and China did not consent, then—the next time a Chinese investor sued Canada—the arbitrators would simply observe that Canada's attempted cancellation was not valid, under the terms of the deal. If Canada tried to frustrate the Chinese lawsuit by refusing to appoint an arbitrator, or by refusing to agree on the presiding arbitrator, then the World Bank officials would use their authority under Article 24(5) of the FIPA to appoint an arbitrator on Canada's behalf. If the arbitrators issued an award against Canada and Canada refused to pay, then the award would be enforceable against Canada's commercial assets and Crown corporations abroad, in the many countries that have agreed—like Canada—to enforce arbitration awards issued under international conventions dating from the 1950s and 1960s (and originally dealing with contractual disputes) that the FIPA and other investment treaties piggyback on. This structure provides an extremely hefty backbone for investment treaties, making them practically unavoidable by countries.

That's the power of the FIPA.

What sorts of issues might trigger FIPA liabilities for Canadians? There are lots of possibilities, as I noted in chapter 8 of this book. One that conveys just how high the stakes could get is climate change.

I do not have expertise in climate change, but, like many Canadians, I see it as a serious threat. Even if the odds of a disastrous scenario are low—though they now seem higher than that—the consequences are potentially so dire that the case for action seems overwhelming to me. Even if one does not share that sense of urgency, I suggest one should consider how even fairly modest steps to respond to climate change—or any other issue—can be hampered by the FIPA.

For example, in Germany, a decision by the Hamburg government to put environmental limits on a power plant was reversed, as part of a settlement of an investor-state lawsuit by the foreign company that proposed the plant. In Canada, two NAFTA lawsuits are ongoing because of disputes about how Ontario implemented its Green Energy Act. Another ongoing NAFTA lawsuit has targeted Quebec's moratorium on oil and gas drilling in the St. Lawrence River basin. Each of these disputes involves tens or hundreds of millions of dollars in public money. They are a big deal. But they are small fries compared to the looming conflict over climate change.

To give a sense of the stakes, the authors of a recent study in the journal *Nature* calculated how much of the world's fossil fuels can be used, if we are to have a 50 per cent chance of keeping average global warming below 2 degrees Celsius, compared to pre-industrial times. To put this in perspective global temperatures rose between 4 and 7 degrees over about five thousand years, as the planet moved out of ice ages in the past million years, according to NASA. In contrast, over the past century, the global temperature has risen 0.7 degrees, which is about *ten times* faster than average warming during ice age recovery.

To meet the widely agreed upon target of 2 degrees Celsius, the authors of the *Nature* study calculated that approximately a third of worldwide oil reserves (not including unconventional oil) should not be used until 2050. The same went for half of gas reserves, and over 80 per cent of coal resources. For Canada, this worldwide limit translated into about 74 per cent of Canadian oil reserves, 24 per cent of gas reserves, and 75 per cent of coal reserves.

Strikingly, for unconventional oil such as the oil sands, the authors calculated that 99 per cent should not be used. The exploitation of these and other new sources of fossil fuels was simply not compatible with the goal of manageable climate change:

> Our results show that policy makers' instincts to exploit rapidly and completely their territorial fossil fuels are, in aggregate, inconsistent with their commitments to this temperature limit. Implementation of this policy commitment would also render unnecessary continued substantial expenditure on fossil fuel exploration, because any new discoveries could not lead to increased aggregate production.

How does this forecast fit with the FIPA? Basically, it means the oils sands, and other parts of Canada's resource sector, should not be expanded over the FIPA's thirty-one-year lifespan.

Yet, a central effect of the FIPA is to open Canada's resources to China, and to protect Chinese-owned assets in Canada. Massive amounts of Chinese-owned resources stand to be affected, therefore, when Canada finally does respond seriously to climate change. If China is not on board, we will have a very big problem. Were Chinese investors to invest hundreds of billions of dollars in the resource sector, they may reasonably expect trillions of dollars in profit, over years.

This ain't lawn darts anymore. Indeed, it sounds crazy. Some would say hysterical, and so on.

Can one expect FIPA arbitrators to award billions against Canada in a dispute with Chinese oil companies, after the federal government changes the rules? Well, recently, there have been massive awards under investment treaties—USD$2 billion against Ecuador, USD$50 billion against Russia—in disputes with oil companies. Other ongoing cases involve resource conflicts, with tens or hundreds of billions of dollars at stake.

True, these cases differ from potential disputes about climate change in Canada's oil sands. But it is not a fantasy to expect that FIPA arbitrators would (1) issue an investor-state award against Canada, since they've done so in NAFTA cases, and (2) award billions to a foreign investor, since they've done so against other countries and the amounts awarded usually reflect the value of the foreign investor's assets, not the Boy Scoutishness of the country.

At the very least, the FIPA makes it more difficult for Canada to take action on climate change, assuming that governments are (sometimes) rational and careful about billions of dollars in public money. Put differently, the oil sands are a huge danger zone under the FIPA because of the likelihood that much of the resources will be owned by China, and because of the evident need for almost all of them to stay in the ground.

With these sky-high stakes, why would the Harper Government mess up Canada's options, as a country, for getting serious on climate change? Why would it move so much power over our future from our legislatures, governments, and courts to Chinese investors and FIPA arbitrators? I think the straightest answer is, Harper seems to have wanted it that way.

If one accepts climate change as a pressing concern, it is hard to imagine a more epic fail than the FIPA. For years, the Harper Government told Canadians it would not act on climate change until China joined in. With the FIPA, on top of all its lopsided elements, the government essentially gave an advance financial bail-out to Chinese investors against steps that future governments in Canada may need to take in order to prevent a climate disaster. At least, there's one topic that maybe should have been studied a bit, before the FIPA was ratified.

CHAPTER 44.

CHANNELLING HOPE

Many thousands of Canadians demanded time to evaluate the FIPA properly, but the federal government and its backers didn't heed them. In September 2014, those of us who opposed the deal, or called for a proper review, lost.

It's easy to get depressed about that. However, it's also possible to do things to limit the damage. In this final chapter, I offer a few hopeful and specific ideas about what governments could be pushed to do to protect Canadians in the era of the FIPA and investor-state arbitration.

Immediately, the federal government should commit to renegotiating the FIPA to address its most serious concessions to China. If China does not agree—which seems likely—the federal government can give notice to terminate the FIPA at the earliest opportunity. That opportunity will not come until October 1, 2030. If the FIPA is terminated on that date, it would apply to existing Chinese investments until 2045. Thus, the termination option gives no relief now. Even so, it should be pursued in order to make clear that the deal is unacceptable.

While termination is pending, Canadians need an independent body to track how the FIPA and similar treaties are affecting our governments. The FIPA is uniquely designed to hide its impacts. It expressly lets the federal government hide

Chinese lawsuits by changing government decisions or by paying out public money, without Canadians knowing that the lawsuit exists. To fix that, governments at all levels should pass laws that require all officials to make public any information they obtain on the use of the FIPA (or Canada's other investment treaties). This requirement for disclosure would allow Canadians to learn when and why the FIPA has been invoked. It would let them decide for themselves what they think about how a government is handling Canada's obligations to Chinese investors, and to hold the government accountable.

The federal government should also commit to rigorous Investment Canada Act reviews of any proposed Chinese takeovers of Canadian companies. This is the best remaining tool to manage Chinese ownership of Canada's resources. As we have seen, the act's usefulness is limited by its thresholds and other conditions, which are locked in by the FIPA. But the act can still play an important role. It may even be possible to tighten how the act is applied to make sure that major takeovers are not hidden from review. The way must be tried, at least.

The FIPA also needs to be monitored closely. This should be done publicly, and independently from the federal government. Perhaps this role could be given to an existing body, such as the office of the Auditor General, or a new entity. Certainly, it should not be given to the usual crowd of promoters in trade ministries and the investor-state legal industry. That crowd got us into this mess and they are not the ones to get us out.

On this, I think we can kiss away any chance of the Harper Government doing the job, since the government failed to do a proper review before ratifying the FIPA. Indeed, Canadians deserve an explanation for why the government accepted a lopsided deal. An independent review could examine this question. More importantly, it should examine how the FIPA will affect Canada's ability to deliver on key economic and environmental goals for Canadians. It should also review the role of investor-state arbitration in Canada's investment treaties. Pending that review, the federal government should decline to accept investor-state arbitration in any more treaties, including the pending Canada-Europe CETA and U.S.-led Trans-Pacific Partnership (TPP), and it should be open to terminating or amending the ones that currently do. Judging from the opposition to investor-state arbitration in more and more countries, nixing this flawed mechanism is not as difficult as its promoters would have us believe.

On the topic of investor-state arbitration, Canada could play a more constructive role in the world. For example, Canada could show diplomatic leadership by promoting a judicial process to resolve sensitive disputes about foreign investment that would be independent, fair, and open. The process should incorporate basic responsibilities for multinational corporations alongside their rights and, to be balanced, the responsibilities and the rights should be equally enforceable. To avoid overloading the international process, it should supplement—not replace—domestic courts or contractually agreed-upon processes. Finally, the international process should be premised on a position of respectful deference to the elected governments of countries, so as not to wipe away our most obvious venues for democracy.

These are not radical ideas, as some promoters of investor-state arbitration would have us believe. The radical idea was to transfer core powers of sovereign nations from their democratic and judicial institutions to large companies and for-profit arbitrators. Canada alone cannot redress that mistake. But we can play a role in making things better, and we can stop making them worse.

Finally, the idea of any treaty having a lock-in period like the FIPA's contradicts basic principles of democracy and sovereignty. One government should not be able to bind future governments in such a powerful and immutable way, regardless of what international law allows. Fortunately, this is also not hard to address. Parliament can pass a law that prohibits federal officials from agreeing to any treaty that has a minimum term going beyond a few years. Anyone who broke the law could face severe criminal penalties.

Even with this restriction, arguably there should be a more careful process to approve treaties that give up core components of Canadian sovereignty. Other countries take more care in this respect. Brazil was saved from many investment treaties in the 1990s because its Congress did not ratify the deals that were negotiated by its national government. To this day, Brazil has not accepted a single treaty that allows for investor-state arbitration.

In Canada, investment treaties should at least have to be approved in Parliament. This should probably extend to provincial legislatures too, given their interest in not having their decisions deterred or their assets seized abroad. For major deals like the China FIPA, it is fair to expect approval only after a national consultation, or even a referendum. Right now, it is just too easy for the federal Cabinet to return Canada to a quasi-colonial legal status. NAFTA's investment chapter was a step in that direction with the United States, the FIPA is another step with China.

I admit that none of these ideas are very satisfying, compared to the stark reality that Canada has been locked in to a lopsided deal. But hope springs eternal, and needs only to be channeled into specific goals. Likewise, Canadians are their own best defence against even more concessions. We can learn about the FIPA and do our best to respond. We can push political parties to commit to reviewing the FIPA, passing a law on FIPA openness, and reforming investor-state arbitration, and we can work with people in other countries who are doing similar things. If nothing else, we can vote with the FIPA in mind, not only in federal elections but in provincial, territorial, and municipal ones too. Casting a vote is one of the easiest and most profound things we can do, and it's what those who disagree most want us to avoid. Turning the FIPA on its head, the lopsided deal should remind us why we have to respond, however we can, for thirty-one years.

NOTES

GENERAL

China FIPA text: *Agreement between the Government of Canada and the Government of the People's Republic of China for the Promotion and Reciprocal Protection of Investments* (signed September 9, 2012; entered into force October 1, 2014), Foreign Affairs, Trade and Development Canada website, accessed March 9, 2012, http://www.international.gc.ca/trade-agreements-accords-commerciaux/agr-acc/fipa-apie/china-text-chine.aspx?lang=eng (China FIPA or Canada-China-FIPA).

Canada's other investment treaty texts: These include both FIPAs and trade deals that allow investor-state arbitration. Their texts are available on the Foreign Affairs, Trade and Development Canada website, accessed March 9, 2015, http://www.international.gc.ca/trade-agreements-accords-commerciaux/agr-acc/a-z.aspx?lang=eng.

China's investment treaties: The texts of China's bilateral investment treaties are available on the United Nations Conference on Trade and Development (UNCTAD) Investment Policy Hub website, accessed March 9, 2015, http://investmentpolicyhub.unctad.org/IIA/CountryBits/42#iiaInnerMenu.

NAFTA: *North American Free Trade Agreement between the Government of Canada, the Government of the United Mexican States, and the Government of the United States of America* (entered into force January 1, 1994), *International Legal Materials* 32 (1993): 296 and 605 (NAFTA).

Foreign investor lawsuits under investment treaties: There is no single official repository for all known cases under investment treaties. Relevant documents for all cases cited in this book are available on websites of Foreign Affairs, Trade and Development Canada (http://www.international.gc.ca/trade-agreements-accords-commerciaux/topics-domaines/disp-diff/gov.aspx?lang=eng), the U.S. State Department (http://www.state.gov/s/l/c3741.htm), or an unofficial academic repository (www.italaw.com). Cases are identified by short names with a precise date for the relevant decision or other document. Formal citations are included where possible.

Court challenge to ratification of China FIPA: The decisions of the Federal Court and Federal Court of Appeal are cited in full in the notes. Other documents in this case are identified by the short name *Hupacasath v Minister of Foreign Affairs*. For all of these documents, the full reference is *Hupacasath First Nation v Minister of Foreign Affairs of Canada and Attorney General of Canada*, Federal Court Case no. T-153-13.

Matthew Fisher, Charles Burton, and William Watson quotes: Matthew Fisher, "What Harper needs to know about trading with China," *Calgary Herald*, February 7, 2012; Jason Fekete and Mark Kennedy, "Canada wary as China raises free-trade talks," *Calgary Herald*, February 10, 2012 (quoting Charles Burton); William Watson, "In China's good books, for now," *Ottawa Citizen*, February 14, 2012.

CHAPTER 1: A PRIME MINISTER BENDS THE KNEE

Prime Minister Harper quote and press releases on signing and ratification of FIPA: Mark MacKinnon, "How Harper's foreign policy focus evolved from human rights to the 'almighty dollar'," *Globe and Mail*, November 27, 2013; Prime Minister of Canada, "Canada-China Foreign Investment Promotion and Protection Agreement (FIPA)," News release, September 8, 2012; Foreign Affairs, Trade and Development Canada, "Canada Ratifies Investment Agreement with China," News release, September 12, 2014.

More than 90 per cent of money awarded appears to have gone to very large companies or very wealthy individuals: This finding is based on a review of the size and wealth of claimants in cases up to the spring of 2014. I elaborate on my blog, http://gusvanharten.wordpress.com/.

CHAPTER 2: PROTECTING CANADIAN INVESTORS, WITH A CATCH

Prime Minister Harper announcement on signing of FIPA: Prime Minister of Canada, "PM announces agreement that will facilitate investment flows between Canada and China," News release, February 8, 2012).

FIPA protections and wide discretion of arbitrators to order compensation for foreign investors: China FIPA, especially articles 4 to 12, 20, and 31.

Canada sued more often than all but four countries: United Nations Conference on Trade and Development, *International Investment Agreements Issues Note – Recent Trends in IIAs and ISDS* (Geneva: UNCTAD, February 2015), 6.

CHAPTER 3: CHINA CAN KEEP ITS DISCRIMINATORY LAWS

Prime Minister Harper quote from press conference on signing of FIPA: "Canada signs investment deal with China," Canadian Press video, February 8, 2012, *Globe and Mail* website, accessed March 9, 2015, http://www.theglobeandmail.com/news/news-video/video-canada-signs-investment-deal-with-china/article544503/.

FIPA exception for existing discriminatory laws and requirement that Canada and China lock in the unevenness between their respective playing fields: China FIPA, articles 1(6) and 8(2). The former article defines "measure" broadly; the latter provides that the FIPA's non-discrimination clauses do not apply to existing discriminatory measures.

U.S.-China Business Council report and Canadian trade official quote: U.S.-China Business Council, *USCBC 2013 China Business Environment Survey Results: Tempered Optimism Continues amid Moderating Growth, Rising Costs, and Persistent Market Barriers* (USCBC, 2013), 5-6 and 11-12; *Hupacasath v Minister of Foreign Affairs*, Cross-Examination on Affidavit of Vernon John MacKay, April 3, 2013, 40-41.

Other countries used China's strategy: Robert Wade, *Governing the Market: Economic Theory and the Role of Government in East Asian Industrialization* (Princeton: Princeton University Press,

2003); Ha-Joon Chang and Duncan Green, *The Northern WTO Agenda on Investment: Do as we Say, Not as we Did* (Geneva: South Centre/ CAFOD (2003).

Risk of losing small and medium Canadian companies: Tavia Grant, Richard Blackwell, and Barrie McKenna, "Vanishing act: Where did Canada's mid-sized companies go?," *Globe and Mail*, July 1, 2012.

Andrew Coyne quote and presentation of himself as champion of parliamentary democracy: Andrew Coyne, "Despite near-suicidal wailing over China trade pact, it's no big deal," *National Post*, November 2, 2012; Andrew Coyne, "A price must be paid—but by whom?," *Maclean's*, April 28, 2011.

John Maynard Keynes and FIPA promoter quotes: Simon Taylor, "The true meaning of 'In the long run we are all dead'," *Simon Taylor's Blog*, May 5, 2013, http://www.simontaylorsblog.com/2013/05/05/the-true-meaning-of-in-the-long-run-we-are-all-dead/; Keith Norbury, "Canada-China FIPA: A good deal for Canadian investors, or not?," *Canadian Sailings*, April 14, 2013 (quoting David Fung).

CHAPTER 4: CANADA PLAYS THE CAPITAL-IMPORTING LOSER

Investment treaties protect foreign investors more powerfully than any other kind of treaty protects anyone: Gus Van Harten, *Investment Treaty Arbitration and Public Law* (Oxford: Oxford University Press, 2007), chapter 5.

Canada as the "safe country" in FIPAs with smaller countries/ uniqueness of the China FIPA: Under the China FIPA, Canada occupies the capital-importing position and is host to large amounts of investment from the other country. This distinguishes the FIPA from all of Canada's other investment treaties except NAFTA. I provide data on capital flows between Canada and its various FIPA partners on my blog, http://gusvanharten.wordpress.com/.

Default arbitrator appointment power given to World Bank officials: e.g. NAFTA, article 1124(1).

Figures on potential China investment outflows: Department of Foreign Affairs and International Trade (Canada), *Responses to Questions submitted through the Chair of the House of Commons Standing Committee on International Trade on behalf of the Liberal Party*, undated, received by author November 9, 2012. I have posted the document on my blog, http://gusvanharten.wordpress.com/.

Prime Minister Harper on Chinese state-owned companies: Prime Minister of Canada, "Statement by the Prime Minister of Canada on Foreign Investment," News release, December 7, 2012.

Takeovers of smaller Canadian companies: Steven Chase, "Inside Ottawa's decision on takeovers," *Globe and Mail*, December 8, 2012.

Drop-off in Chinese investment in 2013: Nathan VanderKlippe, "Investment deal with China coming 'in short order': Baird," *Globe and Mail*, October 16, 2013.

John Baird quote: Tobi Cohen, "Baird talks human rights," *Vancouver Sun*, July 19, 2011.

Rich/ major capital-exporting countries and investment treaties: Gus Van Harten, *Investment Treaty Arbitration and Public Law* (Oxford: Oxford University Press, 2007), 13-14.

Potential seizure of a country's assets abroad: Gus Van Harten, *Investment Treaty Arbitration and Public Law* (Oxford: Oxford University Press, 2007), 117-119.

Investment treaties as public subsidy for foreign investors: Emma Aisbett, Larry Karp, and Carol McAusland, "Compensation for Indirect Expropriation in International Investment Agreements: Implications of National Treatment and Rights to Invest," *Journal of Globalization and Development* 1 (2010): Article 6.

Vetting of government decisions for compliance with foreign investor rights: e.g. Treasury Board of Canada Secretariat, *Guidelines on International Regulatory Obligations and Cooperation* (Ottawa: Queen's Printer, 2007), accessed March 9, 2015,
http://www.tbs-sct.gc.ca/rtrap-parfa/iroc-cori/iroc-cori02-eng.asp.

Principle that one legislature cannot bind another: A.V. Dicey, *Introduction to the Study of the Law of the Constitution*, 3rd ed. (London: Macmillan, 1889), 38; John C. Roberts and Erwin Chemerinsky, "Entrenchment of Ordinary Legislation: A Reply to Professors Posner and Vermeule," *California Law Review* 91 (2003): 1773.

Disparity of investment flows as a cost-benefit measure of investment treaties: e.g. Andrew T. Guzman, "Why LDCs Sign Treaties That Hurt Them: Explaining the Popularity of Bilateral Investment Treaties," *Virginia Journal of International Law* 38 (1997): 639.

CHAPTER 5: THE MAGICAL FIPA: ATTRACTING CHINESE INVESTMENT WITHOUT ANY ENVIRONMENTAL IMPACT!

Andrew Coyne quote: Andrew Coyne, "Despite near-suicidal wailing over China trade pact, it's no big deal" *National Post*, November 2, 2012.

Research on claim that investment treaties encourage investment: e.g. Lauge N. Skovgaard Poulsen, "The Importance of BITs for Foreign Direct Investment and Political Risk Insurance: Revisiting the Evidence," in *Yearbook on International Investment Law and Policy 2009/2010*, ed. Karl P. Sauvant (New York: Oxford University Press, 2010).

Prime Minister Harper quote: Prime Minister of Canada, "Canada-China Foreign Investment Promotion and Protection Agreement (FIPA)," News release, February 8, 2012.

China FIPA environmental assessment and my comment: Foreign Affairs, Trade and Development Canada, *Final Environmental Assessment of the Canada-China Foreign Investment Protection Agreement (FIPA)*, undated, accessed March 9, 2015,
http://www.international.gc.ca/trade-agreements-accords-commerciaux/agr-acc/china-chine/finalEA-pub-EEfinale.aspx?lang=eng. I have posted my comment on this environmental assessment on my blog, http://gusvanharten.wordpress.com/.

Peru FIPA environmental assessment: Foreign Affairs, Trade and Development Canada, *Initial Environmental Assessment of the Canada-Peru Foreign Investment Protection Agreement (FIPA)*, undated, accessed March 9, 2015,
http://www.international.gc.ca/trade-agreements-accords-commerciaux/agr-acc/peru-perou/report-rapport.aspx?lang=eng.

China FIPA definition of investment: China FIPA, article 1(1).

CHAPTER 6: MARKET ACCESS FOR CHINESE INVESTORS, BUT NOT FOR CANADIAN INVESTORS

U.S. versus European policy on market access in investment treaties: e.g. Marie France Houde, "Novel Features in Recent OECD Bilateral Investment Treaties," in *International Investment Perspectives* (Paris: Organisation for Economic Cooperation and Development, 2006), 151-152.

Pre-establishment national treatment in Canada's investment treaties: Gus Van Harten, "The Canada-China FIPPA: Its Uniqueness and Non-Reciprocity," in *Canadian Yearbook of International Law*, eds. John Currie and René Provost (Vancouver: UBC Press, 2013): 17.

FIPA national treatment and most-favoured-nation requirements: China FIPA, article 6, which does not include the terms "establishment" and "acquisition"; China FIPA, article 5, which includes the terms "establishment" and "acquisition."

Post-1994 FIPAs where Canada gave market access to foreign investors: Gus Van Harten, "The Canada-China FIPPA: Its Uniqueness and Non-Reciprocity," in *Canadian Yearbook of International Law*, eds. John Currie and René Provost (Vancouver: UBC Press, 2013): 17.

China's practice of not giving market access to foreign investors: Gus Van Harten, "The Canada-China FIPPA: Its Uniqueness and Non-Reciprocity," in *Canadian Yearbook of International Law*, eds. John Currie and René Provost (Vancouver: UBC Press, 2013): 19-20.

China's consul-general quote: Gordon Hamilton, "Canada-China trade diversifying beyond commodities; Relations now a two-way street, says outgoing Chinese Consul-general," *Vancouver Sun*, November 14, 2011.

Asian, African, and Latin American countries that supply resources to China: e.g. Juan Pablo Cardenal and Heriberto Araújo, *China's Silent Army*, trans. Catherine Mansfield (London: Penguin, 2013).

Canada's trade deficit with China: Pascal Tremblay, *Trade and Investment: Canada-China*, Research Publication No. 2014-54-E (Ottawa: Library of Parliament, 2014).

CHAPTER 7: FAITH IN THE INVESTMENT CANADA ACT

Investment Canada Act: RSC 1985, c 28 (1st Supp).

FIPA promoters stressing Investment Canada Act: e.g. Greg Kanargelidis, Aaron Libbey, and Tamara Nachmani, "Canada-China Investment Treaty: Ratification Process Begins," *Blakes Bulletin*, October 1, 2012.

Carve-out on investment screening: China FIPA, annex D.34. For a FIPA with a broader carve-out on investment screening by Canada, e.g. *Agreement between the Government of Canada and the Government of the Eastern Republic of Uruguay for the Promotion and Protection of Investments*, Canada Treaty Series 1999 no. 31 (entered into force June 2, 1999), annex I(VI)(1).

Limited application of Investment Canada Act to establishment of a new business: *Investment Canada Act*, RSC 1985, c 28 (1st Supp), section 14(1).

Conservative spin on Investment Canada Act: e.g. Conservative Member of Parliament Blake Richards' letter, reproduced in Gus Van Harten, "Taking apart Tories' Party Line on China-Canada Treaty," *The Tyee*, November 5, 2012.

Non-application of Investment Canada Act to Chinese land purchases: Nathan VanderKlippe, "For China, an oil sands investment that can't be blocked," *Globe and Mail*, March 11, 2014; Matthew Fisher, "What Harper needs to know about trading with China," *Calgary Herald*, February 7, 2012. Land grabs are discussed in Lorenzo Cotula et al., *Land Grab or Development Opportunity?* (London/ Rome: International Institute for Environment and Development/ Food and Agriculture Organization/ International Fund for Agricultural Development, 2009).

Limited application of Investment Canada Act based on financial thresholds for review: "Investment Canada Act – Thresholds for Review," Industry Canada website, accessed March 9, 2015, https://www.ic.gc.ca/eic/site/ica-lic.nsf/eng/h_lk00050.html.

China Oil and Gas Group takeover of private Canadian energy company: Jeffrey Jones, "China is still purchasing Canadian oil assets – just smaller ones," *Globe and Mail*, June 20, 2014.

Limited application of Investment Canada Act to expansion of an existing business: "Investment Canada Act: Related-Business Guidelines," Industry Canada website, accessed March 9, 2015, https://www.ic.gc.ca/eic/site/ica-lic.nsf/eng/lk00064.html#p1

Mulcair and Harper on China FIPA and Nexen takeover: Kelly Cryderman, "Ottawa's foreign ownership strategy hurts Alberta, Mulcair argues," *Globe and Mail*, February 19, 2013; John Ivison, "Opponents turning up hysteria over trade deal with China," *National Post*, November 1, 2012.

Provincial steps to block foreign takeover: e.g. Marina Strauss and Bertrand Marotte, "Quebec eyes buying Rona shares to block Lowe's," *Globe and Mail*, July 31, 2012.

European Union Chamber of Commerce in China, David Fung, and federal trade official quotes: European Union Chamber of Commerce (EUCCC), *European Business in China Position Paper 2013/2014* (EUCCC, 2013), 19-20; Keith Norbury, "Canada-China FIPA: A good deal for Canadian investors, or not?," *Canadian Sailings*, April 14, 2013 (quoting David Fung); *Hupacasath v Minister of Foreign Affairs*, Cross-Examination on Affidavit of Vernon John MacKay, April 3, 2013, 39.

CHAPTER 8: POSSIBLE CONFLICTS OVER CANADIAN JOBS, HEALTH, AND THE ENVIRONMENT

Juan Pablo Cardenal and Heriberto Araújo quotes: Juan Pablo Cardenal and Heriberto Araújo, *China's Silent Army*, trans. Catherine Mansfield (London: Penguin, 2013), 6-7.

Premier Wen Jiabao statement on buying Canadian oil: Mark Mackinnon, "PM lands investor protection deal, raises human rights in China," *Globe and Mail*, February 8, 2012.

Prime Minister Harper and federal trade ministry statements on Chinese firms wanting to buy into natural resources in Canada: Prime Minister of Canada, "PM announces signing of new investment agreement with China," New release, September 8, 2012; Foreign Affairs, Trade and Development Canada, "Canada-China Foreign Investment Promotion and Protection Agreement (FIPA) Negotiations," News release, undated, last modified October 1, 2014, accessed March 9, 2015,
http://www.international.gc.ca/trade-agreements-accords-commerciaux/agr-acc/fipa-apie/china-chine.aspx?lang=eng.

Pat Daniel quotes: Carolynne Wheeler, "Chinese 'frustrated' by Northern Gateway regulatory delays," *Globe and Mail*, February 9, 2012.

Use of Chinese workers at Chinese-owned coal mine in Murray River: "Mandarin required in worker permits for B.C. mine project," *Canadian Press*, December 7, 2012; "B.C. mine's temporary foreign workers case in Federal Court," *CBC News*, April 9, 2013; Greg Klein, "695 B.C. coal miners laid off but HD Mining wants workers from China: B.C. minister issues statement on imported labour," *Resource Clips*, April 17, 2014; Wendy Stueck, "Proposed Murray River mine to rely primarily on foreign workers," *Globe and Mail*, January 9, 2015.

Access-to-information requests on temporary foreign workers: Alberta Federation of Labour,

Access to Information and Privacy (ATIP) Documents on Employers with TFW-Dominated Workforces, Backgrounder (Edmonton: Alberta Federation of Labour, 2014).

Chinese coal mine owner quote: Dene Moore, "Mining firm, unions at odds over admission of documents in foreign workers case," *Globe and Mail*, April 9, 2013.

Craig Simons quote: Craig Simons, *The Devouring Dragon* (New York: St. Martin's Press, 2013), 9.

Securities fraud and workplace safety as areas of possible conflict: Barbara Shecter and Peter Koven, "Tracking zungui; Story of Chinese shoemaker illustrates the problems that can arise when a foreign company operating in Canada runs into trouble," *National Post*, February 11, 2012; Ryan Cormier, "Largest workplace fine in Alberta history for oil giant's role in the death of two Chinese workers," *Edmonton Journal*, January 24, 2013.

CHAPTER 9: THE SPECIAL STATUS OF CHINESE INVESTORS

Enforceability of investment treaty awards in many countries around the world: Gus Van Harten, *Investment Treaty Arbitration and Public Law* (Oxford: Oxford University Press, 2007), 117-119.

Ability of Chinese investors to seek compensation for lost future profits: This is discussed in the notes for chapter 29.

Ability of arbitrators to review almost anything Canada does in sovereign role at all levels or branches of the state: This reflects the principle of international law that states are unified entities; e.g. International Law Commission, *Draft Articles on Responsibility of States for Internationally Wrongful Acts*, November 2001, Supplement No. 10 (A/56/10), chp.IV.E.1, article 4(1). It is evident in the China FIPA, articles 1(6) and 2(2).

Principle that one elected government in Canada cannot bind another: This principle of Canadian constitutional law does not apply under the FIPA because a country's international obligations attach to the country, not to any one of its governments. See International Law Commission, *Draft Articles on Responsibility of States for Internationally Wrongful Acts*, November 2001, Supplement No. 10 (A/56/10), chp.IV.E.1, article 12.

FIPA arbitrators not limited by Canada's constitution or other parts of Canadian law/ arbitrators subject to FIPA and other rules of international law: As a principle of international law, a country cannot rely on its own domestic law or constitution to avoid its international obligations. *Vienna Convention on the Law of Treaties*, 1155 United Nations Treaty Series 331 (signed May 22, 1969; entered into force January 27, 1980), article 27; China FIPA, article 30(1).

Limited review and streamlined enforceability of investment treaty awards/ domestic law on award enforcement in different countries: Gus Van Harten, *Investment Treaty Arbitration and Public Law* (Oxford: Oxford University Press, 2007), 154-158; Hazel Fox and Philippa Webb, *The Law of State Immunity*, 3rd ed. (Oxford: Oxford University Press, 2013).

Billions in compensation for foreign investors since 1990s: I have counted just over USD$6.5 billion in total compensation ordered in 76 known awards issued against countries by early summer of 2014 (thus not including the award against Russia noted immediately below). This number does not include payouts from secret awards or from settlements. I elaborate on my blog, http://gusvanharten.wordpress.com/.

USD$50 billion award against Russia: *Yukos Universal v. Russia*, Decision, July 18, 2014, paras.

1847, 1860-1863, 1874, and 1887. This decision and the other two by the tribunal in the case, all issued together, are available on the Permanent Court of Arbitration website, accessed March 9, 2015, http://www.pca-cpa.org/showpage.asp?pag_id=1599.

Caution of courts in ordering monetary compensation against state in its sovereign role: Gus Van Harten, *Sovereign Choices and Sovereign Constraints* (Oxford: Oxford University Press, 2013), 46-47 and 113-114.

Prime Minister Harper quote: Matthew Fisher, "China trade balance on PM's agenda; Harper says he'll press issue with Chinese president at Russia meeting," *Montreal Gazette*, September 8, 2012.

CHAPTER 10: DOES CANADA'S RULE OF LAW PROTECT US?

Milos Barutciski and Matthew Kronby quote: Milos Barutciski and Matthew Kronby, "Investment agreement with China will benefit Canada," *Globe and Mail*, November 2, 2012.

Summary of cases from Canadian Centre for Policy Alternatives report: Scott Sinclair, *NAFTA Chapter 11 Investor State Disputes to January 1, 2015* (Ottawa: Canadian Centre for Policy Alternatives, 2015); Sunny Freeman, "NAFTA's Chapter 11 Makes Canada Most-Sued Country Under Free Trade Tribunals," *Huffington Post*, January 14, 2015.

Reported CDN$17 million award in Mobil / Murphy v. Canada: Jarrod Hepburn, "Canada ordered to pay 17+ million to Exxon Mobil & Murphy Oil – and faces a new claim for imposing R&D requirements on Newfoundland oil project," *Investment Arbitration Reporter*, March 4, 2015.

Canada as 5th-most sued country under investment treaties worldwide: To the end of 2014, Canada was sued under an investment treaty more often than any other developed country and more often than all but four developing or transition countries (Argentina, Venezuela, Czech Republic, and Egypt). See United Nations Conference on Trade and Development, *International Investment Agreements Issues Note – Recent Trends in IIAs and ISDS* (Geneva: UNCTAD, February 2015), 6.

China has more investment treaties than virtually any other country including numerous ones with significant capital-exporting companies: United Nations Conference on Trade and Development (UNCTAD) Investment Policy Hub website, accessed March 9, 2015, http://investmentpolicyhub.unctad.org/IIA/IiasByCountry#iiaInnerMenu.

Only two known lawsuits against China: The first was *Ekran Berhad v China* (documents not public, ICSID Case No. ARB/11/15), an apparently minor case – involving a lease for 900 acres of land – that was filed in May 2011, did not lead to an award, and seems to have been settled off the record in 2013. The second was *Ansung Housing v China* (documents not public, ICSID Case No. ARB/14/25), another apparently minor case – involving the construction of a golf club – that was filed in November 2014 and appears to be ongoing.

Possible reasons for lack of lawsuits against China: Leon Trakman, "China and Investor-State Arbitration," University of New South Wales Law Research Paper No. 2012-48 (2012).

CHAPTER 11: THE EXPLOSION OF FOREIGN INVESTOR LAWSUITS

First known lawsuit under an investment treaty: Asian Agricultural Products Ltd (AAPL) v Sri Lanka, Decision, June 27, 1990, *International Legal Materials* 30 (1991): 577.

Comparison to WTO state-state arbitration: José Augusto Fontoura Costa, "Comparing WTO Panelists and ICSID Arbitrators: The Creation of International Legal Fields," *Oñati Socio-Legal Series* 1, no. 4 (2011).

Average fees of roughly USD$8 million for an investment treaty arbitration: David Gaukrodger and Kathryn Gordon, "Investor-State Dispute Settlement: A Scoping Paper for the Investment Policy Community," *OECD Working Paper on International Investment 2012/03* (Paris: Organisation for Economic Cooperation and Development, 2012).

Boards of journals dominated by investor-state lawyers and arbitrators: Pia Eberhardt and Cecilia Olivet, *Profiting from Injustice* (Brussels: Corporate Europe Observatory and the Transnational Institute, 2012), 66.

Academic statements criticizing investment treaty arbitration in 2010 and 2014: "Public Statement on the International Investment Regime," August 31, 2010, Osgoode Hall Law School website, accessed March 9, 2015,
http://www.osgoode.yorku.ca/public-statement-international-investment-regime-31-august-2010/;

"Statement of Concern about Planned Provisions on Investment Protection and Investor-State Dispute Settlement (ISDS) in the Transatlantic Trade and Investment Partnership (TTIP)," July 17, 2014, University of Kent website, accessed March 9, 2015, http://www.kent.ac.uk/brussels/news/?view=1734.

"Canada is not Ecuador" line of argument: e.g. *Hupacasath v Minister of Foreign Affairs*, Transcript of Hearing, vol. 2, June 6, 2013, 303.

Common features of investment treaties: Gus Van Harten, *Investment Treaty Arbitration and Public Law* (Oxford University Press, 2007), especially chapter 4.

A few dozen individuals sit repeatedly as arbitrators/ personal characteristics of arbitrators: José Augusto Fontoura Costa, "Comparing WTO Panelists and ICSID Arbitrators: The Creation of International Legal Fields," *Oñati Socio-Legal Series* 1, no. 4 (2011): 11; Pia Eberhardt and Cecilia Olivet, *Profiting from Injustice* (Brussels: Corporate Europe Observatory and the Transnational Institute, 2012), 38; Gus Van Harten, "The (Lack of) Women Arbitrators in Investment Treaty Arbitration," *Columbia FDI Perspectives*, February 6, 2012.

Investment treaty lawsuits over the last 15 years: UNCTAD, *International Investment Agreements Issues Note – Recent Trends in IIAs and ISDS* (Geneva: UNCTAD, February 2015); Gus Van Harten, *Sovereign Choices and Sovereign Constraints* (Oxford: Oxford University Press, 2013), 9-15.

CHAPTER 12: FOR-PROFIT ARBITRATORS INSTEAD OF JUDGES

Appointment process for FIPA arbitrators: China FIPA, article 24.

Lack of judicial safeguards of independence and fairness in investment treaty arbitration: Gus Van Harten, "Investment Treaty Arbitration, Procedural Fairness, and the Rule of Law," in *International Investment Law and Comparative Public Law*, ed. Stephan W. Schill (Oxford: Oxford University Press, 2010).

Canadian Judicial Council quote: Canadian Judicial Council, *Ethical Principles for Judges*, 8 (citing *Valente v The Queen*, [1985] 2 SCR 673), CJC website, accessed March 9, 2015, http://www.cjc-ccm.gc.ca/cmslib/general/news_pub_judicialconduct_Principles_en.pdf.

Formal reciprocity of arbitrations under contract or collective agreement as basis for confidence in arbitrator independence: Christopher R. Drahozal, "Judicial Incentives and the Appeals Process," *SMU Law Review* 51 (1998): 501; Alan Scott Rau, "Integrity in Private Judging,"

South Texas Law Review 38 (1997): 523; G. Richard Shell, "Res Judicata and Collateral Estoppel Effects of Commercial Arbitration," *UCLA Law Review* 35 (1988): 633-634.

Canadian investors not having received compensation in any NAFTA lawsuit against U.S.: Relevant documents are available from the U.S. State Department website, accessed March 9, 2015, http://www.state.gov/s/l/c3741.htm.

Arbitrators significantly more likely to take restrictive (country-friendly) approach in NAFTA lawsuits against U.S. compared to Canada and Mexico: This finding has emerged in a follow-up study, not yet published, to Gus Van Harten, "Arbitrator Behaviour in Asymmetrical Adjudication: An Empirical Study of Investment Treaty Arbitration," *Osgoode Hall Law Journal* 50 (2012): 211.

Yves Fortier and George R.R. Martin quotes: *ConocoPhillips v Venezuela*, Decision by Chairman of the Administrative Council, May 5, 2014, ICSID Case No. ARB/07/30, para. 37; George R.R. Martin, *A Dance with Dragons* (New York: Bantam Books, 2011).

CHAPTER 13: NO STANDING FOR CANADIANS

Common law principle of audi alteram partem: J.M. Kelly, "Audi Alteram Partem," *Natural Law Forum* 9 (1964): 103; Gerald Heckman, David Mullan, and Gus Van Harten, *Administrative Law: Cases, Text, and Materials* (Toronto: Emond Montgomery, 2010), chapter 3.

Example of accusations against private individuals: *St. Marys v Canada*, Claimant submission, May 13, 2011, paras. 1 and 33-34.

Example of local company bidding on the same contract: *Eureko v Poland*, Rajski separate opinion, August 19, 2005), para. 11.

Example of province having different interests from Ottawa: *AbitibiBowater v Canada*, Claimant submission, April 23, 2009, paras. 8-9.

Examples of an indigenous people with relevant land claim or cultural traditions: *Pezold v Zimbabwe*, Decision, June 26, 2012, para. 62; *Glamis v U.S.*, Decision, June 8, 2009, *International Legal Materials* 48 (2009): 1035, para. 89-94.

Limited provision for others to participate in FIPA arbitration and limitations on amicus participation in investment treaty arbitration: China FIPA, article 29 and annex C.29(2). Patrick Wieland, "Why the Amicus Curia Institution is Ill-suited to address Indigenous Peoples' Rights before Investor-State Arbitration Tribunals: *Glamis Gold* and the Right of Intervention," *Trade, Law & Development* 3 (2011): 344-345 and 359-360; Alberto Salazar, "Defragmenting International Investment Law to Protect Citizen-Consumers: The Role of *Amici Curiae* and Public Interest Groups," Osgoode Hall Law School Comparative Research in Law & Political Economy Research Paper no. 6/2013 (2013), 4-8.

CHAPTER 14: SECRET DEALS WITH CHINA

Joint statement on openness in NAFTA investor-state arbitration: NAFTA Free Trade Commission, *Notes of Interpretation of Certain Chapter 11 Provisions*, July 31, 2001, article B(1); Meg Kinnear and Robin Hansen, "The Influence of NAFTA Chapter 11 in the BIT Landscape," *UC Davis Journal of International Law and Policy* 12 (2005): 111.

Harper government statement to United Nations body: United Nations Commission on International Trade Law (UNCITRAL), Working Group II (Arbitration and Conciliation), 53rd Sess., UN Doc A/CN.9/WG.II/WP.159/Add.1 (2010).

Narrower FIPA transparency provision: China FIPA, article 28(1) and (2).

Murky cases of apparent NAFTA settlements: *St Marys v Canada* is discussed in the notes for chapter 17. Other cases that appear to have settled with possible payouts by a provincial government are *Greiner v Canada*, Claimant submission, December 2, 2010; and *Trammell Crow v Canada*, Claimant submission, September 7, 2001.

Public policy issues at stake in investment treaty arbitration: Jeswald W. Salacuse, *The Law of Investment Treaties* (Oxford: Oxford University Press, 2010), 354-357; Andreas Kulick, *Global Public Interest in International Investment Law* (Cambridge: Cambridge University Press, 2012), 1-2 and 94-97.

CHAPTER 15: WHAT DO THE TREATIES PROHIBIT?

Issues arising from ambiguous language on expropriation, non-discrimination, and fair and equitable treatment: Peter D. Isakoff, "Defining the Scope of Indirect Expropriation for International Investments," *Global Business Law Review* 3 (2013): 189; Jürgen Kurtz, "The Use and Abuse of WTO Law in Investor-State Arbitration: Competition and its Discontents," *European Journal of International Law* 20 (2009): 749; Peter Muchlinski, "'Caveat Investor'? The Relevance of the Conduct of the Investor Under the Fair and Equitable Treatment Standard," *International and Comparative Law Quarterly* 55 (2006): 527.

Broad interpretations of concept of fair and equitable treatment: Roland Kläger, *'Fair and Equitable Treatment' in International Investment Law* (Cambridge: Cambridge University Press, 2011), 116-119; M. Sornarajah "Evolution or Revolution in International Investment Arbitration? The Descent into Normlessness," in *Evolution in Investment Treaty Law and Arbitration*, eds. Chester Brown and Kate Miles (Cambridge: Cambridge University Press, 2011), 650-652.

Foreign investor rights and protections under the FIPA: China FIPA, article 4 (fair and equitable treatment/ full protection and security), article 5 (no less favourable treatment than is received by third-country investors), article 6 (no less favourable treatment than is received by domestic investors), article 9 (freedom from local content requirements), article 10 (compensation for direct or indirect expropriation), and article 12 (money transfers).

Awards against a country facing financial crisis, unemployment, new health or environmental threats, or corruption: e.g. *BG Group v Argentina*, Decision, December 24, 2007; *Compañía de Aguas del Aconquija & Vivendi v Argentina*, Decision, November 14, 2005, ICSID Case No. ARB/03/19; *SD Myers v Canada*, Decision, November 13, 2000, *International Legal Materials* 40 (2001): 1408; *Siemens v Argentina*, Decision, August 3, 2004, *International Legal Materials* 44 (2005): 138.

FIPA exceptions, reservations, and carve-outs: e.g. China FIPA, articles 8 and 33 and annexes B.8, B.10, and D.34.

Promoters stressing FIPA exceptions: e.g. John Ivison, "Canada's trade deal with China has opponents turning up the hysteria," *National Post*, November 1, 2012; Stephen Gordon, "Don't fear the FIPA," *Maclean's*, September 17, 2014.

Exceptions often do not extend to all foreign investor rights or all areas of regulation: e.g. China FIPA, articles 8 and 33 and annexes B.8, B.10, and D.34.

GATT exception for decisions "relating to the products of prison labour" not in FIPA: *General Agreement on Tariffs and Trade* (entered into force January 1, 1948) (Geneva: World Trade Organization, 1986), article XX(e). Compare the China FIPA, article 33(2).

Arbitrators interpreting "necessity" of exceptions strictly: CMS v Argentina, Decision, May 12, 2005, paras. 316-317, 329, and 331; *Enron v Argentina*, Decision, May 22, 2007, paras. 303-309 and 311-313; *Sempra v Argentina*, Decision, September 28, 2007, paras. 347-355 and 373-374.

Complex most-favoured-nation treatment loophole that undermines FIPA exceptions: Gus Van Harten, "The Canada-China FIPPA: Its Uniqueness and Non-Reciprocity," in *Canadian Yearbook of International Law*, eds. John Currie and René Provost (Vancouver: UBC Press, 2013): 27-34.

CHAPTER 16: THE PRICE TAG FOR DEMOCRACY

Jeremy Caddel and Nathan Jensen study: Jeremy Caddel and Nathan M. Jensen, "Which host country government actors are most involved in disputes with foreign investors?," *Columbia FDI Perspectives*, April 28, 2014.

My coding of 162 investment treaty cases: Gus Van Harten, *Sovereign Choices and Sovereign Constraints* (Oxford: Oxford University Press, 2013), 52-54; the data was posted on the Oxford University Press website for this book, accessed March 9, 2015, http://ukcatalogue.oup.com/product/9780199678648.do.

Misrepresentation of number of investment treaty lawsuits arising from legislative decisions: Christian Tietje, Freya Baetens, and Ecorys, *The Impact of Investor-State Dispute Settlement (ISDS) in the Transatlantic Trade and Investment Partnership*, Doc. no. MINBUZA-2014.78850, June 24, 2014, para. 83.

Investment treaty disputes involving environmental, health, resource, and economic decisions: Gus Van Harten, *Sovereign Choices and Sovereign Constraints* (Oxford: Oxford University Press, 2013), 9-15.

Negative reaction of arbitrators to democratic processes/ example of Tecmed v Mexico: Gus Van Harten, *Sovereign Choices and Sovereign Constraints* (Oxford: Oxford University Press, 2013), 68-76. *Tecmed v Mexico*, Decision, May 29, 2003, *International Legal Materials* 43 (2004): 133, paras. 41, 43, 106-110, 124-132, and 177.

CHAPTER 17: SETTLEMENTS OF LAWSUITS, KNOWN AND UNKNOWN

Secrecy in investor-state arbitration: Gus Van Harten, *Investment Treaty Arbitration and Public Law* (Oxford: Oxford University Press, 2007), 159-164; Gus Van Harten, "A total lack of transparency," *Canadian Lawyer*, October 24, 2011.

International Chamber of Commerce (ICC) arbitration rules and International Centre for Settlement of Investment Disputes (ICSID) arbitration rules: ICC, *Rules of Arbitration of the International Chamber of Commerce*, last revised January 1, 2012, accessed March 9, 2015, http://www.iccwbo.org/Products-and-Services/Arbitration-and-ADR/Arbitration/Rules-of-arbitration/Download-ICC-Rules-of-Arbitration/ICC-Rules-of-Arbitration-in-several-languages/;

ICSID, *Rules of Procedure for Arbitration Proceedings in ICSID*, last revised January 1, 2003, reprinted in *Convention, Regulations and Rules* (Washington: ICSID, 2003); *Rules Governing the Additional Facility for the Administration of Proceedings by the Secretariat of the International Centre for Settlement of Investment Disputes*, last revised January 1, 2003, *ICSID Reports* 1: 213.

Presumption of openness in courts: See Beverley McLachlin, "The Relationship Between the

Courts and the Media – Remarks of the Right Honourable Beverley McLachlin, P.C., Chief Justice of Canada", Carleton University, Ottawa, January 31, 2012.

Exposure of early NAFTA lawsuit against Canada: Report by a confidential source, interviewed for a research project on investment treaties and regulatory change. I elaborate on my blog, http://gusvanharten.wordpress.com/.

NAFTA case of St. Marys v Canada: St Marys v Canada, Claimant submission, May 13, 2011. My description of this case is based partly on a report by a confidential source who was interviewed for a research project on investment treaties and regulatory change, worked for a provincial government ministry, and was involved in the case. I elaborate on my blog, http://gusvanharten.wordpress.com/.

Press releases on St. Marys v Canada settlement: Foreign Affairs, Trade, and Development Canada, "Foreign Affairs and International Trade Canada Issues Statement on St Marys VCNA, LLC, Settlement," News release, March 8, 2013; St. Marys Cement, "Statement by John Moroz, Vice President and General Manager of St Marys Cement," News release, March 8, 2013; Ontario Ministry of Municipal Affairs and Housing, "Ontario Protects Hamilton Land," News release, March 8, 2013.

Ontario government settlements on cancelled power plants: Office of the Auditor General of Ontario, *Mississauga Power Plant Cancellation Costs*, Special Report (Toronto: Queen's Printer for Ontario, 2013); Office of the Auditor General of Ontario, *Oakville Power Plant Cancellation Costs*, Special Report (Toronto: Queen's Printer, 2013).

Proposed deals that would almost completely lock Canada into investor-state arbitration: The other key deals are the Canada-E.U. Comprehensive Economic and Trade Agreement (CETA) and the U.S.-led Trans-Pacific Partnership (TPP).

Constitutional interest of provinces: Mark A. Luz and C. Marc Miller, "Globalization and Canadian Federalism: Implications of the NAFTA's Investment Rules," *McGill Law Journal* 47 (2002): 951; Gus Van Harten, "What if the Canada-China investment treaty is unconstitutional?," *Globe and Mail*, October 23, 2012.

CHAPTER 18: AN EXAMPLE OF REGULATORY CHILL

NAFTA case of Ethyl v Canada: Ethyl v Canada, *International Legal Materials* 38 (1999): 78. My description of the case is based on a review of contemporary press coverage. e.g. Randall Palmer, "Coalition calls for ban on additive MMT," *Calgary Herald*, September 19, 1996; Scott Feschuk, "Marchi advocates ban on MMT," *Globe and Mail*, September 26, 1996; Greg Keenan, "Car dealers join fight to ban gas additive MMT," *Globe and Mail*, September 27, 1996; Bryant Avery, "MMT not an issue in U.S.," *Edmonton Journal*, November 22, 1996; Alan Boras, "Ethyl fights ban on MMT," *Calgary Herald*, January 22, 1997.

Canada's Agreement on Internal Trade: Agreement on Internal Trade, Consolidated Version, 2015 (entered into force July 1, 2005), Internal Trade Secretariat website, accessed March 9, 2015, http://www.ait-aci.ca/en/ait/ait_en.pdf.

Ethyl v Canada settlement and Agreement on Internal Trade panel decision: Andrew Duffy, "Canada drops ban on gas additive: MMT now permitted," *Ottawa Citizen*, July 21, 1998; Ken Traynor, "How Canada Became a Shill for Ethyl Corporation," *Intervenor (Canadian Environmental Law Association)* 23 (1998): 3; Graeme Fletcher, "U.S. bans it; Canada burns it," *National Post*, September 6, 2002. Agreement on Internal Trade, *Report of the Article 1704 Panel Concerning the Dispute Between Alberta and Canada Regarding the Manganese-Based Fuel*

Additives Act, June 12, 1998, International Trade Secretariat website, accessed March 9, 2015, http://www.ait-aci.ca/index_en/dispute.htm.

Eventual phase-out of MMT in Canada: Katherine Blumberg and Michael P. Walsh, *Status Report Concerning the Use of MMT in Gasoline* (International Council on Clean Transportation, September 2004), 8.

Summary on investment treaties and regulatory chill: This is a tentative summary of findings in an ongoing research project on investment treaties and regulatory change, based on about 45 interviews with confidential sources familiar with government decision-making, on access-to-information requests, and on media reports.

Misrepresentation of Ethyl v Canada settlement: Christian Tietje, Freya Baetens, and Ecorys, *The Impact of Investor-State Dispute Settlement (ISDS) in the Transatlantic Trade and Investment Partnership*, Doc. no. MINBUZA-2014.78850, June 24, 2014, paras. 169-170. I elaborate on the inaccuracies in this report on my blog, http://gusvanharten.wordpress.com/.

CHAPTER 19: OUTCOMES OF LAWSUITS

Data on known investment treaty lawsuits: I rely on my own database of investment treaty cases and on United Nations Conference on Trade and Development (UNCTAD), *International Investment Agreements Issues Note – Recent Trends in IIAs and ISDS* (Geneva: UNCTAD, February 2015).

High costs for lawyers and arbitrators: Diana Rosert, *The Stakes Are High: A review of the financial costs of investment treaty arbitration* (Winnipeg: International Institute for Sustainable Development, July 2014).

Extremely limited role for counter-claims by countries: Jean E. Kalicki, "Counterclaims by States in Investment Arbitration," *Investment Treaty News Quarterly* 3, no. 2 (2013).

Ethyl claim for USD$251 million: *Ethyl v Canada*, Claimant submission, October 2, 1997, 13.

Inherent favouritism of investment treaties toward foreign investors: Gus Van Harten, *Sovereign Choices and Sovereign Constraints* (Oxford: Oxford University Press, 2013), 163-164.

CHAPTER 20: WHAT IF IT WAS A JUDICIAL PROCESS?

Arbitrators allowing most cases to go ahead, often when dispute overlapped with a contractually agreed upon forum: Gus Van Harten, *Sovereign Choices and Sovereign Constraints* (Oxford: Oxford University Press, 2013), 125-154; Gus Van Harten, "The Boom in Parallel Claims in Investment Treaty Arbitration," *Investment Treaty News Quarterly* 5, no. 1 (2014).

Tendency of arbitrators to resolve ambiguous legal issues in ways that encourage litigation: Gus Van Harten, "Arbitrator Behaviour in Asymmetrical Adjudication: An Empirical Study of Investment Treaty Arbitration," *Osgoode Hall Law Journal* 50 (2012): 211.

Role of Yves Fortier as repeat player among the arbitrators: In the coding for the *Osgoode Hall Law Journal* study mentioned immediately above, it emerged that Fortier was the most active arbitrator in the resolution of contested jurisdictional issues.

First example of Fortier tribunal: *Compañia de Aguas del Aconquija & Vivendi v Argentina*, Annulment decision, July 3, 2002, *International Legal Materials* 41 (2002): 1135. See Gus Van Harten, *Sovereign Choices and Sovereign Constraints* (Oxford: Oxford University Press, 2013), 136-143.

Second example of Fortier tribunal: Occidental v Ecuador (no. 2), Decision, September 9, 2008, ICSID Case No. ARB/06/11.

Third example of Fortier tribunal: Yukos Universal v. Russia, Decision, July 18, 2014, paras. 1847, 1860-1863, 1874, and 1887. This decision and the other two decisions by the tribunal in the same case, on the same date, are available on the Permanent Court of Arbitration website, accessed March 9, 2015, http://www.pca-cpa.org/showpage.asp?pag_id=1599.

Preclusion or limitation of judicial review of investment treaty awards: Gus Van Harten, *Investment Treaty Arbitration and Public Law* (Oxford: Oxford University Press, 2007), 154-158.

European Court of Human Rights ruling on Yukos v Russia dispute: European Court of Human Rights, *Case of OAO Neftyanaya Kompaniya Yukos v Russia*, Decision, July 31, 2014, ECHR website, accessed March 9, 2015,
http://hudoc.echr.coe.int/sites/eng/pages/search.aspx?i=001-145730.

CHAPTER 21: THE ROLLER COASTER CONTINUES

Philip Morris lawsuits against Australia and Uruguay: Philip Morris v Australia, Claimant submission, November 21, 2011; *Philip Morris v Uruguay*, Decision, July 2, 2013, ICSID Case No. ARB/10/7.

Bloomberg Foundation funding of Uruguay defence: Luke E. Peterson, "Uruguay hires law firm and secures outside funding to defend against Philip Morris claim," *Investment Arbitration Reporter*, October 20, 2010.

Withdrawal of proposed plain packaging law in Canada and apparent delays of similar laws in other countries: David Schneiderman, *Constitutionalizing Economic Globalization* (Cambridge: Cambridge University Press, 2008), chapter 4. Tariana Turia, "Government moves forward with plain packaging of tobacco products," News release (New Zealand Government), February 19, 2013; Michael Safi, "Big Tobacco's Lawsuits of Mass Destruction," *Global Mail*, December 2, 2013.

Roughly 2500 investment treaties now in force: United Nations Conference on Trade and Development (UNCTAD) Investment Policy Hub website, accessed March 9, 2015, http://investmentpolicyhub.unctad.org/IIA.

Limited coverage of investment treaty arbitration at present/ more than half of cases brought under just 17 treaties: I elaborate on my blog, http://gusvanharten.wordpress.com/.

Other deals locking Canada into investment treaty arbitration: For 20 years, Canada has been the Western developed country whose economy is most subject to investor-state arbitration, due to the amount of U.S.-owned assets in Canada covered by NAFTA. Canada's submission to investor-state arbitration expanded significantly with the China FIPA and would expand further with the Canada-E.U. Comprehensive Economic and Trade Agreement (CETA) and the U.S.-led Trans-Pacific Partnership (TPP).

CHAPTER 22: THE FIPA AND THE COURTS

USD$35 million order against Czech Republic: Eastern Sugar v Czech Republic, Decision, March 27, 2007, paras. 297-314.

Example of Eli Lilly v Canada/ annual revenue of Eli Lilly: Eli Lilly v Canada, Claimant submission, June 13, 2013, paras. 37 and 43. See also *Eli Lilly v Canada*, Claimant submissions, September 12, 2013 and September 29, 2014. Eli Lilly and Company reported about USD$23.1

billion in revenue for 2013: Eli Lilly website, accessed March 9, 2015, https://investor.lilly.com/annuals.cfm.

Special right of foreign investors to sue without going to a country's courts: Gus Van Harten, *Investment Treaty Arbitration and Public Law* (Oxford: Oxford University Press, 2007), 110-113.

Only a handful of other treaties allow private lawsuits against sovereign countries before an international tribunal with binding and enforceable powers: Gus Van Harten, *Investment Treaty Arbitration and Public Law* (Oxford: Oxford University Press, 2007), chapter 5.

John Manley quotes: John Manley, "We need not fear the FIPA," *Ottawa Citizen*, November 9, 2012.

Corporate members of Canadian Council of Chief Executives whose parent companies benefited from investor-state arbitration: e.g. *Chevron v Ecuador*, Decision, March 30, 2010, *World Trade and Arbitration Materials* 22, no. 3 (2010): 455; *Cargill v Mexico*, Decision, September 6, 2010, ICSID Case No. ARB(AF)/04/2; *Chevron v Ecuador*, Decision, February 27, 2012.

Dow lawsuit under NAFTA after Quebec banned chemical pesticide: *Dow AgroSciences v Canada*, Claimant submission, March 31, 2009; *Dow AgroSciences v Canada*, Settlement, May 25, 2011.

Federal government's description of Dow settlement as a win: Foreign Affairs, Trade and Development Canada, "Canada Welcomes Agreement with Dow AgroSciences," News release, May 27, 2011.

Chief Justices Margaret Marshall and Ronald George quotes: Adam Liptak, "Review of U.S. Rulings by Nafta Tribunals Stirs Worries," *New York Times*, April 18, 2004.

South Korea Supreme Court quote and South Korean judges' statement: Jung Eun-joo, "Supreme Court recommends renegotiation of ISD clause," *Hankyoreh*, April 26, 2012.

U.S. Supreme Court decision and Chief Justice John Roberts quote: *BG Group PLC v Republic of Argentina*, Decision of the U.S. Supreme Court, March 5, 2014.

Intervention in U.S. Supreme Court case by members of investor-state legal industry: *BG Group PLC v Republic of Argentina*, "Brief of Amici Curiae Professors and Practitioners of Arbitration Law in Support of Reversal," August 30, 2013.

Chief Justice Robert French quotes: R.S. French, "Investor-State Dispute Settlement – A Cut Above the Courts?," Presentation to the Supreme and Federal Courts Judges' Conference, July 9, 2014.

NAFTA-related cases before Canadian courts: e.g. *Canada (Attorney General)* v. *SD Myers*, [2004] 3 FCR 368 (Federal Court of Canada); *United Mexican States v Marvin Roy Feldman Karpa* (2005), 248 DLR (4th) 443 (Ontario Court of Appeal); *Council of Canadians v Canada (Attorney General)* (2006), 2006 CanLII 40222 (Ontario Court of Appeal).

Recent decision on duty to consult with aboriginal peoples: *Tsilhqot'in Nation v British Columbia*, [2014] 2 SCR 256 (Supreme Court of Canada).

Three-year limitation period for Chinese investor to challenge Canadian court decision: China FIPA, article 21(2)(f).

CHAPTER 23: THE LEGAL CHALLENGE TO THE FIPA, PART ONE

Constitutional challenge to ratification of the FIPA and Federal Court of Canada decisions: *Hupacasath v Minister of Foreign Affairs*, Notice of Application, January 18, 2013; *Hupacasath v Minister of Foreign Affairs*, Memorandum of Fact and Law of the Applicant, April 29, 2013. *Hupacasath First Nation v Canada (Foreign Affairs)* (2013), 2013 FC 900 (CanLII), paras. 22, 26, and 134.

Quote by spokesperson for trade minister: Dene Moore, "Canada-China FIPA Challenge By Hupacasath First Nation Rejected," *Canadian Press*, August 27, 2013 (quoting Rudy Husny).

Legal test of "possible" adverse impact on aboriginal rights: A key issue in the case was whether the FIPA's ratification would have "possible" and not "merely speculative" adverse impacts for the Hupacasath First Nation. *Hupacasath First Nation v Canada (Attorney General)* (2015), 2015 FCA 4 (CanLII), para. 86.

My expert opinion on international investment law: *Hupacasath v Minister of Foreign Affairs*, Affidavit of Gus Van Harten, February 13, 2013, 2, 13-14, and 19.

CHAPTER 24: THE LEGAL CHALLENGE TO THE FIPA, PART TWO

Government expert J. Christopher Thomas' expert opinion on international investment law: *Hupacasath v Minister of Foreign Affairs*, Affidavit of J. Christopher Thomas, March 13, 2013, paras. 57 and 119.

Judge preferred government expert on all issues: The judge stated that he "generally accepted [Thomas'] evidence over Mr Van Harten's when they did not agree" but, in his judgment, did not rely on any statement in my opinion, with the possible minor exception of the point that investor-state arbitrators also work as investor-state lawyers. *Hupacasath First Nation v Canada (Foreign Affairs)* (2013), 2013 FC 900 (CanLII), paras. 42, 86, and 100.

Reliance by judge on government expert's misleading portrayal: The most important examples are in *Hupacasath First Nation v Canada (Foreign Affairs)* (2013), 2013 FC 900 (CanLII), paras. 73, 95, 129, and 134. I elaborate on my blog, http://gusvanharten.wordpress.com/.

Government expert's selective reference to cases: J. Christopher Thomas' opinion focused on a few NAFTA cases that are exceptionally country (usually U.S.)-friendly. He put special emphasis on *Glamis v U.S.*, mentioning it nine times in his expert opinion. Because of its handling of fair and equitable treatment, however, *Glamis* is probably the single most country-friendly decision under NAFTA and arguably the most country-friendly tribunal decision under any investment treaty. I elaborate on my blog, http://gusvanharten.wordpress.com/.

My opinion based on systematic study: *Hupacasath v Minister of Foreign Affairs*, Affidavit of Gus Van Harten, February 13, 2013, 2.

Appeals court deferred to judge's factual findings and agreed with his conclusions: *Hupacasath First Nation v Canada (Attorney General)* (2015), 2015 FCA 4 (CanLII), especially paras. 18, 74-78, 89, 101-102, 108, and 115-118.

Appeals court said Canadian courts can put aboriginal rights ahead of FIPA in future: *Hupacasath First Nation v Canada (Attorney General)* (2015), 2015 FCA 4 (CanLII), especially paras. 103-104.

Some modern treaty rights of First Nations are subject to Canada's international obligations: e.g. *Tsawwassen First Nation Final Agreement* (between the federal government, the Tsawwassen

First Nation, and the British Columbia government), Aboriginal Affairs and Northern Development Canada website, accessed March 9, 2015, https://www.aadnc-aandc.gc.ca/eng/1100100022706/1100100022717.

Brief mention by appeals court that FIPA was ratified while appeal was pending: Hupacasath First Nation v Canada (*Attorney General*) (2015), 2015 FCA 4 (CanLII), para. 28.

CHAPTER 25: A REPLY TO THE CHARGES OF BIAS, PART ONE

Open letter to Prime Minister Harper: This was sent on 16 October 2012. It remains available on *The Tyee* website, for example, and I have posted it on my blog, http://gusvanharten.wordpress.com/.

Investigation of my personal history of political donations: This occurred at the House of Commons trade committee's meeting on 27 March 2013. Canada, Parliament, House of Commons Standing Committee on International Trade, *Evidence*, 1st Sess., 41st Parliament, Meeting no. 70, March 27, 2013, Parliament of Canada website, accessed March 12, 2015, http://www.parl.gc.ca/HousePublications/Publication.aspx?-DocId=6069885&Language=E&Mode=1&Parl=41&Ses=1.

Denunciation in Parliament of questioning on political donations: Canada, *House of Commons Debates*, No. 231, Vol. 146, 1st Sess., 41st Parliament, March 28, 2013 (Wayne Easter, Liberal, and Don Davies, NDP), Parliament of Canada website, accessed March 12, 2015, http://www.parl.gc.ca/HousePublications/Publication.aspx?Language=E&Mode=1&Parl=41&Ses=1&DocId=6072129.

Chief Justice Crampton quote dismissing my expert opinion: Hupacasath First Nation v Canada (*Foreign Affairs*) (2013), 2013 FC 900 (CanLII), paras. 37-38 and 42.

Federal government argument that I was partial because I previously criticized investor-state arbitration and the China FIPA before my appointment as an expert: Chief Justice Crampton did not explain in his judgment why he thought that I was partial. He referred instead to the federal government's submission on this issue. I reproduce the government's submission and relevant evidence from my cross-examination on my blog, http://gusvanharten.wordpress.com/.

Government expert's previous criticism of investor-state arbitration: Hupacasath v Minister of Foreign Affairs, Cross-Examination on Affidavit of John Christopher Thomas, April 5, 2013, 30-33.

Certification that I would assist the court impartially: Hupacasath v Minister of Foreign Affairs, Certificate of Gus Van Harten concerning Code of Conduct for Expert Witnesses, February 13, 2013; *Federal Courts Rules* (SOR/98-106), Schedule (Rule 52.2), Code of Conduct for Expert Witnesses.

CHAPTER 26: A REPLY TO THE CHARGES OF BIAS, PART TWO

Appointment and promotion of Mr. Paul Crampton: The Harper Cabinet appointed Mr. Crampton to the Federal Court on November 26, 2009 and made him chief justice of that court on December 15, 2011. He was previously a partner at Osler, Harkin & Harcourt from 2004 to 2009 and at Davies, Ward, Phillips and Vineberg from 1992 to 2002, where he worked on takeovers of Canadian companies. His biographical statement is available on the Federal Court website, accessed March 9, 2015, http://cas-ncr-nter03.cas-satj.gc.ca/portal/page/portal/fc_cf_en/Crampton.

Mr. Crampton's reported past donations to Conservative Party: Janice Tibbetts and Glen McGregor, "Dozens of judges appointed by Tories also donated money to Conservative party," *Ottawa Citizen*, March 2, 2010.

Mr. Crampton's past work on Investment Canada Act deals: e.g. Jim Middlemiss, "Competition lawyer Paul Crampton moves to the federal bench," *National Post*, December 2, 2009.

Mr. Crampton previous criticism of Canadian foreign investment law: Paul Crampton, "A critical step forward," *Globe and Mail*, July 2, 2008). See also Janet McFarland, "The Americanization of Canada's Competition Act," *Globe and Mail* February 11, 2009.

Chief Justice Crampton's authority over case assignment: The chief justice of a court in Canada conventionally has final authority over the assignment of individual cases to judges on the court. e.g. *Courts of Justice Act*, RSO 1990, c. C.43, sections 14(1) and 75(1); *Federal Courts Act*, RSC 1985, c. F-7, sections 14(3) and 15(2).

Evident political sensitivity of the constitutional challenge to the FIPA's ratification: e.g. Les Whittington, "First Nations seek to hold up ratification of Canada-China foreign investment treaty," *Toronto Star*, January 3, 2013; "B.C. First Nation asks court to block Canada-China deal," *Canadian Press*, January 22, 2013.

Chief Justice Crampton's statement that I did not provide examples to prove MFN treatment loophole: Hupacasath First Nation v Canada (Foreign Affairs) (2013), 2013 FC 900 (CanLII), paras. 100 and 104. I elaborate on the MFN treatment loophole in Gus Van Harten, "The Canada-China FIPPA: Its Uniqueness and Non-Reciprocity," in *Canadian Yearbook of International Law*, eds. John Currie and René Provost (Vancouver: UBC Press, 2013): 27-34. See also my blog, http://gusvanharten.wordpress.com/.

Hupacasath First Nation argument that I, unlike the government expert, refused paid work in investor-state arbitration to maintain claim of objectivity: Hupacasath v Minister of Foreign Affairs, Reply of the Applicant, May 28, 2013, para. 45.

My disclosure of previous criticism in my expert opinion: Hupacasath v Minister of Foreign Affairs, Affidavit of Gus Van Harten, February 13, 2013, 3-4.

Canadian Judicial Council quote: Canadian Judicial Council, *Ethical Principles for Judges*, "Impartiality" (Comment A.4), CJC website, accessed March 9, 2015, http://www.cjc-ccm.gc.ca/cmslib/general/news_pub_judicialconduct_Principles_en.pdf.

Investor-state lawyer's cutting and pasting of excerpt from judgment: Email of December 3, 2013 on fee-based mailing list called OGEMID [on file with author].

CHAPTER 27: THE FIPA MEDIA BLITZ

Government promotion of FIPA and Globe and Mail editors quote: e.g. Prime Minister Harper, "PM announces agreement that will facilitate investment flows between Canada and China," News release, February 8, 2012; "In China, a leap forward by Canada," *Globe and Mail*, February 8, 2012.

Stockwell Day interview: The Agenda with Steve Paikin, "Stockwell Day: Canada's Dance with China" *TV Ontario*, December 3, 2012, TVO website, accessed March 9, 2015, http://tvo.org/video/185840/stockwell-day-canadas-dance-china.

Paul Wells opinion article and Globe and Mail article: Paul Wells, "Canada-China investment: Big risk in the fine print," *Maclean's*, September 27, 2012; Bill Curry and Shawn McCarthy, "Tories quietly table Canada-China investment treaty," *Globe and Mail*, September 27, 2012.

Government announcement that FIPA would be ratified after 21 sitting days in Parliament: Prime Minister of Canada, "Canada-China Foreign Investment Promotion and Protection Agreement (FIPA)," News release, September 8, 2012.

My opinion articles: e.g. "Canada-China investment deal allows for confidential lawsuits against Canada," *Toronto Star*, September 29, 2012; "Why rush Canada-China investment deal?," *Calgary Sun*, October 16, 2012; "Canadians blindly submitting to harmful Canada-China treaty," *Sudbury Star*, October 30, 2012; "FIPA: It's just not a very good deal," *New Brunswick Telegraph-Journal*, November 20, 2012; "Early Christmas present for Chinese government," *Winnipeg Sun*, December 11, 2012; "What if the Canada-China investment treaty is unconstitutional?," *Globe and Mail*, October 22, 2012.

Open letter to Prime Minister Harper: This was sent on 16 October 2012. It remains available on *The Tyee* website, for example, and I have posted it on my blog, http://gusvanharten.wordpress.com/.

Other commentators who raised concerns: Lawrence Martin, "Why aren't we debating the Canada China investment pact?," *Globe and Mail*, October 23, 2012; Michael Den Tandt, "Conservative plan would tie Canada to China in hush-hush elopement," *National Post*, October 22, 2012; Diane Francis, "Canada-China trade deal is too one-sided," *Financial Post*, November 2, 2012; Rick Mercer, Rick Mercer Report, "Rick's Rant – China Trade Agreement," *CBC Television*, November 7, 2012.

CHAPTER 28: ANDREW COYNE, PART ONE

Andrew Coyne opinion article attacking Sergio Marchi: Andrew Coyne, "Trade Tempest," *National Post*, June 21, 1999.

Andrew Coyne on The National's At Issue panel: The National, "Canada's Relationship with China," *CBC Television*, October 31, 2012, CBC website, accessed March 9, 2015, http://www.cbc.ca/player/News/TV+Shows/The+National/At+Issue/ID/2298905631/.

CHAPTER 29: JOHN IVISON

John Ivison opinion article: John Ivison, "Canada's trade deal with China has opponents turning up the hysteria," *National Post*, November 1, 2012.

Ability of Chinese companies to sue Canada for provincial, territorial, and municipal decisions: This is not a controversial point; see the notes for chapter 9.

Arbitrators award compensation for foreign investors' lost profits: This is not a controversial point; it is common for investor-state arbitrators to award compensation for a foreign investor's economic loss including reasonably-expected lost profits. Sergey Ripinsky and Kevin Williams, *Damages in International Investment Law* (London: British Institute of International and Comparative Law, 2008), chapter 7.

FIPA does not require discrimination to establish a violation: This is not a controversial point. e.g. Roland Kläger, 'Fair and Equitable Treatment' in International Investment Law (Cambridge: Cambridge University Press, 2011), 304.

Simon Lester quote: Simon Lester, "How Not to Defend ISDS," *International Economic Law and Policy Blog*, September 17, 2014, http://worldtradelaw.typepad.com/ielpblog/2014/09/how-not-to-defend-isds.html.

Andrew Coyne (first) opinion article: Andrew Coyne, "Despite near-suicidal wailing over China trade pact, it's no big deal," *National Post*, November 2, 2012. Coyne's article also ran in the *Edmonton Journal, Montreal Gazette, Ottawa Citizen, Regina Leader Post, Saskatoon Star-Phoenix, Windsor Star*, and *Victoria Times Colonist*.

Major transformation of international law marked by investment treaties: Gus Van Harten, *Investment Treaty Arbitration and Public Law* (Oxford: Oxford University Press, 2007), chapter 5.

China began to open up its outbound investment only in 1999: This is the year that China adopted its Going Out strategy, which began the liberalization of China's outward investment flows. The liberalization process is ongoing, suggesting that China's purchases of major assets in Canada over the last five years may be the beginning. Joe Zhang, "China's New Outward Investment Measures: Going Global in a Sustainable Way?," *Investment Treaty News Quarterly* 5, no. 4 (2014).

TRIMs Agreement: Agreement on Trade-Related Investment Measures, April 15, 1994, Marrakesh Agreement Establishing the World Trade Organization, Annex IA, *Final Act Embodying the Results of the Uruguay Round of Multilateral Trade Negotiations* (1994), 1868 United Nations Treaty Series 186 (entered into force 1 January 1995) 139 (TRIMS Agreement).

"Fair" compensation in historical debates about international law on expropriation: Investment treaties tend to adopt the more aggressive Hull standard of compensation, historically supported by capital-exporting countries, instead of alternative standards supported by newly independent countries. Resolution on Permanent Sovereignty Over Natural Resources, General Assembly Res. 1803, UN GAOR, 17th Sess., Supp no. 17, UN Doc A/5217 (1962) 15, article 4; Frank G. Dawson and Burns H. Weston, "'Prompt, Adequate and Effective': A Universal Standard of Compensation?," *Fordham Law Review* 30 (1962): Article 4.

Canadian expropriation law compared to NAFTA (and the FIPA): Raymond E. Young, "A Canadian Commentary on Constructive Expropriation Law Under NAFTA Article 1110," *Alberta Law Review* 43 (2006): 1001.

Many arbitrators have decided that a merely substantial or significant reduction triggers duty of full compensation for indirect expropriation: I elaborate on my blog, http://gusvanharten.wordpress.com/.

Performance requirements prohibit a country from requiring foreign investors to use local materials and suppliers: e.g. *Canada – Certain Measures Affecting the Renewable Energy Generation Sector/ Canada – Measures Relating to the Feed-In Tariff Program* (2013), WTO Docs WT/DS412/AB/ R, WT/DS426/AB/R, para. 5.6 (Reports of the Appellate Body).

NAFTA prohibition on performance requirements: NAFTA, article 1106.

Andrew Coyne (second) opinion article and response from me: Andrew Coyne, "What does Canada's investment deal with China actually say?," *National Post*, November 5, 2012; Gus Van Harten, "Don't be fooled by the spin on the Canada-China treaty," *Troy Media*, November 7, 2012.

CHAPTER 31: MILOS BARUTCISKI AND MATTHEW KRONBY, PART ONE

Milos Barutciski and Matthew Kronby opinion article: Milos Barutciski and Matthew Kronby, "Investment agreement with China will benefit Canada," *Globe and Mail*, November 2, 2012.

Barutciski and Kronby, and their firm, apparently positioned to profit from FIPA: I say this because, as providers of investor-state legal services, they apparently stood to earn income from the demand of foreign investors or governments for legal advice due to the new litigation opportunities and public liabilities created by the FIPA's entry into force.

David Schneiderman and Gus Van Harten opinion article: David Schneiderman and Gus Van Harten, "Self-interested lawyers and the Canada-China FIPA," *Toronto Star*, November 25, 2012.

NAFTA case of AbitibiBowater v Canada: I elaborate on my blog, http://gusvanharten.wordpress.com/.

CHAPTER 32: MILOS BARUTCISKI AND MATTHEW KRONBY, PART TWO

Milos Barutciski and Matthew Kronby opinion article: Milos Barutciski and Matthew Kronby, "Investment agreement with China will benefit Canada," *Globe and Mail*, November 2, 2012.

Milos Barutciski listed as top lawyer for NAFTA lawsuit: Lone Pine Resources v Canada, Claimant submission, November 8, 2012, 17.

McCarthy Tétrault overview of the FIPA: John W. Boscariol et al., "A Primer on the New China-Canada Bilateral Investment Treaty," October 4, 2012, McCarthy Tétrault website, accessed March 9, 2015, http://www.mccarthy.ca/article_detail.aspx?id=6023.

Goodmans update on the FIPA: "Canada-China Agreement to Promote and Protect Reciprocal Investment Coming into Force" *Goodmans Update*, September 16, 2014. See also e.g. Susan Hutton and Erin Dand, "The Canada-China FIPA: Energizing Canadian oil & gas investment in China," *The Competitor*, September 24, 2014.

CHAPTER 33: THE TRADE SPECIALISTS

Andrew Coyne quote: Andrew Coyne, "Despite near-suicidal wailing over China trade pact, it's no big deal," *National Post*, November 2, 2012.

Academic statements criticizing investment treaty arbitration in 2010 and 2014: "Public Statement on the International Investment Regime," August 31, 2010, Osgoode Hall Law School website, accessed March 9, 2015, http://www.osgoode.yorku.ca/public-statement-international-investment-regime-31-august-2010/; "Statement of Concern about Planned Provisions on Investment Protection and Investor-State Dispute Settlement (ISDS) in the Transatlantic Trade and Investment Partnership (TTIP)," July 17, 2014, University of Kent website, accessed March 9, 2015, http://www.kent.ac.uk/brussels/news/?view=1734.

CHAPTER 34: LAWRENCE HERMAN

Globe and Mail editorial: "In China, a leap forward by Canada," *Globe and Mail*, February 8, 2012.

Example of inaccurate paraphrasing in my own case: Shawn McCarthy, "Free trade with China still a decade away, Mulroney says," *Globe and Mail*, October 3, 2012 (statement that I "said the [FIPA] signed by Mr. Harper is one-sided because it only protects investors currently operating in the other country"). This paraphrase was not accurate if one reads it to mean the FIPA does not protect future foreign investors. The intended point was that the FIPA does not provide for market access by Canadian investors.

Larry Herman and Daniel Schwanen opinion article: Larry Herman and Daniel Schwanen, "China investment: Deal a big step forward," *Financial Post*, October 26, 2012.

China-U.S. investment treaty negotiations: Vicki Needham, "U.S., China still talking on investment treaty," *The Hill*, November 10, 2014.

FIPA arbitrators can order compensation for Canadian tax measures on grounds of indirect expropriation unless China agrees otherwise: China FIPA, articles 10 and 14(4) and (5).

FIPA arbitrators can order compensation for Canadian environmental regulations, with limited exceptions: China FIPA, article 33(2).

FIPA moderating language on indirect expropriation: China FIPA, annex B.10. One limitation of this moderating language is the MFN treatment loophole that I discuss on my blog, http://gusvanharten.wordpress.com/.

China-Germany investment treaty: Agreement between the People's Republic of China and the Federal Republic of Germany on the Encouragement and Reciprocal Protection of Investments (signed December 1, 2003), article 15.

Germany and China, unlike Canada, have not given market access rights to foreign investors: Marie France Houde, "Novel Features in Recent OECD Bilateral Investment Treaties," in *International Investment Perspectives* (Paris: Organisation for Economic Cooperation and Development, 2006), 151-152.

Minimum terms and survival clauses in FIPAs: The minimum terms, if any, and the survival clauses in Canada's FIPA are outlined on my blog, http://gusvanharten.wordpress.com/.

Barrick Gold's mine in Tanzania: Geoffrey York, "Deadly clashes continue at African Barrick gold mine," *Globe and Mail*, August 26, 2014.

John Baird's hiring by Barrick Gold and Richard Li: Kristy Kirkup, "John Baird, ex-foreign affairs minister, to advise Barrick Gold," *CBC News*, March 28, 2015; Steven Chase, "John Baird lands yet another job as adviser to Hong Kong billionaire," *Globe and Mail*, April 2, 2015.

Larry Herman opinion article after FIPA was ratified: Larry Herman, "China investment treaty no sell-out," *Financial Post*, October 2, 2014).

Acknowledgment of independence issues in investor-state arbitration: David Gaukrodger and Kathryn Gordon, "Investor-State Dispute Settlement: A Scoping Paper for the Investment Policy Community," *OECD Working Paper on International Investment 2012/03* (Paris: Organisation for Economic Cooperation and Development, 2012); European Commission, "Public consultation on modalities for investment protection and ISDS in TTIP," undated, European Union website, accessed March 9, 2015, http://trade.ec.europa.eu/doclib/docs/2014/march/tradoc_152280.pdf.

Herman got his numbers wrong: He said there was only one registered arbitration claim by a Chinese investor, when there were at least three to that point. Besides the claim against Belgium which Herman mentioned, there was *China Heilongjiang v Mongolia*, documents not public, noted on Permanent Court of Arbitration website, accessed March 10, 2015, http://www.pca-cpa.org/showpage.asp?pag_id=1378; and *Tza Yap Shum v Peru*, Decision, July 7, 2011, ICSID Case No. ARB/07/6.

CHAPTER 35: A LEFT-WING HOBBY HORSE?

The Economist, Cato Institute, Marine Le Pen, and Australian Productivity Commission quotes: "Investor-state dispute settlement: The arbitration game," *The Economist*, October 11, 2014; Daniel J. Ikenson, "A Compromise to Advance the Trade Agenda: Purge Negotiations of Investor-State Dispute Settlement," *Cato Institute Free Trade Bulletin* no. 57, March 4, 2014; C. Willy, "Final EU-Canada trade text includes transnational investment courts," *dpa Insight*, December 15, 2014; Australian Productivity Commission, *Bilateral and Regional Trade Agreements* (Canberra: APC, 2010), 276-277.

CHAPTER 36: THE GOVERNMENT'S SPIN, PART ONE

Prime Minister Harper quote and backgrounder on signing of FIPA: Prime Minister of Canada, "Canada-China Foreign Investment Promotion and Protection Agreement (FIPA)," News release, September 8, 2012; Prime Minister's Office, "Canada-China Foreign Investment Promotion and Protection Agreement (FIPA)," Backgrounder, September 8, 2012.

Charles Burton quote: Mark MacKinnon, "PM lands investor protection deal, raises human rights in China," *Globe and Mail*, February 8, 2012.

Blake Richards answers and my replies: Gus Van Harten, "Taking apart Tories' Party Line on China-Canada Treaty," *The Tyee*, November 5, 2012.

Australian Productivity Commission quote and Australian government positions on investor-state arbitration: Australian Productivity Commission, *Bilateral and Regional Trade Agreements* (Canberra: APC, 2010), 276-277 and 285; Department of Foreign Affairs and Trade (Australia), *Gillard Government Trade Policy Statement: Trading our way to more jobs and prosperity* (DFAT, April 2011); Mike Seccombe, "Abbott: Open for Business – and Multinational Lawsuits," *Global Mail*, September 20, 2013.

CHAPTER 37: THE GOVERNMENT'S SPIN, PART TWO

Conservatives blocking study and debate on the FIPA: The Conservatives did not allocate time to debate the FIPA in Parliament and evidently used their majority to frustrate a study or debate of the FIPA in the House of Commons trade committee, beyond a short briefing by federal trade officials. Canada, Parliament, House of Commons Standing Committee on International Trade, *Evidence*, 1st Sess., 41st Parliament, Meeting no. 70, 2012 (October 16 and 18), Parliament of Canada website, accessed March 12, 2015, http://www.parl.gc.ca/HousePublications/Publication.aspx?-DocId=5756675&Language=E&Mode=1&Parl=41&Ses=1 and http://www.parl.gc.ca/HousePublications/Publication.aspx?-DocId=5767586&Language=E&Mode=1&Parl=41&Ses=1.

Inaccurate or misleading claims by federal trade officials: Canada, Parliament, House of Commons Standing Committee on International Trade, *Evidence*, 1st Sess., 41st Parliament, Meeting no. 51, October 18, 2012, Parliament of Canada website, accessed April 6, 2015, http://www.parl.gc.ca/HousePublications/Publication.aspx?-DocId=5767586&Language=E&Mode=1&Parl=41&Ses=1. I elaborate on my blog, http://gusvanharten.wordpress.com/.

Wayne Easter questions and replies from trade officials: Canada, Parliament, House of Commons Standing Committee on International Trade, *Evidence*, 1st Sess., 41st Parliament, Meeting no. 51, October 18, 2012 – *Questions submitted to government officials through the Chair on behalf of the Liberal Party*; Department of Foreign Affairs and International Trade

(Canada), *Responses to Questions submitted through the Chair of the House of Commons Standing Committee on International Trade on behalf of the Liberal Party*, undated, received by author November 9, 2012. I have posted these documents on my blog, http://gusvanharten.wordpress.com/.

Wang Xinping quote: Jeff Lewis and Carrie Tait, "Canada's immigration policies hurt bottom line, China says," *Globe and Mail*, November 17, 2014.

CHAPTER 38: THE GOVERNMENT'S SPIN, PART THREE

Quote from federal trade official: *Hupacasath v Minister of Foreign Affairs*, Cross-Examination on Affidavit of Vernon John MacKay, April 3, 2013, 9. Mr. MacKay was Canada's lead negotiator of the China FIPA.

China FIPA departures from Canada's other treaties including narrower carve-out on aboriginal rights: Gus Van Harten, "The Canada-China FIPPA: Its Uniqueness and Non-Reciprocity," in *Canadian Yearbook of International Law*, eds. John Currie and René Provost (Vancouver: UBC Press, 2013): 3. China FIPA, annex B.8, which omits FIPA article 9 from the list of articles to which the annex B.8 reservations apply.

Prohibition on requirements for foreign investors to use local materials and suppliers: Davies Ward Phillips & Vineberg LLP, *Investment Canada Act – Guide for Foreign Investors in Canada* (undated), 16, Davies website, accessed March 9, 2015, http://www.dwpv.com/en/Resources/Publications/2013/Investment-Canada-Act-Guide-for-Foreign-Investors-in-Canada.

Opposition by multinational companies to performance requirements and U.S. pressure for other countries to give up performance requirements: e.g. Maria Isabel Studer Noguez, *Ford and the Global Strategies of Multinationals* (London: Routledge, 2001), 86; U.S. Trade Representative (USTR), *2014 National Trade Estimate Report on Foreign Trade Barriers* (Washington: USTR, 2014), 1-2. For Canada, the U.S. attained this goal primarily in NAFTA, article 1106.

Closure of plants in Canada due to U.S. multinational priorities and Buy America policy: Steve Arnold, "Does the former Stelco have a future in Hamilton?," *Hamilton Spectator*, February 4, 2012.

Evidence that performance requirements can benefit a country's economy/ "kicking away the ladder" phrase: e.g. Robert Wade, *Governing the Market: Economic Theory and the Role of Government in East Asian Industrialization* (Princeton: Princeton University Press, 2003). Ha-Joon Chang, *Kicking Away the Ladder: Development Strategy in Historical Perspective* (London: Anthem Press, 2003), borrowing the phrase from German economist Friedrich List.

FIPA prohibition on performance requirements and missing exception for aboriginal peoples: China FIPA, article 9 and annex B.8. Specifically, annex B.8 omits FIPA article 9 from the list of articles to which the annex's reservations apply.

Extension of expanded prohibition on performance requirements to U.S. investors: NAFTA has a most-favoured-nation treatment clause (article 1103) which entitles U.S. investors to no less favourable treatment than that received by Chinese investors in Canada.

FIPA incorporation of TRIMs obligations that prohibit local content requirements: The FIPA incorporates article 2 and the annex of the Agreement on Trade-Related Investment Measures, April 15, 1994, Marrakesh Agreement Establishing the World Trade Organization, Annex IA, *Final Act Embodying the Results of the Uruguay Round of Multilateral Trade Negotiations*

(1994), 1868 United Nations Treaty Series 186 (entered into force 1 January 1995) 139 (TRIMS Agreement).

Significance of transfer of WTO obligations into treaty that allows investor-state arbitration: Martin Molinuevo, *Protecting Investment in Services: Investor-State Arbitration Versus WTO Dispute Settlement* (Alphen aan den Rijn: Wolters Kluwer, 2012), 72-74 and 233-34; Simon Lester, "The Sad State of the Investor-State Debate," *Huffington Post*, October 22, 2014.

Federal government claim that reservations not needed because the FIPA reproduced TRIMS obligations: *Hupacasath v Minister of Foreign Affairs*, Affidavit of Vernon MacKay, March 13, 2013, paras. 42-43 and 49.

Divergence from standard carve-out in Canada's other treaties: Gus Van Harten, "The Canada-China FIPPA: Its Uniqueness and Non-Reciprocity," in *Canadian Yearbook of International Law*, eds. John Currie and René Provost (Vancouver: UBC Press, 2013): 36-40. e.g. NAFTA, annex II (Schedule of Canada – aboriginal affairs).

Impact and benefit agreements in Canada: Federal, Provincial and Territorial Social Licence Task Group, *Mining Sector Performance Report: 1998-2008* (Ottawa: Government of Canada, 2010), 27; Sandra Gogal, Richard Riegert, and Joann Jamieson, "Aboriginal Impact and Benefit Agreements: Practical Considerations," *Alberta Law Review* 43 (2005): 129; Courtney Fidler and Michael Hitch, "Impact and Benefit Agreements: A Contentious Issue for Environmental and Aboriginal Justice," *Environments Journal* 35, no. 2 (2007) 49.

Lack of specific consultation with aboriginal peoples or other constituencies: *Hupacasath v Minister of Foreign Affairs*, Cross-Examination on Affidavit of Vernon John MacKay, April 3, 2013, 9-11.

Potential for conflict and ongoing liability: *Mobil Investments Canada Inc and Murphy Oil Corp v Canada*, Decision, May 22, 2012, ICSID Case No. ARB(AF)/07/4. The research and development spending requirements in this case had been upheld in *Hibernia Management and Development Company Ltd. v Canada-Newfoundland and Labrador Offshore Petroleum Board* (2008), 2008 NLCA 46 (CanLII) (Newfoundland & Labrador Court of Appeal). I elaborate on my blog, http://gusvanharten.wordpress.com/.

CHAPTER 39: LAURA DAWSON'S LAWN DARTS

Short press release on ratification: Foreign Affairs, Trade and Development Canada, "Canada Ratifies Investment Agreement with China," News release, September 12, 2014.

Laura Dawson promotion of FIPA: Laura Dawson, "Time to dial back the hysteria surrounding the China FIPA," *The Province*, October 30, 2012.

Dawson reportedly has clients that may use investor-state arbitration: Andy Blatchford, "Canada has faced most NAFTA claims: report," *Canadian Press*, January 14, 2015.

Description of Dawson as former senior economic advisor at U.S. Department of State: Laura Dawson, "TPP: Now the hard part," *Financial Post*, June 21, 2012.

FIPA secrecy point conveyed in open letter to Prime Minister: This was sent on 16 October 2012. It remains available on *The Tyee* website, for example, and I have posted it on my blog, http://gusvanharten.wordpress.com/.

Technical details on limited judicial supervision of investor-state lawsuits: Gus Van Harten, *Investment Treaty Arbitration and Public Law* (Oxford: Oxford University Press, 2007), 154-158.

FIPA allowance for confidentiality of business information: China FIPA, article 28(2).

Real issue that FIPA allows federal government to keep documents secret until award issued: China FIPA, article 28(1).

Diane Francis description of FIPA: Diane Francis, "Canada-China trade deal is too one-sided," *Financial Post*, November 2, 2012.

Dawson reportedly co-authored report and appears to have written several reports commissioned by Canadian Council of Chief Executives: Barrie McKenna, "Ottawa could face lawsuits for strict corruption rules: report," *Globe and Mail*, November 24, 2014. See also Laura Dawson, *Canada's trade with Mexico: Where we've been, where we're going and why it matters* (CCCE, February 2014); Brian Staples and Laura Dawson, *Made in the world: Defragmentation rules of origin for more efficient global trade* (CCCE, June 2014).

Siemens lawsuit/ subsequent corruption scandal and settlement: *Siemens v Argentina*, Decision, February 6, 2007, *World Trade and Arbitration Materials* 19, no. 2 (2007): 103. Jason Webb Yackee, "Investment Treaties and Investor Corruption: An Emerging Defense for Host States?," *Virginia Journal of International Law* 52 (2012): 723.

CHAPTER 40: THE STRANGE CASE OF STEPHEN GORDON

Stephen Gordon opinion article: Stephen Gordon, "Don't fear the FIPA," *Maclean's*, September 17, 2014.

Correction from Simon Lester: Simon Lester, "How Not to Defend ISDS," *International Economic Law and Policy Blog*, September 17, 2014,
http://worldtradelaw.typepad.com/ielpblog/2014/09/how-not-to-defend-isds.html.

Haiti compensation of former slave owners: David Whitehouse, "Haiti's Ex-Slaves Demand Land and Mule From France's CDC," *Bloomberg*, May 27, 2013; Isabel Macdonald, "France's debt of dishonour to Haiti" *The Guardian*, August 16, 2010; Kim Ives, "Haiti: Independence Debt, Reparations for Slavery and Colonialism, and International 'Aid'," *Global Research*, May 10, 2013.

NAFTA case of SD Myers v Canada: *SD Myers v Canada*, Decision, November 13, 2000, *International Legal Materials* 40 (2001): 1408.

Relative power of investment treaty arbitrators: Gus Van Harten, *Investment Treaty Arbitration and Public Law* (Oxford: Oxford University Press, 2007), chapter 5.

CHAPTER 41: "THE LARGEST ENERGY PROJECT IN THE ENTIRE WORLD"

Government support for new pipelines and oil shipments by rail: e.g. Shawn McCarthy, Steven Chase, and Brent Jang, "Canadian government approves Enbridge's controversial Northern Gateway pipeline," *Globe and Mail*, June 17, 2014; Murray Brewster and Benjamin Shingler, "Lac Megantic: Oil shipments by rail have increased 28,000 per cent since 2009," *Canadian Press*, July 8, 2013.

Government overhaul of environmental and fisheries laws: Gloria Galloway, "Don't gut Fisheries Act, scientists urge Harper," *Globe and Mail*, March 22, 2012; Keith Stewart, "What the oil industry wants, the Harper government gives," *Greenpeace Canada Blog*, January 9, 2013, http://www.greenpeace.org/canada/en/Blogentry/what-the-oil-industry-wants-the-harper-govern/blog/43617/.

Government cutbacks and layoffs of science and research capacity: e.g. Ed Struzik, "Oh Canada: the government's broad assault on the environment," *The Guardian*, July 2, 2012; John Dupuis, "The Canadian War on Science: A long, unexaggerated, devastating chronological indictment," *Confessions of a Science Librarian Blog*, May 20, 2013, http://scienceblogs.com/confessions/2013/05/20/the-canadian-war-on-science-a-long-unexaggerated-devastating-chronological-indictment/.

Government rejection of concerns about high Canadian dollar: Maria Babbage, "Mulcair's 'logic is off' on oil sands, Flaherty says," *Globe and Mail*, May 11, 2012.

Government lobbying campaign in U.S. and Europe: e.g. Martin Lukacs, "The Harper Offensive: Selling Tar Sands to Europe and the USA," *Canadian Dimension* 45, no. 6 (November/December 2011); Mike De Souza, "Stephen Harper's cabinet personally approved ads," *Mike De Souza's Blog*, December 13, 2014, http://mikedesouza.com/2014/12/13/stephen-harpers-cabinet-personally-approved-ads/.

Oil sands need for over CDN$500 billion in investment: Canadian Energy Research Institute (CERI), *Canadian Economic Impacts of New and Existing Oil Sands Development in Alberta (2014-2038)* (Calgary: CERI, November 2014), 2-4.

China expected to invest as much as CDN$1 trillion by 2020: Department of Foreign Affairs and International Trade (Canada), *Responses to Questions submitted through the Chair of the House of Commons Standing Committee on International Trade on behalf of the Liberal Party*, undated, received by author November 9, 2012. I have posted the document on my blog, http://gusvanharten.wordpress.com/.

John Carruthers and Campbell Clark quotes: Shaun Polczer, "Canada urged to look to Asia for oilsands trade," *Calgary Herald*, April 5, 2011; Campbell Clark, "On upcoming visit to Beijing, Harper has bargaining power," *Globe and Mail*, January 19, 2012.

Chinese government gung ho on Canadian oil when FIPA announced: Mark Mackinnon, "PM lands investor protection deal, raises human rights in China," *Globe and Mail*, February 8, 2012.

Chinese ambassador Junsai Zhang and Deborah Yedlin quotes: Claudia Cattaneo, "Is Canada taking China for granted?," *National Post*, May 5, 2012; Deborah Yedlin, "Chinese reality check for energy industry," *Calgary Herald*, May 8, 2012). See also Jordan Press, "Keystone failure not an issue, PM says," *Ottawa Citizen*, December 20, 2011.

Chinese ownership in Canadian oil and Northern Gateway pipeline: Nathan VanderKlippe, "China's new play for Canada's oil and gas," *Globe and Mail*, October 10, 2011; "Who Owns Our Oil Sands? Foreign corporations stake their claims to our resources," April 22, 2011, Alberta Federation of Labour website, accessed April 6, 2015, http://www.afl.org/index.php/May-2011/who-owns-our-oil-sands-foreign-corporations-stake-their-claims-to-our-resources.html; Alberta Federation of Labour, *China's Gas Tank* (Edmonton: AFL, 2012).

John Baird and Ed Fast quotes: Tobi Cohen, "Tories review foreign policy goals," *Calgary Herald*, August 17, 2011; Tobi Cohen, "Canada has 'entered a new era' in relations with China, Baird says," *Calgary Herald*, July 21, 2011; Wenran Jiang, "Sino-Canadian relations: 'Strategic Partnerships' II," *Toronto Star*, July 24, 2011; Mike Raptis, "Feds seek China trade boost; Minister wants to further tap Asia-Pacific potential," *The Province*, July 15, 2011.

Newspaper reports on FIPA: "China, Canada talk investor protection," *National Post*, August 17, 2011. See also Andy Hoffman, "Canada-China ties 'very warm,' envoy says," *Globe and Mail*, August 30, 2011; Jason Fekete, "Canada closes in on trade pact with China," *Ottawa Citizen*, October 4, 2011.

National Post report on FIPA trip/ Joseph Caron and Charles Burton quotes: Jason Fekete, "Oil sales, human rights (and pandas) on Stephen Harper's China agenda," *National Post*, February 7, 2012; Jason Fekete, "Stephen Harper in China," *National Post*, February 10, 2012.

Prime Minister Harper speech in Guangzhou and Joe Oliver quotes: Prime Minister of Canada, "PM Delivers Remarks at a Business Dinner in Guangzhou," February 10, 2012; Theophilos Argitis, "Oil sands need China, Oliver says on visit," *National Post*, February 13, 2012.

CHAPTER 42: OTHER EXPLANATIONS FOR A LOPSIDED DEAL

Ideological reasons for spread of trade deals: e.g. Robert W. Benson, "Free Trade As an Extremist Ideology: The Case of NAFTA," *University of Puget Sound Law Review* 17 (1994): 555.

Wenran Jiang quote: Lee Anne Goodman, "Canada ratifies investment deal with China," *Toronto Star*, September 12, 2014.

Kevin and Julia Garratt detention / Globe and Mail report when FIPA ratification was announced: Terry Pedwell, "Canadian spy agency says Chinese hacked into NRC computers," *Canadian Press*, July 30, 2014; Giuseppe Valiante, "Canadian couple detained: Diplomacy at work?," *Toronto Sun*, September 2, 2014; Nathan VanderKlippe, "Ottawa threatens to snub Beijing over Garratt couple's arrest," *Globe and Mail*, September 12, 2014.

Billions in legal fees from investor-state lawsuits: I base this on reports of over 600 known cases under investment treaties at an average cost of about USD$8 million in legal fees per case. United Nations Conference on Trade and Development, *International Investment Agreements Issues Note – Recent Trends in IIAs and ISDS* (Geneva: UNCTAD, February 2015); David Gaukrodger and Kathryn Gordon, "Investor-State Dispute Settlement: A Scoping Paper for the Investment Policy Community," *OECD Working Paper on International Investment 2012/03* (Paris: Organisation for Economic Cooperation and Development, 2012).

Lawyers at the Canadian Bar Association and Canada's ratification of the ICSID Convention: I elaborate on my blog, http://gusvanharten.wordpress.com/.

Interests of Canadian investors versus interests of Canadians: e.g. Joseph E. Stiglitz, "Regulating Multinational Corporations: Towards Principles of Cross-Border Legal Frameworks in a Globalized World Balancing Rights with Responsibilities," *American University International Law Review* 23 (2007): 455-456.

Prime Minister's push for market access when FIPA was announced and press reports on Scotiabank bid: Prime Minister of Canada, "PM Delivers Remarks at a Business Dinner in Guangzhou," February 10, 2012; Grant Robertson, "Scotiabank takes stake in Chinese bank," *Globe and Mail*, September 9, 2011; John Greenwood, "Scotiabank waits turn after Nexen approval; Guangzhou stake," *National Post*, December 11, 2012; Doug Alexander and Katia Dmitrieva, "Scotiabank Drops Bid to Buy Bank of Guangzhou Stake," *Bloomberg*, July 12, 2013.

FIPA promoters who flagged market access as priority for Canadian investors: e.g. John Ivison, "Ottawa eyeing full-blown free trade agreement with China," *National Post*, September 11, 2012.

Treaties are binding under international law according to their terms: Vienna Convention on the Law of Treaties, 1155 United Nations Treaty Series 331 (signed May 22, 1969; entered into force January 27, 1980), articles 7(2) and 11-12.

Most treaties can be terminated on six months' or one year's notice: Laurence R. Helfer, "Terminating Treaties," in *Oxford Guide to Terminating Treaties*, ed. Duncan Hollis (Oxford: Oxford University Press, 2012): 643.

Harper government withdrawal from Kyoto Protocol and United Nations Convention to Combat Desertification: "Canada under fire over Kyoto protocol exit," *BBC News*, December 13, 2011; "Canada quietly pulls out of UN anti-droughts convention," *Canadian Press*, March 27, 2013.

China FIPA has longest lock-in period among Canada's relevant treaties: China FIPA, article 35(1)-(3). I elaborate on my blog, http://gusvanharten.wordpress.com/.

NAFTA can be terminated on six months' notice: NAFTA, article 2205. This is another point on which a government expert gave inaccurate testimony in the Hupacasath First Nation's constitutional challenge to the FIPA, as I elaborate on my blog, http://gusvanharten.wordpress.com/.

Canada's model FIPA: *Agreement Between Canada and [other country] for the Promotion and Protection of Investments* (2004), article 38, ITA website, accessed March 10, 2015, http://italaw.com/documents/Canadian2004-FIPA-model-en.pdf.

Foreign investor lawsuits against Hamburg restrictions on power plant, Ontario implementation of Green Energy Act, and Québec moratorium on oil and gas drilling: *Vattenfall v Germany*, Claimant submission, March 30, 2009, ICSID Case No. ARB/09/6; *Mesa Power v Canada*, Claimant submission, July 6, 2011; *Windstream Energy v Canada*, Claimant submission, November 6, 2013; *Lone Pine Resources v Canada*, Claimant submission, November 8, 2012.

Study on unburnable fossil fuels and comparison to global warning during ice-age recovery: Christophe McGlade and Paul Ekins, "The geographical distribution of fossil fuels unused when limiting global warming to 2 °C," *Nature* 517 (2015): 187. NASA Earth Observatory, "How is Today's Warming Different from the Past?," undated, NASA website, accessed March 10, 2015, http://earthobservatory.nasa.gov/Features/GlobalWarming/page3.php.

Billion dollar-plus awards against Ecuador and Russia: *Occidental v Ecuador (no. 2)*, Decision, September 9, 2008. *Yukos Universal v. Russia*, Decision, July 18, 2014; this decision and two others by the *Yukos* tribunal are available on the Permanent Court of Arbitration website, accessed March 9, 2015, http://www.pca-cpa.org/showpage.asp?pag_id=1599.

Other cases involving tens or hundreds of billions in assets: e.g. Khaleeq Kiani, "Govt may go for deal rather than wait for verdict on Reko Diq," *Dawn.com*, October 13, 2014 (estimated USD$150 billion to $3 trillion in disputed assets).

Blaming China for Canada's inaction on climate change: Shawn McCarthy, "U.S.-China climate deal presents challenges for Harper," *Globe and Mail*, November 12, 2014.

CHAPTER 44: CHANNELLING HOPE

Brazil's avoidance of investment treaties: Daniela Campello and Leany Barreiro Lemos, "The non-ratification of bilateral investment treaties in Brazil: a story of conflict in a land of cooperation" *Review of International Political Economy* 22 (2015) (online version), accessed

April 6, 2015,
http://www.tandfonline.com/doi/abs/10.1080/09692290.2014.987154?journalCode=r-rip20#.VSLmAOH19Ui.

INDEX

China Investment Corporation, 284
China National Offshore Oil
    Corporation (CNOOC), 47, 284, 294
China Oil and Gas Group Limited,
    47–48, 284
China's Silent Army (Cardenal and
    Araújo), 50
Chinese strategy
    asset acquisition, 50–51
    China, Inc., 50
    FIPA, 4, 11
    foreign investors, 10–11
    industrialization, 17
    investment treaties, xiv
    natural resources, 4, 42–43, 51–52
    oil industry, 282–283
    protectionism, 17–18
cigarette packaging, 125–126
Clark, Campbell, 283
Clayton/Bilcon v. Canada, 65, 147
climate change. *see* environmental
    protection and policy
colonialism, 20–21, 306
compensation
    academic statements against, 220
    backward-looking compensation,
    59, 255–256
    broad interpretation of treaties,
    58, 91
    enforcement of, 56–59, 117,
    297–298
    environmental assessments, 65
    expropriation, 11, 64–65, 90, 92,
    148, 199–200, 272–273
    fair and equitable treatment,
    11–12, 58, 91–92, 120–121, 123,
    151–152, 192–193, 198
    fair compensation, 199, 203
    health and safety issues, 265–266
    Hull standard, 199
    indirect expropriation, 198, 200,
    202–203, 216, 228
    levels of government, 184,
    191–192
    NAFTA, 63–66, 103–105, 108–
    110, 115–116, 258–259
    parliamentary supremacy, 93,
    133, 248
    safe countries, 21–22
    secrecy, 5
    World Trade Organization
    (WTO), 255–256
    see also liability
compromise. *see* Canadian strategy
confidential information. *see* secrecy
constitutional issues. *see* sovereignty
counterclaims, 114
Coyne, Andrew, 18, 29, 185, 187–189,

197–202, 211, 219
Crampton, Paul, 161–163, 166–175
Curry, Bill, 183
Czech Republic, 131–132

D
damages. *see* compensation
Davies, Don, 194, 195, 246
Dawson, Laura, 185, 260–270
Day, Stockwell, 181–183
Den Tandt, Michael, 185
discriminatory laws
    environmental protection,
    273–274
    grandfathering of existing rules,
    12, 14–19, 48, 200
    Investment Canada Act, 44–49
    investor protection, 90
    market access, 38–42
    most-favoured-nation (MFN),
    39–42, 171, 198, 207–208
    national treatment provision,
    38–39, 198
    permits, 15, 16
    promotion of FIPA, 14, 48–49,
    198–199, 202, 225
    rule of law, 15, 62–66, 207
    tax rates, 15
dismissal of public concerns, promotion
    of FIPA, 188–189, 196
Dow AgroSciences v. Canada, 147
Dow Chemical, 136

E
Easter, Wayne, 246–251
Eastern Sugar, 131–132
economic policy, 99
Eli Lilly, 132–133
Enbridge Northern Gateway, 282
environmental protection and policy
    cause and effect, 31–35, 54
    Chinese resources, 54
    climate change, 299–301
    discriminatory rules, 273–274
    environmental assessments, 65
    environmental treaties, 63, 274
    exceptions, 94–95
    FIPA, 29–35, 54
    international treaties, 63
    investor-state arbitration, 63, 99,
    100, 102–105, 107–110, 147
    oil sands projects, 282
    promotion of FIPA, 227–228
    regulatory chill, 32–33, 106–112
    sovereignty, 63–65
Ecuador, 122
Ethyl v. Canada, 63, 107–110, 115–116,
    147